Fifty Years of the Formula One World Championship

Fifty Years of the Formula One World Championship

In the words of those who were there

Geoff Tibballs

Robson Books

First published in Great Britain in 2000 by Robson Books, 10 Blenheim Court, Brewery Road, London N7 9NT

A member of the Chrysalis Group plc

British Library Cataloguing in Publication Data
A catalogue record for this title is available from the British Library

ISBN 186105 309 6

Printed by Butler and Tanner, Frome, Somerset

Contents

Introduction

Forget the train sets and football boots – probably my most cherished Christmas present as a boy was Jack Brabham's motor-racing book. It was published in 1960, I think, and couldn't have been more gratefully received if it had been delivered by the man himself. Similarly, for all the trips to the zoo, the seaside and Wembley, one of my most memorable days out was when my parents took me to watch him race at Brands Hatch one Bank Holiday. It was less than ten miles away but it was like being transported to a different world from staid suburbia where a game of Junior Scrabble constituted excitement. You see, Brabham was my hero. He was quiet, unassuming, hard-working, rarely had accidents and was a double world champion by 1960 – the perfect role model for a nine-year-old. Formula 1 is a sport of heroes. And these days I take my own offspring – one a Villeneuve fan, the other an Irvine follower – on the annual pilgrimage to Silverstone.

F1 remains a tremendous spectacle, whether you're trackside or watching ITV's excellent coverage, enhanced by the presence of Murray Walker, one of our genuine national treasures. Like all sports, it has had its ups and downs – periods when the races have been labelled 'dull' and the drivers 'colourless'. But who could describe the likes of Stirling Moss, Graham Hill, James Hunt, Alan Jones or Ayrton Senna as 'colourless'? True, if you listen to the post-race press conferences, you could be forgiven for thinking that the leading drivers possess all the charisma of a speak-your-weight machine. But for every Mika Hakkinen, there is an Eddie Irvine. And even Hakkinen showed glimpses of emotion when he broke down in tears in the bushes at Monza. Although the organised conferences rarely reveal any insights into the drivers' personalities, thanks to the motor-racing press and numerous biographies and autobiographies, their most poignant words down the years have been captured in print. So here they are – the compliments, the insults, the agonies, the ecstasies and the philosophies, from Ascari to Schumacher, Fangio to Mansell, Hawthorn to Hill – and all relayed faster than a flat-out Minardi.

In addition to the books named, I have found the following publications to be invaluable sources of material: *Autosport*, *F1 Racing*, *Chequered Flag*, *Motor Sport*, *Motor Racing*, *Autocar*, *The Motor*, the *Times*, *The Sunday Times*, the *Daily Mail*, the *Guardian* and the *Daily Telegraph*. I would also like to thank the British Newspaper Library at Colindale; the public libraries at Marylebone, Victoria, Westminster, Sheffield and Derby; Nottinghamshire Library Services for unearthing ageing motor-racing books; my daughters Nicola and Lindsey for their boundless enthusiasm and considerable expertise on the subject; and, above all, Jeremy Robson for supporting this project.

Geoff Tibballs, 1999

Chapter One

Driving Forces

'Drivers are just interchangeable light bulbs – you plug them in and they do the job.' – Former McLaren team boss Teddy Mayer

'The driver is crucial. He is our interpreter, he translates the car for us.' – Frank Williams, 1983

'Today's drivers are athletes who hire out their capacities for profit. The old drivers didn't risk their lives for nothing, but the sport came before the cash.' – Enzo Ferrari, 1977

'I always say the drivers are mad – anyone who drives one of those cars has to be.' – Professor Sid Watkins, Formula 1's chief medical officer, 1999

Michele Alboreto

'A smooth and stylish man without some of the more histrionic traits of his fellow countrymen.' – Author Steve Small, from *The Guinness Complete Grand Prix Who's Who* (Guinness Publishing, 1994)

'He is arguably the best Italian driver around – a reasonably intelligent man who is, however, prone to the occasional mistake on the track.' – John Watson, 1984

Jean Alesi

'Unlike others, he saves his arrogance and aggression for the car. When he takes his helmet off, he's a little honey.' – Eddie Jordan, 1990

'He isn't sitting on a pile of gold and he hasn't got fifteen kids.' – Tyrrell designer Harvey Postlethwaite explaining the reasons behind Alesi's success, 1990

'He has the hot blood that this sport needs. When Alesi sits at the wheel of his car he does not mind who is in front or who is behind. All he cares about is to do the best he can, without worrying whether the other guy is a world champion or not. This will give him a lot of problems...' – Ayrton Senna, 1990

'He has said that Schumacher's presence is not compatible with him. Alesi knows how much I admire him, but I have told him this and I say it again: it is important not to make accusations about treachery and not to behave like a little baby.' – Ferrari president Luca di Montezemolo rounding on Alesi after the Frenchman had expressed his concerns about the prospect of Michael Schumacher joining the team, 1995

'I don't understand what was going on in his brain. Was it switched off?' – Michael Schumacher after a coming-together at the 1995 Australian Grand Prix

'We were level, wheel to wheel, but he just banged into me.' – Jacques Villeneuve, unhappy with Alesi's driving at the 1996 San Marino Grand Prix

'It was totally unacceptable. I would go and have a word with him, but I don't think there would be any point. He wouldn't take any notice.' – David Coulthard, rammed by Alesi on the final lap of the 1997 French Grand Prix when lying in fifth place

'I try to be a calm person. Sometimes when I am very angry I want to explode, but I try to remember the English way.' – Alesi, from *Grand Prix People* by Gerald Donaldson (MRP, 1990)

'Jean is quicker than Michael in pure speed but that is not so important. One quick lap means nothing – you need consistency.' – Benetton boss Flavio Briatore comparing Alesi and Schumacher, 1996

'Once again, I'm going to be taken for an idiot.' – Alesi after running out of fuel on lap 35 while lying second in the 1997 Australian Grand Prix. Alesi had failed to see the pit-board hung out by the Benetton team, ordering him to come in and refuel.

Chris Amon

'He was endowed with tremendous natural talent, but he was never sufficiently organised to take best advantage of his own ability. He was always signing for the wrong team at the wrong time.' – Jackie Stewart, from *Jackie Stewart's Principles of Performance Driving* (Hazleton Publishing, 1986)

Mario Andretti

'I kind of like to have someone looking up my arse.' – Andretti endeavouring to explain how he didn't mind having another car on his tail, 1978

'His reputation among his fellow drivers isn't one of great virtuosity but rather of great determination. He still has that youthful drive. He runs a car hard – heck, he runs it off the road a lot. He still breaks cars, but that's part of the game.' – Dan Gurney, 1968

'When somebody is one and a half seconds faster in practice than the next fastest, you shouldn't react to a bad start so that you are straightaway in a collision. With this, he threw away the biggest superiority any driver had in any race this year.' – Niki Lauda, unimpressed by Andretti's performance at the 1977 Belgian Grand

Prix, from *For The Record: My Years With Ferrari* (William Kimber, 1978)

Michael Andretti

'Car racing is too dangerous. Me, I'm too old to change, but Michael is going to go to college, become a lawyer or a businessman.' – Mario Andretti revealing his career plans for his son, 1978

'My son has been exposed to racing, to speed in all forms, since he was an infant. I'm guilty of that.' – Mario Andretti giving up trying to persuade Michael to do a sensible job, 1983

'I think Michael is probably in that small band of perhaps five drivers in the world who have the necessary aggression in traffic and the desire to win.' – McLaren boss Ron Dennis signing IndyCar star Michael Andretti, son of Mario, for 1993. Nine months later, Andretti was on his way back to the States with seven points and a string of retirements.

Elio de Angelis

'He came from an extremely wealthy family, and fundamentally he was not hungry enough. We never quite knew how he was going to perform.' – Lotus chief engineer Tony Rudd

René Arnoux

'He brakes like a bloody old woman in that thing. Those Renaults always brake early.' – A frustrated John Watson mocking Arnoux at the 1981 San Marino Grand Prix

'He is a pain in the backside on the race-track. He is so very inconsiderate, particularly in qualifying. His driving etiquette is consistently poor and he seems to have this idea that he cannot allow himself to be overtaken.' – John Watson, 1984

'A highly nervous individual, over-tense and over-wound. You only need to look at his eyes; they dart, the pupils always seem to be enlarged.' – Jackie Stewart, from *Jackie Stewart's Principles of Performance Driving* (Hazleton Publishing, 1986)

'He's just a total bloody idiot. Always was, always will be.' – Derek Warwick, 1987

Peter Arundell

'Jimmy was so good that every other driver was mesmerised by him. But when I spoke to Arundell, he said: "Give me an equal car and I can beat him!" This is why I signed him up. I felt he had the correct mental approach.' – Lotus chief Colin Chapman choosing the virtually unknown Arundell to partner Jim Clark for 1964. Sadly Arundell never fulfilled that early promise

Alberto Ascari

'He was the fastest driver I ever saw – faster even than Fangio.' – Mike Hawthorn

'When he put his goggles on, those warm and friendly eyes suddenly became like steel, intense and concentrated.' – Fellow Italian driver Luigi Villoresi

'I deeply admired the graceful, pleasant style of Alberto's driving. He was a real champion, worthy in every way of his father Antonio.' – Juan Manuel Fangio

'He was a man who had to lead from the start. In that position he was hard to overtake, almost impossible to beat. Alberto was secure when playing the hare. That was when his style was at its most superb. In second place, or further back, he was less secure.' – Enzo Ferrari, from *Grand Prix Greats* by Nigel Roebuck (Patrick Stephens Ltd, 1986)

'My game is going wrong – the star is setting.' – The superstitious Ascari to Juan Manuel Fangio at the 1955 Monaco Grand Prix. Four days later Ascari was killed at the wheel of a sports car

'I have lost my greatest opponent.' – Fangio after Ascari's death

Lorenzo Bandini

'His attitude to other drivers during a race leaves a certain amount to be desired. Pointless balking can only merit censure. He should remember that the sport can be lethal. Those who play with fire are sometimes themselves burnt.' – BRM supremo Louis T. Stanley, from *Grand Prix* (Macdonald, 1965)

'I liked Lorenzo a lot. He was uncomplicated, cheerful and non-political. I don't think he was really number one material or, come to that, ever wanted to be. He liked somebody in the team to relate to, to aim for, and to satisfy himself against an established bench-mark.' – John Surtees on his 1963 Ferrari team-mate, from *John Surtees: World Champion* (Hazleton Publishing, 1991)

'He virtually cried and pleaded with me not to leave Ferrari. I said to people in the team: "Look, you will kill the lad because the sort of responsibility he'll face – an Italian in a Ferrari car – isn't on."' – John Surtees. The Englishman left Maranello in 1966 and Bandini was killed driving a Ferrari at the 1967 Monaco Grand Prix

Carel de Beaufort

'A tall, heavy, jolly, flabby individual not good enough to drive in any other Grand Prix, but he never misses the Dutch one where organisers permit him to enter his own car because they are thus given the excuse to fly a Dutch flag and play the Dutch anthem. De Beaufort in his Porsche or Cooper is ten seconds a lap slower at Zandvoort than other cars, so slow that he is perpetually blocking cars, and he causes drivers like Stirling Moss to walk about muttering "bloody silly that".' – Author Robert Daley on the last of the amateurs, from *Cars at Speed* (Foulis, 1961)

Jean Behra

'I saw in him something of myself. He lived for his motor racing and he was a real fighter.' – Stirling Moss

'A magnificent racing driver and a charming man, but devastatingly temperamental.' – BRM chief Raymond Mays

'When things went well he was on top of the world, but if things were not quite right he was dreadfully depressed and just did not try.' – BRM chief engineer Tony Rudd, from *It Was Fun!* (Patrick Stephens Ltd, 1993)

Derek Bell

'I never re-warm cold soup.' – Enzo Ferrari on why he hadn't given Bell a second chance, 1971

Jean-Pierre Beltoise

'A tough little blighter with a lot of courage.' – James Hunt's assessment of the French driver who raced with a crippled left arm as a result of a horrendous accident at Reims early in his career, 1974

Gerhard Berger

'He has pace, courage and lots of aggression. He likes a fight and isn't afraid to bang wheels from time to time.' – Nigel Mansell, 1992

'The whole idea of Gerhard as a joker is a misconception. He recognises the risks of his business. He wants to minimise them as much as anybody else, but he is capable of departmentalising things in his mind. He is responsible about his career, but for him, life when you are not in the car is about having fun.' – Lotus managing director Peter Collins who worked with Berger at Benetton, 1994

'He does not show it like Alesi, but Gerhard needs reassurance. He needs to be told how much he is wanted.' – Ferrari sporting director Jean Todt, 1995

Jo Bonnier

'He handles cars with poker-faced assurance, but he lacks the spirit of ruthless determination to keep up maximum pressure until the chequered flag... One of the fairest drivers in motor racing and certainly one of the friendliest.' – Louis T. Stanley, 1965

Thierry Boutsen

'I was Boutsened.' – Johnny Herbert, squeezed out by the Belgian at the 1992 Brazilian Grand Prix

Jack Brabham

'He seemed to have forgotten that he was no longer on a dirt-track in Australia and insisted on coming round the corners sideways in a power slide.' – Stirling Moss on Brabham's F1 debut at the 1955 British Grand Prix

'He was one of the few very complete racing drivers the world has known. Others may have received more acclaim, but few more success.' – Graham Hill, 1971

'He was a damn good driver because he used his nut. Later when Bruce McLaren joined the team, what Bruce didn't know, Jack taught him. They were both good engineers. They could set up the cars and they didn't mind getting their hands dirty and working on them.' – John Cooper, from *Brabham* by Phil Drackett (Arthur Barker Ltd, 1985)

'Few can equal Brabham in race-craft. He is a master of Grand Prix tactics.' – Louis T. Stanley, 1965

'His style may not satisfy the purist, but it is ruthlessly effective. The car is always under control. Few men have such a knack of nursing an ailing machine.' – Louis T. Stanley, 1966

'I decided to have a bit of a go at the press for labelling me the old man of motor racing. They were giving me a hard time. My wife Betty went off shopping and bought me a false beard and I got hold of a jack handle. Just prior to the start of the race I went out to the car with the beard, leaning heavily on the jack handle. I just had to win after that.' – Forty-year-old Brabham making his point before the 1966 Dutch Grand Prix. Brabham duly won and went on to clinch his third world championship

'Jack could give the impression that he was a bit vague at times. He was quite good at that, particularly with anyone who wanted to talk about money! But he knew *exactly* what he was doing and in which direction he wanted to travel.' – Denny Hulme, from *British Grand Prix* by Maurice Hamilton (Crowood Press, 1990)

Tony Brooks

'The greatest "unknown" racing driver there's ever been.' – Stirling Moss

'He was very underrated. He was not as ruthless as Stirling, but just as fast when he was happy with the car.' – BRM chief engineer Tony Rudd, from *It Was Fun!* (Patrick Stephens Ltd, 1993)

Andrea de Cesaris

'His attitude is that if someone's on his tail trying to get by, he should prevent it by any means. If it had been possible I would have got out of the car in the middle of the straight and hit him as hard as I could straight in the face, climbed back in the car and gone on.' – Keke Rosberg after being held up by de Cesaris at the 1982 French Grand Prix

'What really worries me about Andrea is his unwillingness to learn. This is his fourth year in Formula 1 and he's still doing the same things, making the same mistakes.' – Keke Rosberg, 1984

'Formula 1 was never meant to be easy. We have to fight, we know that. But today was a complete joke. Every time I got alongside him, he drove straight at me. He is mad, de Cesaris, crazy.' – René Arnoux after the 1984 British Grand Prix

'Fast on his day. Otherwise he usually connects with the scenery.' – Unnamed driver on de Cesaris

'If you come into F1 too early, you cannot cope with the pressure and your mind goes a little crazy.'– de Cesaris, 1991

François Cevert

'It's the best decision you ever made. He's as handsome as a Greek god.' – Norah Tyrrell to husband Ken on signing Cevert in 1970

Jim Clark

'Jim races because he loves it. Naturally he likes making a lot of money out of it too, but to him it is a sport, not a business. If he had his way, at the end of a meeting he would creep away into obscurity until it was time for the next race. He's not interested in the glamour or the frills.' – Lotus boss Colin Chapman, 1965

'Nobody ever knew what was going on inside him. He was an incredibly private person. He isolated himself. You could see the anxiety in his shoulders. He had a stiffness in his shoulders. He was never what you could call a loose guy and it got worse as he got older.' – Jackie Stewart, from *Jim Clark* by Eric Dymock (Dove Publishing, 1997)

'His nails were bitten almost to the core. He was the coolest, calmest, most calculating racing driver in the world, and he continually bit his nails and chewed his fingers with nervousness. If there was anybody who was going to have an ulcer it would have been Jim Clark. In a way he was a terribly highly-tensed man and yet... the moment he slipped into a racing car he changed.' – Jackie Stewart, from *Champions!* by Christopher Hilton and John Blunsden (Motor Racing Publications Ltd, 1993)

'If you want to see Jim explode, just listen to a so-called professional journalist asking him a completely asinine and irrelevant question, and wait for the reaction. It can be quite impressive!' – Colin Chapman, 1965

'Jimmy was no longer the Border farmer depending on Colin. I saw the change. He was a different man. He was more independent, more vocal about what he wanted. I thought Colin was going to have more and more trouble with him.' – Jackie Stewart detecting a change in Clark in 1967, from *Jim Clark* by Eric Dymock (Dove Publishing, 1997)

'Jimmy ranked with, perhaps even out-ranked, Nuvolari, Fangio and Moss, and I think we all felt that he was in a way invincible. To be killed in an accident with a Formula 2 car is almost unacceptable.' – Bruce McLaren following Clark's death at Hockenheim in 1968

'His ability was so much greater than he ever revealed. He hardly ever drove to the limits of his capacity. He only used nine-tenths of his talent, which makes the gulf between him and other drivers even bigger.' – Colin Chapman

'What he did was build up an enormous lead and simply try and sap your will to win by making it seem impossible.' – Graham Hill on Clark's tactic of going flat out in the opening laps of a race

'It was very touching to find somebody who wasn't hard and cynical who basically was a warm, honest person.' – Graham Hill

'Jimmy Clark was never a bighead. He would never speak loudly to anybody. He shared information on the car. He was a good lad.' – Clark's Lotus team-mate Trevor Taylor

'Jimmy was always a driver you could really drive hard against and be quite confident that he wasn't going to do something stupid.' – Jack Brabham

'He drove in a very clean way – you never saw him wasting precious time by throwing the car sideways.' – Jackie Stewart, 1969

'I never heard a word of criticism of Jim Clark's driving technique or his methods in a race.' – Colin Chapman

'He could jump in darn near anything and drive the wheels off it.' – Dan Gurney

'For me, Jimmy will always be the best driver the world has ever known.' – Colin Chapman, 1980

Peter Collins

'A brash, smug young man...While he had the skill of a great driver, Collins never had the right emotions. He appeared to love the idea of being a famous racing driver, but he didn't want the responsibilities of being a great racing driver.' – Author Robert Daley, from *Cars at Speed* (Foulis, 1961)

David Coulthard

'I got a bit cheesed off being behind Coulthard, because I was able to go quicker. I'll be having a word with him later.' – Damon Hill stuck behind his Williams team-mate for part of the 1994 Canadian Grand Prix

'I've heard he had a moan about me, but I think he'd be better just sorting out his own problems.' – Damon Hill after Coulthard had complained that Hill wouldn't move over to let Coulthard lap him at the 1999 Spanish Grand Prix

'I know a lot of people would love me to kick the wing mirror of my car in frustration when things go wrong, like Nigel did. But, in my opinion, to show your emotions to a competitor is a great weakness.' – Coulthard refusing to follow Mansell's example, 1999

'David has a high level of integrity.' – McLaren boss Ron Dennis, 1999

Derek Daly

'When Derek flew twenty feet over a billboard in Zandvoort, he saw the pictures and thought it was good stuff. He was utterly fearless, but it seemed he couldn't learn what you need to be successful in F1 – a little patience and a little discipline. It was as though he had this huge bubble in his brain and it was always about to burst. He is a much better driver than his performance in 1982 showed, but he didn't last in F1 because of his temperament. He just could not cope with the pressures he put on himself.' – Keke Rosberg discussing his team-mate at Williams in 1982, from *Keke* by Keke Rosberg and Keith Botsford (Stanley Paul, 1985)

Christian Danner

'Bloody Danner ruined my best lap. Not looking in his mirrors, as usual. I had to change down before I got round him. I'm on my way to see him now.' – An irate Stefan Johansson berating the young German driver following an incident in qualifying for the 1987 Belgian Grand Prix

Patrick Depailler

'Patrick was a little boy all his life. That was why you could never be angry with him for long. He was always wanting to go skiing or hang-gliding. I offered him a third car for the North American races in 1973. This was a big chance for him – and ten days before, he goes and breaks his leg falling off a motorbike! Later when he was driving full time for me, I had it written into his contract that he had to keep away from dangerous toys.' – Ken Tyrrell on Depailler's accident shortly before the 1973 Canadian Grand Prix

Pedro Diniz

'I just happened to come upon one of those few idiot drivers who shouldn't be in Formula 1.' – Jacques Villeneuve after Diniz had inadvertently forced him on to the grass at Monza during practice for the 1996 Italian Grand Prix

Juan Manuel Fangio

'I am satisfied to run second. Fangio is a master.' – Froilan Gonzales, 1951

'It is hard to say how much I respect him as a man and as a driver, and how much I have learned from him. At Spa in particular we would come past the grandstands as though tied together by a piece of string, but on the back of the course he would go really fast on a certain section, a good deal faster than I could at that time, just to show me what could be done. And then after we had duly made our twin-like public appearance, he would do it again on the next lap but over a different part of the course.' – Stirling Moss in praise of his Mercedes team-mate for 1955, from *Design and Behaviour of the Racing Car* by Moss and Laurence Pomeroy (William Kimber, 1963)

'He was the one who could always go that little bit quicker, for that little bit longer.' – Stirling Moss

'I have never been a spectacular racer. If there was some crazy guy around I let him overtake and then tried to follow him, never letting him get out of sight. A lot of people would have beaten me if they had followed me. They lost because they overtook me.' – Fangio

'I don't think I knew a more softly spoken man, yet he still had real presence. You were always aware of him when he entered a room, even if you couldn't see him.' – Phil Hill

'He treated all those he met, from the highest to the lowest, with equal dignity and importance. When he was talking to you, you were the only one who mattered.' – Stirling Moss

'We certainly didn't treat him any differently because he was older than us. We looked at Fangio and saw him as a bloody fast driver.' – Stirling Moss on his old adversary, 1997

'The great thing about him is that he won five world titles in four different cars and he never had a row with anyone.' – John Cooper

'Although he had been beaten he had never, ever, been outdriven in a Grand Prix car.' – Author Doug Nye, from *Great Racing Drivers* (Hamlyn, 1977)

'Fangio, the man, is even greater than the myth.' – Stirling Moss

Giuseppe Farina

'A man capable of any performance demanded of him; a man of steel, inside and out, a man who was a racing champion in every sense of the word.' – Enzo Ferrari on the 1950 world champion

'Fearless, flamboyant, he was a "natural" driver with a distinctive style. His outstretched arms method had many imitators, but few could equal his skill.' – Louis T. Stanley, 1966

'I could never help feeling apprehensive about him, especially at the start of a race and one or two laps from the end. At the start he was not unlike a highly strung thoroughbred, liable to break through the starting tape in its eagerness. Nearing the finish he was capable of committing the most astonishing follies although it must be admitted in all justice that he risked only his own safety and never jeopardised that of others. As a consequence he was a regular inmate of hospital wards.' – Enzo Ferrari

'All the drivers said that only the Holy Virgin was capable of keeping him on the track, because of the crazy way he used to drive, and that one day the Virgin would get tired of going along behind him.' – Juan Manuel Fangio after Farina had been killed in a road accident in 1966

Giancarlo Fisichella

'His mental stability is as good as any Italian I have ever seen.' – Jordan technical director Gary Anderson, 1997

'He's young, simpatico and very quick.' – Gerhard Berger, 1997

Emerson Fittipaldi

'Emerson created the sport of motor racing in Brazil.' – Nelson Piquet, 1981

'To see him "psyching" his opponents, and even his team-mates, was a revelation. He was a young man who had drawn in experience like a magnet; a young man with an old and mature head on his shoulders.' – Author Doug Nye, from *Great Racing Drivers* (Hamlyn, 1977)

'Emerson had already been world champion in 1972 and was now assuming the attitude consistent with that high office. He was no longer the "tiger" he had been when he first joined the team.' – Lotus team manager Peter Warr discussing Fittipaldi's approach to the 1973 season

'The talk of Emerson coming back shows the man hasn't really matured. A man who's really grown up would know a return isn't on.' – Keke Rosberg pouring scorn on Fittipaldi's plans to return to F1, 1984

Heinz-Harald Frentzen

'They tell me I can't handle the pressure, that I am a weak egg.' – Frentzen, pilloried in the press after some disappointing results for Williams, 1997

'If I say I am going to win a race or a championship, people will say I am arrogant. If I explain what happens when things go wrong, they say I am making excuses. I can't win.' – Frentzen, 1997

'Heinz-Harald is very talented, but I think he relies on that a bit too much.' – Williams' technical director Patrick Head, 1997

'Frentzen just came out of the pits and pushed me off the track. He was being an idiot. I was very annoyed to say the least, but it is hopeless talking to him. He is one brick short of a full load.' – Damon Hill after an incident with Frentzen at the 1998 Spanish Grand Prix

'He's very mellow. Nothing perturbs him. He doesn't get on a high, but he doesn't get on a low either.' – Jacques Villeneuve, 1999

'Some people thought I was loopy taking him on. But I never had any doubts because he was with me in Formula 3000 and I know his qualities.' – Eddie Jordan, 1999

'A year ago he was shop-soiled goods; now he's a star.' – John Watson after Frentzen's triumph at the 1999 Italian Grand Prix

'H-H has been the revelation of the season. Like Lazarus he's back from the dead.' – Eddie Jordan, 1999

Bruno Giacomelli

'I don't know what Bruno was doing. I was alongside him, and he just moved over on me. It was very dangerous.' – Andrea de Cesaris hitting out at Giacomelli after the 1981 San Marino Grand Prix

'We were level, eyeball to eyeball. We looked across at each other and then he just drove into me. I couldn't believe it. He'd made a mistake at the previous corner, and he just seemed ready to do *anything* to defend his place. I felt like punching him.' – Eddie Cheever nearly coming to blows with the Italian just two laps later at the same San Marino Grand Prix, 1981

Richie Ginther

'Ginther may be small, but he has exceptional staying-power and a tenacious will to win. He always reminds me of a freckled little boy attending what, if his behaviour does not improve, will surely be his last party.' – Louis T. Stanley, from *Grand Prix* (Macdonald, 1965)

Masten Gregory

'I expect Masten Gregory to get killed any day. I tell him this to his face. I've said to him, "Masten, you're going to kill yourself." He acts as if he doesn't even hear me.' – Stirling Moss, 1960

'He has survived more crashes in the last six years than any living driver of race cars. To break down in a Grand Prix is, for Gregory, a most prosaic ending to a race.' – Author Robert Daley, from *Cars at Speed* (Foulis, 1961)

'A young American who had made the big league with no other help than an enormous determination, great courage and a gradual honing of his skills through some crashes no other man would have survived. Masten was a charger, but outside a race car, a quiet, soft-spoken and very pleasant individual.' – John Cooper, from *John Cooper: Grand Prix Carpetbagger* (Foulis, 1977)

Dan Gurney

'At the funeral Jim's father told [Clark's] great friend and rival, the smiling tall American Dan Gurney, that he had been the only driver Jimmy truly feared. Gurney never forgot it, but typically kept it to himself.' – Author Eric Dymock, from *Jim Clark* (Dove Publishing, 1997)

'Dan won himself a reputation as a "meddler", always juggling with his car's settings at the last moment and usually introducing some problem which foiled him time after time.' – Author Doug Nye, from *Great Racing Drivers* (Hamlyn, 1977)

Mika Hakkinen

'He comes up to you on the grid and shakes you by the hand, which is very sporting and makes him seem like a normal person. But when he gets into the car and puts his helmet on, he turns into some sort of demon.' – Damon Hill after Hakkinen had taken him out of the 1994 Pacific Grand Prix

'Mika gave me a bit of a driving lesson all this weekend.' – Honest David Coulthard after finishing second to team-mate Hakkinen at the 1998 Spanish Grand Prix

'Have you noticed Hakkinen makes mistakes when he's alone and leading without any pressure on him? When he's threatened he never makes a mistake.' – Eddie Irvine turning up the heat on the Finn on the run-in to the 1999 world championship

'I don't know if I would have done what Mika did. I think I would have hidden it. When you are a boy and cry in Ireland, you don't last very long.' – Eddie Irvine after Hakkinen burst into tears after spinning out of the 1999 Italian Grand Prix

Mike Hawthorn

'As British as the Royal Family and roast beef.' – Journalist Denis Jenkinson

'He was always laughing and sticking two fingers up, very much alive.' – Roy Salvadori

'While Mike was quite likely to be seen in the bar on the eve of a race, I was more likely to be tucked up in bed.' – Stirling Moss

'He had a *Boy's Own* image of a racing driver, the flying neck scarf, the distinctive bow tie...the type of hero who enjoyed life and did motor racing as a diversion, an interesting pastime.' – Tony Brooks

'Everyone liked Hawthorn, and indeed how could one help doing so? He was full of fun and loved practical jokes and gave his all to driving fast cars. He was perhaps blessed by the fact that nothing went really deep with him, nothing left a lasting scar, physical or mental. In fact, nothing bothered him with any degree of permanence.' – John Cooper, from *John Cooper: Carpetbagger* (Foulis, 1977)

'I was really very upset. I really reckoned that I deserved to win it. To lose to a guy you are sure you can beat is obviously pretty disturbing.' – Stirling Moss after losing the 1958 world drivers' championship by a single point to Hawthorn despite winning four Grands Prix to Hawthorn's one

'On his day he had that rare ability to beat Fangio in a straight fight in a way that somehow eluded Moss in Grands Prix.' – Author William Court in *Grand Prix Requiem* (Patrick Stephens Ltd, 1992)

Johnny Herbert

'He's such a nice bloke, which is very good for racing, but he lacks a winner's instinct.' – Stirling Moss, 1998

'I don't get fed up with the cheeky-chappie image because people know that when I am in the back of the motor home or in the debrief, that is when the happy, jokey side disappears. That is when you have to be damn serious about it.' – Herbert, 1996

'I've been criticised at times for being too cheerful and not appearing to take things seriously but that's a mask I adopted after the accident. Before the accident I wasn't a bubbly sort of guy.' – Herbert on how his 1988 crash at Brands Hatch altered his outlook, 1998

'Before the accident I had got a reputation for not talking to anyone else, of being a little bit miserable and stuck-up. That was because I was super-confident. I felt invincible – I could take on anybody, in any car, any time, anywhere and beat them.' – Herbert, 1999

'If I walk slowly I look very normal, if I walk quicker the limp comes back. It's all mental. I have shrunk. I don't really know where it's gone but I've shrunk maybe an inch. I used to be taller than my girlfriend.' – Herbert, 1989, from *Johnny Herbert: The Steel Behind the Smile* by Christopher Hilton (Patrick Stephens Ltd, 1996)

'When you're at my end of the grid, nobody wants to know you.' – A struggling Herbert ignored by the media, 1994

Damon Hill

'He should take a few boxing tips over the winter and if he's not had lessons in self-defence, he should take some.' – Nigel Mansell's advice to Hill on learning that Ayrton Senna was to be Hill's team-mate at Williams for 1994

'He craves recognition. I think his placid character doesn't go with his results. If his character was slightly more vivacious or sparkling, perhaps he would be held in higher esteem.' – McLaren team chief Ron Dennis, 1994

'I don't get any credit for being polite and diplomatic so I'm going to ditch that tack because it's not getting me anywhere.' – Damon gets tough, 1994

'I won't be the first or the last driver to make a mistake. I would love to have a perfect c.v., but show me a driver who has.' – Hill following his collision with a trackside tyre barrier at the 1996 Italian Grand Prix

'I've never seen anyone go to so much trouble to lose the world championship.' – Niki Lauda after Hill's failure to clinch the title at the 1996 Portuguese Grand Prix

'He's proved himself to have more integrity and dignity in his little finger than most people have got in their whole body.' – Georgie Hill as husband Damon becomes world champion, 1996

'He is always determined about everything. He wants to do it quickly, get it done. It's not just racing. He's like that when he gets the breakfast cereals out.' – Georgie Hill, 1996

'I feel like I'm on a rocket that's just taken off.' – Damon Hill's reaction to clinching the title, 1996

'I think Damon has done it the same way as his dad did. I don't think Graham had any great talent, but he won Monaco five times as well as Indianapolis and Le Mans. Damon has slogged away at it. He's not a Clark, a Senna or a Stewart, but he's done a great job.' – Ken Tyrrell, from *Damon Hill: On Top of the World* by Alan Henry (Patrick Stephens Ltd, 1996)

'He's climbed the mountain, and now he's at the top.' – Frank Williams on Hill's title triumph, 1996

'It was nice to work with a driver who didn't treat all of the talented people who work at Williams as if they were just minions here to do his bidding.' – Williams' technical director Patrick Head singing Hill's praises, 1996

'If you really want to know why we're replacing Hill, it's because he can't bloody pass people.' – Unnamed Williams team member on the axing of Hill, 1996

'Damon had the chance to drive a McLaren, which everyone thinks is going to be the car we all have to beat, and he turned it down because he wanted more money. If Ron Dennis offered me the chance to drive his McLaren, I would have taken it for free. So far as I can see, Damon is just trying to secure his pension.' – Eddie Irvine as Hill rejects McLaren in favour of Jordan, 1998

'Constructive criticism is fine, but destructive criticism isn't. We've got 165 people at Jordan, all working their nuts off. But they need motivation. Instead, they've been reading in the press that the product they're making is not good. I'm not saying that the criticism is unjustified – because the car isn't perfect – but it's been made in the wrong way. The really top drivers – the Schumachers, the Sennas – know how to lift an entire team.' – Jordan's technical director Gary Anderson advising Hill to stop complaining in public, 1998

'Damon would be a very sick puppy if he does the race, drives into a wall and has a bad limp for the rest of his life.' – Eddie Irvine urging Hill not to take part in what was to be his farewell race, the 1999 British Grand Prix

'Damon's retiring like he overtakes. Will he? Won't he? It's not a very good way to walk away, is it?' – Irvine puzzled by Hill's change of heart, 1999

Graham Hill

'He did not suffer fools gladly and was not afraid to show it. But he was a great ambassador for our sport.' – Jackie Stewart

'He had a compulsion for minute adjustment and recording every roll-bar setting, every tyre pressure, every roll centre in his wee black book.' – Jackie Stewart

'Graham stimulated, prodded and generally kept everyone up to fever pitch with his enthusiasm. Graham inspired us to make his car go faster.' – BRM chief engineer Tony Rudd

'He was one of the first guys who breathed, ate and slept motor racing and he spent a lot of time at the BRM factory. He put an awful lot of effort into the technical side.' – Tony Brooks

'Graham was deadly serious about the job of racing. In fact, you couldn't even speak to him before a race – he simply wouldn't communicate. He was as withdrawn and tense at that particular moment as he was gregarious and relaxed afterwards.' – Stirling Moss, from *Racing and All That* by Stirling Moss and Mike Hailwood (Pelham Books, 1980)

'Drivers such as Fangio, Moss, Clark and Stewart were natural drivers. I've never been described as this. I had to work at it.' – Graham Hill

'He was the sort of driver that I'd want to get behind me pretty quickly because he made quite a few mistakes in his earlier years, but developed his technique to a stage where he became very, very competitive.' – Tony Brooks, from *Champions!* by Christopher Hilton and John Blunsden (Motor Racing Publications, 1993)

'Butter wouldn't melt in Graham's mouth – he could charm snakes out of the trees. A great showman, a great ambassador but a wretched man to work for. He wouldn't listen to anyone's advice. He was stubborn and inflexible.' – Alan Jones who drove for Hill's Lola Embassy team in 1975

'Hill was never short of what some would have called "brass", "neck" or "bull", and others, more politely, charisma.' – Author William Court, from *Grand Prix Requiem* (Patrick Stephens Ltd, 1992)

'I must have been eight years old at the time and I remember coming in and watching Dad coming round the old Gasworks hairpin in the red and gold Lotus 49, and sort of finishing the race and that was it. It didn't impress me at all.' – Damon Hill left unmoved by dad Graham's win at Monaco in 1968, from *Williams: Triumph Out of Tragedy* by Alan Henry (Patrick Stephens Ltd, 1995)

'When he died, well, I had no interest at all in Formula 1 after that.' – Damon Hill on the death of his father in 1975. Damon was fifteen at the time

Phil Hill

'At times, when the mood took him, he was a brilliant driver, especially in sports cars. But I don't think he had anything like the same virtuosity in a Grand Prix car. I don't think Phil would have won the 1961 world championship had not von Trips been killed in the Monza accident.' – John Cooper, from *John Cooper: Carpetbagger* (Foulis, 1977)

'Phil took the view that Grand Prix cars did get written off and if they did, so what? It happened all the time. It was a risk that the entrant had to accept in the same way that a driver lives with the risk of injuring or killing himself. Fair enough, I suppose, but what really got my goat was having a driver make precisely the same mistake at the same spot twice running, then treating the whole thing as a mere incident.' – John Cooper after Hill crashed twice – once in practice, once on the first lap of the race – at the same corner at the 1964 Austrian Grand Prix, from *John Cooper: Grand Prix Carpetbagger*. Cooper was so enraged by Hill's laid-back reaction that the pair had a very public slanging match in full view of the Austrian crowds

Denny Hulme

'Beneath a rugged exterior is a quietly spoken, dedicated man. There is nothing subtle about him. He is completely genuine.' – Louis T. Stanley, 1966

James Hunt

'He was very quick and had big balls.' – Alan Jones, 1981

'If he really wanted to win, he wouldn't keep falling off the road while leading motor races.' – Hesketh team boss Bubbles Horsley after Hunt spun off in the 1975 Argentine Grand Prix. He recovered to finish second behind Emerson Fittipaldi

'Of all the drivers we've had, James has the greatest talent – by far. Possibly he makes more mistakes than, say, Emerson Fittipaldi, but he certainly is quicker than Emerson ever was when he drove for us and I think James is as consistently fast a driver as anyone I've ever seen.' – McLaren boss Teddy Mayer, 1976

'He does what amuses him and I like that.' – Niki Lauda, 1976

'Life is too short to be bound by regulations when it isn't absolutely necessary.' – Hunt

'I can talk to James about women and backgammon, tennis, taxes, Spain, food, childhood, but I can't get him to talk to me about cars.' – McLaren boss Teddy Mayer complaining about the lack of feedback from Hunt, 1978

'I don't get involved in the technical side of motor racing. I'm not interested in it.' – James Hunt, 1977

'You get some calm with experience, but you use that in setting up the car. I'm not a calm man when I get into it.' – James Hunt, 1977

'He opens his mouth very quickly, which is unfortunate.' – Jochen Mass following a collision with McLaren team-mate Hunt at the 1977 Canadian Grand Prix. Having been forced to retire, Hunt angrily shook his fist at Mass by the side of the track for several laps afterwards before punching a marshal who tried to stop him running across the circuit.

'When James wakes up I'm sure he will be trying to work out

what happened and will think of the excessively high number of accidents and incidents he has been involved in. He must examine what is going on.' – Jackie Stewart's view of Hunt's behaviour at the 1977 Canadian Grand Prix

'You lust after the wench for years, then she's yours and you can't make it.' – John Watson on world champion Hunt's struggles in the first part of 1977

'My ego's got shagged out.' – Hunt on his declining fortunes, 1978

'Sometimes he was not unintelligent but childish. James wasn't difficult, just an extrovert and basically he knew what he wanted. I found it difficult to tell what he was and how he was because at the time I didn't know whether this was the real James or James chasing the image which he wanted to create for himself.' – Jochen Mass, from *James Hunt: Portrait of a Champion* by Christopher Hilton (Patrick Stephens Ltd, 1993)

'James had a maverick lifestyle and was very contradictory in many ways, but this was one of his charms. He made his statement and he lived with it.' – Jackie Stewart

'James was a total non-conformist who was a curious mixture of wit, intelligence and unparalleled stubbornness – someone who stood firmly behind his actions and beliefs. Whatever else he may have been, James was not boring. Never.' – Stirling Moss at Hunt's memorial service, 1993

Jacky Ickx

'Ickx is first and foremost a fighter. He is forever giving his all, whatever the car. He is a conqueror – a very brave man and very, very clever.' – François Cevert, 1973

'Ickx was well past his best by then. He just could not come to terms with a bad car and, believe me, we gave him a bad car.' – Frank Williams who took on Ickx for 1976

Taki Inoue

'People like Inoue should not have a licence. He was clueless.' – Damon Hill laying into the Japanese driver at the 1995 Italian Grand Prix

Innes Ireland

'One of the great flamboyant personalities of motor racing. But although always ready to have a good time, he took his sport very seriously.' – Jack Brabham

'I could never concentrate totally. I would find myself in the middle of a race thinking about the party we would have that night.' – Innes Ireland

Eddie Irvine

'He should be banned from Formula 1. He is always driving like this and causing trouble.' – Johnny Herbert after Irvine shunted him at the 1994 Italian Grand Prix

'The idiot screwed it up again. It just annoys me that he won't admit that he's done anything wrong. I just wish he would sometimes think what he's doing.' – Johnny Herbert after Irvine shunted Jacques Villeneuve and Herbert out of the 1997 Australian Grand Prix

'Irvine must have been looking in the wrong mirror. He started coming out and I was on the kerb. He kept going and ended up driving over my front wheel. That was the end for me.' – Despondent Stewart driver Jan Magnussen after the 1997 Brazilian Grand Prix

'If it were not for the fact I knew it would cost me a $10,000 fine, I would have put my fist in his face.' – Jean Alesi after a collision with Irvine at the 1997 Austrian Grand Prix

'I've got a nutter's reputation that isn't fully deserved. But if I can intimidate my rivals with it, if I can scare them off a bit, it's to my advantage.' – Irvine, 1998

'Eddie is a driver who just drives. It seems to come naturally. Sometimes he doesn't know what gear he's in.' – Rubens Barrichello, 1999

'I have fallen in love with him easily and fallen out of love with him easily.' – Eddie Jordan, 1999

'He's brash and can be abrasive. He goads people. He's the Ian Paisley of Formula 1.' – Damon Hill, 1999

'He's a hard nut.' – Damon Hill, 1999

'There have been some who everyone agreed were worthy of the title. In some ways Eddie will be worthy but in some ways maybe not. With his character…probably not.' – Johnny Herbert on whether Irvine would make a suitable world champion, 1999

Alan Jones

'Every motor racing fan's common man.' – Journalist Keith Botsford, 1980

'A hard, no-nonsense Aussie who carried the spirit of Williams on to the track.' – Nigel Mansell

'I wouldn't say he's the quickest driver around but he has a very good understanding of motor racing and a first-class tactical brain. He's physically tough, has a lot of stamina and makes very few mistakes.' – James Hunt, 1981

'He has this natural force when it comes to driving: he's on the mark from the start, he's single-minded about being best. He's the sort of driver who puts in the fast laps you need. He responds best when he's really got to hang it out.' – Frank Williams, 1981

'The great thing about Alan was his ability to lift everybody's morale when things were going badly. He acted as an inspiration to the team and that is not a quality displayed by many drivers.' – Williams' technical director Patrick Head

'Like a dog after a rat.' – Jackie Oliver watching Jones testing for Arrows, 1983

Karl Kling

'He had an extraordinarily high opinion of himself.' – Juan Manuel Fangio on German driver Karl Kling

Jacques Laffite

'Jacques is as good as his car. Give him a good chassis and he'll be up with the leaders, but he won't lift an uncompetitive machine further up the grid than it wants to go.' – Keke Rosberg, 1984

'He does not make waves and I'm afraid that may handicap him; it makes it possible for a team to ignore him.' – Rosberg, 1984

Niki Lauda

'He is hardly likely to go down in history as a great champion.' – Journalist Denis Jenkinson on Lauda's first title win, 1975

'He was 100 per cent determined, to the same sort of level as Graham Hill had been. There was no doubt at all in his own mind that he would make the grade.' – Tim Parnell, team manager at BRM for whom Lauda drove in 1973, from *Niki Lauda* by Alan Henry (Hazleton, 1989)

'He is a real thinker, a master tactician and he doesn't make mistakes under pressure.' – James Hunt, 1974

'His thought processes are governed entirely by logic. Everything he does is based on playing percentages, not gambling.' – John Watson, 1982

'A tremendous character and personality and completely single-minded. A living legend. But he does have a reticence to overtake, indeed a lack of ability to do that.' – John Watson, 1984

'He kept his easygoing side well hidden. He was an unpopular world champion, but when he came back after his terrible accident, we had to respect him.' – Alan Jones, 1981

'I don't think I have any real friends in the sport.' – Lauda, 1984

'He had no right to be driving there because he was nowhere near healed. It was the most courageous thing I have ever witnessed in sport.' – Jackie Stewart on Lauda's comeback at Monza just six weeks after his near-fatal crash at the Nürburgring in 1976

'He's the best driver in the car and the best driver out of the car. He has a total commitment to what he's doing and – as long as the team is behind him – that means results. We provide the ingredients and Niki mixes the cake.' – McLaren's Ron Dennis, 1982

'It's been a season of stress and obsession. I've been under constant challenge and that's hard to take. I've never had it before from inside the same team.' – Lauda, pushed to the limit by his new McLaren team-mate Alain Prost, 1984

'He's had Prost so big in his eyes. I've been with Niki in a few corners and I've been given a very clear picture; either I move, or something's going to happen.' – Keke Rosberg on Lauda's renewed drive following the arrival of Prost in 1984, from *Niki Lauda* by Alan Henry (Hazleton, 1989)

'I've had fantastic relationships with John Watson, with Keke Rosberg, with Stefan Johansson and with Niki Lauda, but the only one who taught me something, who dominated his subject, was Lauda.' – Alain Prost

'There were times when he drove like a racer and there were other times when he didn't want to drive at all. I find that difficult to understand.' – Stirling Moss

Nigel Mansell

'It's no use denying it, the similarities are there. Even at this stage I instinctively know I've got a boy who is going to go all the way to the top. I can already feel he and I are developing the kind of relationship Jimmy and I shared.' – Lotus boss Colin Chapman comparing his new boy Mansell to Jim Clark, 1981

'What he did was unbecoming of a member of the same team.' – Lotus team-mate Elio de Angelis taking exception to Mansell's bullish approach to the 1984 United States Grand Prix at Dallas

'He'll never win a Grand Prix as long as I have a hole in my arse.' – Lotus team manager Peter Warr, 1984

'He's unfit to be a Formula 1 driver.' – Keke Rosberg, 1984

'He had created a lot of problems at Lotus and that's why I was a bit negative of him joining – well, not a bit, but very negative.' – Rosberg, learning that Mansell was to be his future team-mate at Williams, 1984

'The human being I can get along with; the professional person I'm not so sure about.' – Rosberg, 1984

'I couldn't understand what Frank Williams was up to when he took on Nigel. He used to go off and make mistakes. Then he won the Grand Prix of Europe at Brands Hatch and it was like turning a switch. All of a sudden he became a racing driver.' – Ken Tyrrell

'I am doing my best to stay serene. Just do my job and bring the car home.' – Mansell at Ferrari, 1990

'When the lights go green, he goes red!' – Frank Williams on Mansell's gritty determination, 1991

'The one thing you absolutely knew about Nigel is that he always gives 100 per cent when he is in the cockpit.' – Williams' technical director Patrick Head, 1992

'I don't know if Nigel is the only driver Senna hasn't psyched out but he's certainly one of them.' – Frank Williams

'I'm at peace with myself. The politics are gone. No one is trying to screw me.' – Mansell enjoying a temporary lull at Williams before open warfare broke out with Nelson Piquet, 1986

'I'll miss him as a driver, not as a bloke.' – Frank Williams as Mansell leaves for Ferrari, 1988

'People hang on his every word and he thinks he is a superstar. In fact, he is just a lot richer and a bit quicker than when he first joined us.' – Frank Williams following Mansell's return to the fold, 1992

'I don't think that being the new world champion and winning 26 races for the Williams team counts for anything these days. The team doing as well as it has with Riccardo [Patrese] has made everyone extremely happy, yet they have to destroy the good feeling. It is mind-boggling for any blue-chip company. They don't need to do that, but they have deemed to do that.' – Mansell on the impending split from Williams, 1992

'To say I have been badly treated is, I think, a gross understatement.' – Mansell announcing his decision to retire from Formula 1 after failing to reach agreement with Williams, 1992

'It was a matter of two hard-headed idiots who couldn't make a deal, couldn't communicate at the right time.' – Frank Williams perhaps admitting that he was partly to blame for the second split with Mansell at the end of 1992

'He has a very strong persecution complex, thinks that everybody is trying to shaft him at all times. On a day-to-day basis that became extremely wearing.' – Patrick Head, 1993

'No question – Nigel was a whinger. He was a difficult man. But he would never give up. On race day he was somebody you really had to look out for.' – Gerhard Berger

'Basically I am an old crock. I have broken my neck, my back twice, smashed toes, fractured wrists and a whole lot of other stuff. I feel like a man of 90 some days.' – 38-year-old Mansell, 1992

'I hate being weighed. I am always the heaviest. Somehow it's disheartening.' – Mansell citing the pre-race weigh-in as the worst part of the F1 weekend, 1991

'If some people want to believe I am overweight and unfit let them do so, because it is pathetic.' – Mansell, 1994

'He has burnt his boats with every team he has been involved with. I don't even know if he is fit enough for F1's rigours. He has all the money he needs, beautiful homes, a boat and a jet. It is time for him to make way for the new generation.' – Jackie Stewart, 1994

'Given the opportunity, the motivation, the encouragement, I can win another world title without batting an eye. I can beat Schumacher, I can beat anyone.' – Mansell pushing for a return to Formula 1, 1994

'Nigel went out of his way to be co-operative. It was a pleasure to have him around. Nothing was too much trouble for him. Of course, he tends to be rather different when he's got his feet under the table. If we take him next year, I know what's going to happen – it will be wall-to-wall aggravation between him and Damon.' – Frank Williams declining the option to extend Mansell's race contract into the 1995 season

Jochen Mass

'I think I have got to the stage where I really have to prove that I'm a bit more than a lazy sailing boy.' – Mass contemplating leaving McLaren, 1977

Bruce McLaren

'I thought Bruce would become world champion because he had the ability to think about it. He wasn't going to be the world's quickest driver, but then the world's quickest driver isn't always world champion.' – Ken Tyrrell on signing the 22-year-old New Zealander in 1959, from *McLaren: The Man and His Racing Team* by Eoin S. Young (Patrick Stephens Ltd, 1995)

'He drove well, damned hard, and I think hung it out a bit if he thought there was a good chance to win. On the other hand if he was running fifth or sixth he would set a reasonable pace for himself which I sometimes felt was below his limit, and wait to see what would happen.' – Former McLaren team manager Teddy Mayer, from *McLaren: The Man and His Racing Team*

'Bruce had the kind of technical know-how that can be of enormous help to mechanics before and during a race. It's an ability to communicate clearly with the pit crew and draw their attention to whatever may be wrong with the car. Not many drivers have this gift, but those who do usually turn out to be brilliant people in the race game.' – *John Cooper, from John Cooper: Carpetbagger* (Foulis, 1977)

'He had an amazing ability to learn quickly.' – John Cooper

Stirling Moss

'British people are all for the underdog and most of my career I was that – but an underdog with a chance of winning.' – Moss

'He was a better driver than anyone in motor racing at the time. Everything he did was absolutely at maximum – all the time. If the race lasted for 30 minutes, he concentrated on it at maximum for 30 minutes. If it was three hours, he blanked everything else out of his mind for three hours.' – Innes Ireland comparing Moss's total concentration at the wheel to his own somewhat more cavalier approach, from *All Arms and Elbows* (Pelham Books, 1967)

'He had an uncanny ability to get the best out of any motor car he stepped into. I am sure he got more out of the cars he drove than even the designer thought it possessed, or indeed intended it to possess. He could beat very good drivers, top-rank men, even with an inferior car. He would just out-drive them.' – Innes Ireland, from *All Arms and Elbows*

'Stirling was the man to beat in those days. He was easily the quickest driver around, and there was only one catch; he didn't really know how to save the car. While he was going he used to get the utmost out of the car, but it rarely got to the finishing line. If the car lasted he generally used to win.' – Jack Brabham, from *When the Flag Drops* (William Kimber, 1971)

'There ought to be someone who can build a car capable of taking all he can give it.' – Phil Hill, 1960

'I don't think I ever passed a driver in my life without thanking him or shaking my fist at him.' – Moss

'Stirling had no nervous signs whatsoever. The only time I thought he showed the slightest sign of nerves was in his first Formula 1 race after his crash at Spa. He went to the lavatory before the race.' – Team owner Rob Walker

'What Moss needed was to be in a team ruled by a firm manager. Rob Walker was far too easy-going to adopt the role of disciplinarian. It needed someone to tell the driver that his job was to drive and not pretend to be chief engineer or designer.' – Former BRM team patron Louis Stanley

'If Stirling Moss had put reason before passion, he would have been world champion. He was more than deserving of it.' – Enzo Ferrari on Moss's decision not to join a factory team

'Being the name of a chap who won the title a certain year is less important to me than being the chap who many say should have won it but never did – it gives me a sort of uniqueness.' – Moss

Luigi Musso

'He was too conscious of the fact that he was the only Italian driver of note; it made him try too hard. He felt that he must press on for the sake of national honour.' – Mike Hawthorn, from *Champion Year* (Aston Publications, 1959)

Carlos Pace

'If Pace had lived, I would not have needed Niki Lauda.' – Bernie Ecclestone, then boss at Brabham, paying tribute to the Brazilian driver killed in a flying accident in 1977

'He got a bit over-excited once in a while but he was one tough, mean character in the car – a bit like Alan Jones. And, like Jones, he was never designed to take physical exercise. A bit overweight perhaps, but one tough bastard in a car.' – Frank Williams

Riccardo Patrese

'Patrese is an idiot. There was no way through that gap – anyone could have seen that. But he goes for it, spins and causes the whole thing. Later I asked him what he was doing. Knowing him, I guess I was stupid to expect an apology. What I got was abuse. I'm through with trying to get along with him.' – An irate Eddie Cheever following a pile-up at the 1984 British Grand Prix

'You call Riccardo up, ask him to test at a moment's notice, and he'll say: fine, no problem, I'll be there. He's not a selfish man, which is quite rare as a driver. His ego is under control too...which is also quite rare.' – Williams' technical director Patrick Head, 1990

'I don't play politics and maybe that is one of my problems, because in Formula 1 sometimes you win with politics. I play my cards on the table, not under the table.' – Patrese, from *Designs On Victory: On the Grand Prix Trail With Benetton* by Derick Allsop (Stanley Paul, 1993)

Ronnie Peterson

'He was considered *the* talent, pure and simple. His ability to drive with cars that were handling badly was enormous. He had a quite special gift of driving flat out in all circumstances.' – Niki Lauda on Peterson's 1971 season in Formula 2, from *For the Record: My Years With Ferrari* (William Kimber, 1978)

'He's had fourteen accidents with us this year, and frankly we can't afford him. I only hope that Chapman has plenty of cars for him to use up.' – March boss Max Mosley as Peterson signs for Lotus, 1972

'We signed a contract for two seasons with him. I am confident that Ronnie will be world champion at the end of one of these two seasons.' – Colin Chapman, 1972

'Without doubt they were the most outstanding combination I ever had.' – Chapman on the Lotus teaming of Peterson and Mario Andretti for 1978

'I've made all my number one drivers world champions, and I'd have done the same for Ronnie if he'd been willing to wait.' – Chapman announcing in the summer of 1978 that Peterson would be leaving Lotus for 1979. A few weeks later, Peterson was killed at Monza

'Ronnie was every man's dream of a racer. He just breathed, walked and talked motor racing the whole time.' – Lotus team manager Peter Warr

'Even in the hard-bitten world of Formula 1 you would have been hard-pressed to find anyone who didn't like Ronnie Peterson.' – Journalist Alan Henry, 1978

Nelson Piquet

'I don't give a shit for fame, I don't give a shit for society. I don't want to make friends with anybody who is important.' – Piquet, 1989

'Nelson had an unbelievable natural talent but he didn't really have respect for other people, and this I never liked.' – Gerhard Berger

'I am consistent. It is very easy to do a good year and be world champion. Well, not easy, but not so difficult. If you are in Formula 1, you have the talent already. So if you have the right team and the right car, you win. To win three times, that means I am very, very consistent.' – Piquet, 1989

'You mean some 55-year-old washed-up Indy driver can blow you off the track?' – Disbelieving Brabham boss Bernie Ecclestone to his number one driver, Piquet, after the reborn Mario Andretti had snatched a surprise pole at the 1982 Italian Grand Prix

'The reason my relationship with Nelson Piquet is so profitable is that we speak the same language; we talk to each other through the machine. He is an instrument on which I play.' – Brabham chief designer Gordon Murray, 1983

'You wouldn't think he had a care in the world. He sleeps before a race, relaxes, and tells silly jokes all the time in shocking English.' – Frank Williams, 1986

'It was a masterstroke. In one move, he's screwed Williams, he's screwed Mansell, he's screwed Senna – and kept Honda.' – Williams team member on Piquet's decision to sign for Lotus before the 1987 Hungarian Grand Prix. In 1987 Mansell had been Piquet's team-mate at Williams while Senna was at Lotus. Senna swiftly departed for McLaren

'If I have a criticism of Nelson, it is communication. He will say, I want the car two millimetres lower, I want this changed, or that changed. He never says *why*.' – Lotus team manager Peter Warr, 1989

'A hell of a talented driver, a real natural and a very nice guy.' – John Watson, 1984

Didier Pironi

'There are one or two drivers who never give up. Pironi's one of them. You think you've lost him, you ease up, look in your mirror and there he is again.' – Alan Jones, 1980

Alfonso de Portago

'Every time he comes in from a race the front of his car is wrinkled where he has been nudging other cars out of the way at 130 mph.' – Fellow driver Ed Nelson on the gung-ho approach of the colourful Spanish nobleman. The pair were killed when Nelson acted as de Portago's co-driver in the 1957 Mille Miglia

Alain Prost

'Alain Prost is the only driver for whom I feel absolute veneration – both for the man and the driver.' – Fellow countryman Jean Alesi

'Alain has a great tactical brain and is brilliant at working with the car. I can learn so much from him on tactics and car set-ups. Speed, I know about. I was born with that.' – Alesi teaming up with Prost at Ferrari, 1991

'I don't think Senna developed as a driver until he drove with Prost. I am sure he learned a lot just by watching, keeping his eyes open, seeing how Prost worked with the car.' – Swedish driver Stefan Johansson, from *Alain Prost* by Christopher Hilton (Partridge Press, 1992)

'I thought I was the fastest driver in the world until I went to McLaren with Alain Prost.' – Keke Rosberg disappointed at his inability to keep up with Prost in 1986

'My God, usually he's only quickest on Sundays!' – Eddie Cheever as race maestro Prost excelled in testing at Imola, 1987

'He is the most complete driver there is. You could say that Senna is the fastest, but that is only one aspect of driving in F1. Alain's knowledge is phenomenal, in terms of setting up a car, motivating the pits, race tactics and psychology. Senna is the racer, but Prost is the racing driver.' – Stirling Moss, 1990

'There is no doubt in my mind that he is the best race driver of the generation.' – Jackie Stewart, 1987

'He is very sympathetic to his car. He allows it to survive where others may suffer some breakdown. He knows how to nurse cars, bully them, but never abuse them.' – Jackie Stewart, 1990

'The mark of his brilliance is that the faster he drives, the smoother he looks. You just cannot tell when he is on the limit.' – Frank Williams, 1993

'His concentration over a weekend is total and he barely spends a second without thinking what needs to be done, or what can be done, to win the race.' – Damon Hill, 1993

'He bites his fingernails so deeply that it must be very painful for him but he cannot stop it. He's just concentrating on his job all the time.' – Patrick Tambay, 1983

'The classic "I want this, I want that" man.' – John Watson, 1984

'If I am a whinger, so be it. That is better than being taken for an idiot.' – Prost responding to criticisms that he complained too much at McLaren, 1989

'It is obvious that Alain made a very clever tactical change on to dry tyres, but threw it away with a vastly premature change back to wets, and that was the end of the race. It surprised me that a driver of Alain's experience should make those mistakes, but he doesn't like the wet and he is cautious.' – Frank Williams criticising Prost after the 1993 European Grand Prix at Donington. Arguably their relationship never recovered and Prost announced his retirement at the end of the year

'He retired once to suit himself and he came back to suit himself. Now he has retired again and let's hope this time it is on a permanent basis. I think he must walk down the pit lane and think he sees a sign saying Public Convenience.' – F1 supremo Bernie Ecclestone shedding few tears over Prost's retirement, 1993

'I am disappointed that we got used by somebody. We do not want people who keep popping in and popping out all the time. He had been written off anyway. Nobody even asked him for autographs.' – Bernie Ecclestone wouldn't let it lie, 1993

Clay Regazzoni

'To the Italian public he was the original macho man, a no-holds-barred womaniser.' – Niki Lauda on his Ferrari team-mate

'A superb number two and a happy, uncomplicated man.' – Frank Williams

Carlos Reutemann

'When his head's in the right place, he's a fantastic driver.' – James Hunt, 1981

'Carlos had a problem. He lived in a kind of box. The box consisted of a few drivers and himself and inside that box, for some reason, there was always someone ahead of Carlos. "Oh," he'd say, "Hulme is quicker than I am. Emerson is quicker than I am. I think I am number four."' – Brabham designer Gordon Murray on Reutemann's inferiority complex, 1981

'He needed psychological support more than most drivers. He needed to be aware that everyone in the team was wearing a Reutemann lapel badge and an Argentine scarf.' – Frank Williams, from *Grand Prix Greats* by Nigel Roebuck (Patrick Stephens Ltd, 1986)

'He came up like an express train, like he was heading for Acapulco.' – Mario Andretti, stunned by Reutemann's charge into the first corner at the 1977 United States West Grand Prix at Long Beach, a move that caused a collision which took out Hunt, Peterson and Mass

Peter Revson

'It was all there, but was he ever temperamental! The slightest thing and he would go up like a balloon!' – Former Vanwall team manager David Yorke who ran a sports car team in the United States for which Revson drove

Jochen Rindt

'What am I going to do with this bloke? He has lightning reflexes, is bloody quick, but keeps telling me how to design my cars.' – Colin Chapman, 1970

'I followed in fear and trepidation because I thought, "Any minute now I'll be running over pieces of debris."' – Jackie Stewart recalling Rindt's hairy reputation during a Formula 2 race at Pau

'As I driver I thought Jochen was the sort of person who tended to drive at ten-tenths most of the time. Not that I was worried about him from the point of view of flying off the road. But he was always driving that near the edge that something was liable to happen to him through no real fault of his own.' – Jack Brabham

'He drove so hard and put his car through so much there was always a chance that one day he wouldn't be able to put it all back together again.' – Graham Hill following Rindt's death at Monza in 1970

Pedro Rodriguez

'If anybody offered him a wheelbarrow to race, he would go and race it. He was just a racer all the way.' – Jo Ramirez

'In common with most drivers from tropical countries, Pedro did not understand that wet roads were slippery and dangerous and that you should slow down.' – BRM chief engineer Tony Rudd

Keke Rosberg

'Long blond hair, Gucci briefcase, Rolex gold identity bracelet...Frank, I think he is very quick.' – Carlos Reutemann asked by Frank Williams what he thought of Rosberg, his new team-mate for 1982

'An aggressive driver, highly talented and a modern-style businessman who wheels and deals tremendously hard and competitively.' – John Watson, 1984

'He is still a little over-aggressive; he still has trouble restraining his exuberance, his flair, his tendency to drive around problems rather than eliminating them.' – Jackie Stewart, from *Jackie Stewart's Principles of Performance Driving* (Hazleton Publishing, 1986)

'He had charisma. He'd be drinking schnapps or smoking cigarettes, but he'd also do a race distance at a street circuit in boiling-hot temperatures and not collapse.' – Gerhard Berger

Jody Scheckter

'Jody has probably got the greatest innate talent we shall ever see in motor racing.' – Jackie Stewart, 1974

'The first time I really appreciated that I'd won the world championship was when I got home to Monaco a few days after Monza. I found that my laundry was returned in two days rather than four!' – Scheckter, 1979

'Jody was always extremely combative. He had incredible car control – pure, natural, undiluted talent.' – John Watson

'Temperamental, argumentative, sulky at times...he was outspoken but at the same time had a charming touch of innocence and a shy sense of humour.' – Professor Sid Watkins, Formula 1's chief medic, from *Life at the Limit: Triumph and Tragedy in Formula 1* (Macmillan, 1996)

'At the beginning I thought I was the fastest driver in the world. At the end I thought I was the cleverest driver.' – Scheckter

Harry Schell

'He wasn't really as good a driver as he could have been. Every year people would write him off, then at the very last race old Harry would pull out all the stops and turn in a remarkably good performance as if to say, "Look, I can be this good, and next year I will be!" Someone would then sign him up, but always he would slip back.' – Stirling Moss, from *Racing and All That* by Stirling Moss and Mike Hailwood (Pelham Books, 1980)

'When the flag comes down you let in the clutch and go. Unless you are Harry Schell, in which case you let in the clutch and go about three seconds before anybody else.' – Stirling Moss

Michael Schumacher

'The thinking man's racing driver.' – Murray Walker

'I realised he was an exceptional talent and that there was no point in blowing my brains out over it.' – Martin Brundle accepting that he would have to play second fiddle to Schumacher at Benetton in 1992, from *Michael Schumacher: Defending the Crown* by Christopher Hilton (Patrick Stephens Ltd, 1995)

'Age for age, experience for experience, he is the best Grand Prix driver I have ever seen.' – Jackie Stewart, 1997

'In the wet, in the dry, he believes he's the best. We all think we are, but Michael *knows* it.' – Johnny Herbert, 1999

'I don't want to be treated as special because I'm not. I just drive a racing car round in circles a bit faster than anyone else.' – Schumacher trying his hardest to sound modest, from *Ferrari: The Passion and the Pain* by Jane Nottage (CollinsWillow, 1998)

'He wins races he shouldn't and, more importantly, doesn't lose races he shouldn't.' – Ferrari's technical director Ross Brawn, 1997

'Overtaking back markers is something Schumacher does very well. When he comes up to them, people acquiesce more than they do for others.' – Frank Williams, 1996

'Perhaps I was too successful too early. I had no time to learn.' – Schumacher, 1997

'Sometimes the way people talk, you would think I have had a picture of Michael up on my wall to throw darts at in the years since we last raced.' – Heinz-Harald Frentzen, Schumacher's old adversary in Formula 3, 1997

'No, we are not friends and I'm sick of Michael trying to claim we are.' – Jacques Villeneuve after Schumacher had told the media that he and Villeneuve had enjoyed a few drinks and were pals despite their controversial collision at Jerez in 1997

'The most selfish driver I have ever worked with. He was happy enough to choose me as a partner, but when he realised I could drive quickly our friendship changed. He saw me as a threat and he didn't like it.' – Johnny Herbert on his Benetton team-mate, 1995

'Michael Schumacher gives the impression that he races for the love of it but he is the biggest money-grabber of the lot. He is obsessed with cash and it still grieves him that he had to pay us £150,000 for his first drive while his brother came straight in as a paid racer. We gave Michael his first break. We took him from sports cars when no one else would take a chance. But after one race, he left us in the lurch because he was offered a better deal by Benetton.' – Eddie Jordan, 1998

'Schumacher is spitting in the plate he eats from.' – Goodyear's Italian chief Antonio Corsi following Schumacher's criticism of the tyres, 1998

'He makes quite a lot of small mistakes, but that is because he is fighting a car at the limit more often than everybody else. He really is flat out all the time – into the pits, out of the pits, giving it everything.' – Alain Prost, 1998

'I make mistakes and I do not think mistakes are wrong. But Michael is a person who does not like anyone to make mistakes.' – Heinz-Harald Frentzen, 1994

'He has a serious relaxation problem – he doesn't know how to do it.' – Eddie Irvine, 1996

'There has never been anyone so head and shoulders above the rest like Michael, but it's not because the rest of us are crap, it's because he's so unbelievably quick.' – Eddie Irvine, 1999

'The worst bit about Michael is that he gains on you everywhere. He exerts this constant pressure. He's on the knife edge all the time. Keke Rosberg says Michael makes too many mistakes. But look at how fast he's going – are you surprised?' – Eddie Irvine, 1999

'He's the fastest. With equal cars, no one can beat him, but speed is not enough. You need to avoid mistakes and he makes a lot. Too many.' – Eddie Irvine changing tack to put the boot into his incapacitated team-mate before the 1999 Hungarian Grand Prix

'Michael is not only the best number one, but the best number two.' – Eddie Irvine after Schumacher, in a supporting role on his comeback from injury, had helped Irvine to victory at the controversial 1999 Malaysian Grand Prix

'We are just really good friends. We hang out, play sports, train in the gym and usually talk about everything except motor racing.' – Ralf Schumacher dismissing rumours of brotherly rivalry, 1999

'Michael would remain a formidable challenge if he was driving a pram.' – Frank Williams as Schumacher tried to concede the world championship to Damon Hill after the 1996 Canadian Grand Prix

Ralf Schumacher

'I thought the world could only bear one Schumacher. Now we have two!' – Damon Hill learning that Michael's brother Ralf would be joining F1 in 1997

'This guy does not realise he must give others some room. What he did was pointless and unacceptable. It shows he is just a novice with no experience of racing at high speed.' – An irate Johnny Herbert after being pushed off the track by Ralf Schumacher at the 1997 Italian Grand Prix

'Ralf has tremendous potential; he's incredibly quick. He just needs to come at it with a bit more patience.' – Jordan technical director Gary Anderson, 1997

'Ralf has tended to become too flustered on the starting grid, and we worked on relaxing. The five seconds before the lights go out can seem like a lifetime and it's important not to get psyched up until the last two.' – Gary Anderson, 1998

'For his current performance, Ralf is too expensive.' – Eddie Jordan, 1998

'It is fairly difficult to be his friend as he is a very competitive person.' – Alex Zanardi trying to get closer to his Williams team-mate on and off the track, 1999

Ayrton Senna

'He was a fantastic driver, but he had an immense number of collisions. And they could not all have been everybody else's fault.' – Jackie Stewart, 1998

'Senna is a genius. I define genius as just the right side of imbalance. He is highly developed to the point where he is almost over the edge. It's a close call.' – Martin Brundle, from *Ayrton Senna: The Second Coming* by Christopher Hilton (Patrick Stephens Ltd, 1994)

'He's an enigma, he's not something that anybody is going to handle or understand.' – Toleman's Alex Hawkridge, Senna's first F1 boss

'I could never be just another Formula 1 driver.' – Senna

'Once in a blue moon, someone comes along who is simply

special. I don't know how you define it; it's just something you know. I saw him in '81 in Formula Ford and I thought, "The rest are going to have to watch out for this one."' – Lotus team manager Peter Warr, 1985

'Perhaps one way you can tell a real champion is that his mind is never off it. Other drivers will come in when a light goes on in the cockpit, but Ayrton will work out how to beat whatever trouble he's in. He'll persist. He works at his job.' – Peter Warr, 1985

'I've never seen Prost sweat in a race and Ayrton doesn't sweat much. The racing comes so naturally to them.' – McLaren team co-ordinator Jo Ramirez, from *Ayrton Senna: The Second Coming*

'I'm sorry, I'm nearly 37 and I don't have the balls to bang wheels at 170 mph. What I need is a month in Formula 3, I guess, to learn how to race him.' – Keke Rosberg after locking horns with Senna at the 1985 European Grand Prix at Brands Hatch

'The more I win, the more I want it.' – Senna, 1991

'Somebody said you need two lives – one to make mistakes in, the other to enjoy. I feel I could do with three or four.' – Senna, 1993

'The shame is that he is such a good driver he doesn't need to do that.' – Michele Alboreto criticising Senna for weaving on the straights at Hockenheim, 1987

'He is a madman.' – Michele Alboreto

'Senna missed a gear, and when I got alongside him he just drove me off the road.' – Andrea de Cesaris blowing his top after the 1987 Mexican Grand Prix

'He was slowing down and speeding up. If he had a problem he should have got out of the way. I don't know what game he was playing but it was not a game I like. He is the world champion and he should behave better.' – New boy Michael Schumacher having a go at Senna after the 1992 Brazilian Grand Prix

'I was a bit angry. He turned left, which wasn't necessary. I went wide and nearly on to the grass, otherwise I would have hit him. It was not a very nice thing to do.' – Michael Schumacher after Senna's exit from the pit lane forced Schumacher's Benetton wide at the 1993 Belgian Grand Prix

'The era of one driver saying "After you, Claude" is long gone and that is as much due to Senna as anybody else. He started being very aggressive and everybody else has copied him.' – Damon Hill after Senna accused Eddie Irvine of driving recklessly at the 1993 Japanese Grand Prix. To Senna's fury, Irvine, in his first Grand Prix, had the nerve to unlap himself at the Brazilian's expense. The incident ended with Senna thumping Irvine in the face

'I told him that I was driving the way I had learned from watching him. I don't think there was much he could say about that.' – Damon Hill after Senna complained that Hill had got in his way during the 1993 San Marino Grand Prix

'I will drive for 23 million dollars less than the retainer Mansell is demanding.' – Senna cheekily offering his services to Williams for free during their protracted dispute with Nigel Mansell, 1992

'His financial demands were excessive. Our friendship was very deep. That made it difficult for us to go in different directions, but it was time for us to have a trial separation. We were hurting each other too much.' – McLaren team boss Ron Dennis on seeing Senna join Williams for 1994

'Ayrton and I fought a lot, argued even more and at times even ignored each other. This is because we were both consumed by the same will to win and to do so fairly. Out of our shared passion grew mutual respect.' – Ron Dennis

'People in the outside world don't know me and make assumptions – wrong assumptions.' – Senna

'What do you think he's going to do, put me in a Vulcan mind grip?' – Damon Hill to journalists when asked about Senna's liking for employing psychology on team-mates, 1994

'He taught me a lot about racing. I taught him how to laugh.' – Gerhard Berger in the wake of Senna's death at Imola, 1994

'Ayrton's driving style didn't exist. He didn't really have one. When it was time for qualifying, he tailored his driving style to the problems of his car. And he'd put it on pole.' – Gerhard Berger

'Ayrton wasn't a saint. He was in the business to win, and he was pretty ruthless.' – Damon Hill, 1995

'He was no ordinary person. He was very clever, shrewd, focused, tough – all the things I admired. He was actually a greater man out of the car than in it.' – Frank Williams, from *Williams: Triumph Out Of Tragedy* by Alan Henry (Patrick Stephens Ltd, 1995)

'The only driver I respected . . . with his death, half my career has gone.' – Old enemy Alain Prost, 1994

'When Ayrton lost his life, it was like losing your own child.' – Ron Dennis, 1994

Johnny Servoz-Gavin

'When he gave a big party to celebrate his non-qualification I should have realised that something was up.' – Ken Tyrrell on the charismatic young French driver who failed to qualify at Monaco in 1970 and retired from motor racing shortly afterwards

Jo Siffert

'He was a real charger who drove purely by the seat of his pants.' – Derek Bell summing up the dashing Swiss driver of the 1960s

Mike Spence

'He tries very hard, but it seems to get him nowhere, rather like watching a first-rate squash player hammering away at a court without walls.' – Louis T. Stanley on the young Briton who drove for Lotus, 1966

Alan Stacey

'He got a great deal of fun out of that leg. Many a chambermaid had run from his room at the sight of an apparently dismembered leg hanging over a chair, complete with shoe and sock.' – Innes Ireland on Lotus team-mate Stacey who drove with a tin leg, from *All Arms and Elbows* (Pelham Books, 1967)

Jackie Stewart

'Given reasonable luck, Stewart's driving will ripen into a masterpiece – not of the superficial kind, but the real thing, a structure of rare natural skill and cool judgement.' – Louis T. Stanley, boss of BRM who gave Stewart his chance in F1, 1965

'At the moment he has more verve than Clark, more natural skill than Surtees, and more youth than Graham Hill or Brabham: he is, in short, the best *jeune premier* in Formula 1 racing.' – Louis T. Stanley after Stewart's second season in F1, 1966

'"Don't make any mistakes" is his theme song. According to Jackie one should not try to go too fast – good times will come naturally when there are no mistakes and the car is well set up.' – François Cevert, 1973

'Jackie was the first of the modern-style drivers – a man who drove fast enough to win, but at the slowest possible speed.' – Stirling Moss

'On one occasion we found a small fuel leak in the tank breather on the start-line at Monza. I told him we could not fix it in time, but that it should clear up after two or three laps when the fuel level dropped; but it was up to him. He just shrugged his shoulders, got in the car and got on with it. It was this quality, in particular, that to my mind set him above Jimmy Clark ... The prime difference was when things were not quite right, such as a wet Nürburgring: Jimmy would hold back a little – there was always another day and another race – but Jackie would give every race his maximum effort.' – BRM chief engineer Tony Rudd, from *It Was Fun!* (Patrick Stephens Ltd, 1993)

'The outstanding driver of his day.' – James Hunt

John Surtees

'I was a bit nuts, really.' – Surtees reflecting on his life of speed, two wheels and four, 1996

'I sparked off some quite prickly feelings among some members of the Grand Prix fraternity. Not from people like Stirling, on the whole, but from the likes of Jo Bonnier who did not seem particularly receptive to a young man coming straight into Formula 1 and going faster than them after only a handful of races.' – John Surtees, from *John Surtees: World Champion* (Hazleton Publishing, 1991)

'He had a really hard time breaking into the car world. I think many of the established stars of Formula 1 resented someone coming in from what they felt was an inferior sport and showing them the way.' – Fellow biker-turned-F1 driver Mike Hailwood, 1980

'That stark take-it-or-leave-it glare has not mellowed. It is an instinct, not a pose.' – Louis T. Stanley, 1966

Tora Takagi

'Tora is very quick over a single lap but he lacks consistency over a race distance.' – Arrows boss Tom Walkinshaw, 1999

Wolfgang von Trips

'He knew what spark plugs were and that was about the end of it.' – Phil Hill on the lack of mechanical expertise of his Ferrari team-mate, from *Grand Prix Showdown* by Christopher Hilton (Patrick Stephens Ltd, 1992)

Jarno Trulli

'Trulli's often been almost a second slower than Nakano. So why does everybody think he's bloody good? I don't know!' – Mika Salo, 1997

'He's been known to throw his toys out of the pram from time to time.' – ITV pundit Tony Jardine, 1999

Gilles Villeneuve

'Everything in Gilles's life moved at 200 mph, whether it was driving, playing Monopoly, flying helicopters or spending!' – Patrick Tambay

'When they presented me with this tiny Canadian, this minuscule bundle of nerves, I instantly recognised in him the physique of the great Nuvolari. I said to myself, "Let's give him a try."' – Enzo Ferrari

'I reckoned I was as quick as anyone at that time and I couldn't get near him.' – James Hunt's first glimpse of Villeneuve in 1976

'He is a genuine speed freak and he drives with enormous aggression and flair, but he seems unable to combine that with common sense.' – James Hunt, 1981

'The man who never knew fear.' – Didier Pironi

'He indulged in some of the most hair-raising acrobatics I have ever seen. Transmissions, gear-boxes, differentials, drive-shafts – all were subjected to the utmost punishment. Gilles was the high priest of destruction.' – Enzo Ferrari

'Gilles is good, very good, but I see things in his driving that I used to do when I was younger. He regularly drops wheels into the dirt, but I try to keep the car off the kerbs.' – Jody Scheckter, 1979

'He's not like the rest of us. He's on a separate level.' – Jacques Laffite, 1979

'I had never seen Gilles angry like that...he was stunned. There had always been this innocence about Gilles. He didn't have a trace of maliciousness in him and he couldn't quite believe what had happened to him. It was awful that the last days of his life were so tormented and disillusioned.' – Jackie Stewart, 1982. Villeneuve had been robbed of that year's San Marino Grand Prix when his Ferrari team-mate Didier Pironi stole victory from him on the last lap. Villeneuve was still seething two weeks later when he crashed fatally during practice for the Belgian Grand Prix at Zolder

'He'd never deliberately block you. If he thought you'd won the corner, he'd give you room – maybe only a foot more than you needed, but never a foot less – and consequently I'd do the same for him. A totally honourable racing driver.' – Alan Jones, 1982

'Gilles was the hardest bastard I ever raced against, but completely fair.' – Keke Rosberg, from *Gilles Villeneuve* by Nigel Roebuck (Hazleton Publishing, 1990)

'You can only race like that with someone you trust completely. He beat me but it didn't worry me – I knew I'd been beaten by the best driver in the world.' – René Arnoux after his epic duel with Villeneuve at the 1979 French Grand Prix

'He was one of our type – the people who race because we love racing.' – Stirling Moss

'He never gave up. If it had been Piquet or Reutemann, that would have been the end of it, but it was Gilles. He was without doubt the best driver I ever raced against.' – Alan Jones recalling Villeneuve's superb drive to take second place at the 1979 Canadian Grand Prix

'He had the best talent of all of us. In any car he was quick.' – Niki Lauda, 1982

'He could only drive one way and that was flat out.' – John Watson

'Gilles had an extraordinary inbred flair for outstanding car control but his whole mental attitude caused him to over-drive too often during his career. If he had tried a little less, he might have achieved a great deal more.' – Jackie Stewart, from *Jackie Stewart's Principles of Performance Driving* (Hazleton Publishing, 1986)

'Fantastic driver though he was, he was not necessarily a champion in the making. First or nothing is not the attitude of a champion.' – Keke Rosberg, 1984

'Winning races was everything to him, but he didn't care that much about titles. For him, the important thing was to *know* his car could not have been driven faster.' – Jody Scheckter, from *Gilles Villeneuve* by Nigel Roebuck (Hazleton Publishing, 1990)

'Gilles has gone, and with him the light of genius in Grand Prix racing.' – Journalist Nigel Roebuck, 1982

'No human being can do a miracle, but Gilles made you wonder.' – Jacques Laffite

Jacques Villeneuve

'When most drivers start racing, nobody knows who they are until they make a name for themselves. But when you start racing with a name like mine, everybody knows who you are and expects you to succeed.' – Jacques Villeneuve, son of Gilles, 1996

'He is the only one who can give Schumacher some stick. He is like Senna as a person and Prost as a driver.' – Bernie Ecclestone building up the new boy, 1996

'We took a stab in the dark with Jacques but it paid off. I do like to see the car have its neck wrung and he certainly does that.' – Williams technical director Patrick Head happy with the team's latest recruit, 1996

'He is young and quick and he's taken to Formula 1 like a duck to water. I'm certain that he's a future world champion.' – Damon Hill, 1996

'He's mentally very strong, very confident, very aggressive. He is very tough, a good little racer.' – Eddie Irvine, 1996. Within twelve months Irvine was being less complimentary about the Canadian

'It wasn't my fault. I know that Jacques must be under a lot of pressure, but I think I was a good excuse for him. I am an easy target. As a driver, Jacques is quick but as a person I have no time for him.' – Ricardo Rosset replying to Villeneuve's assertion that Rosset shouldn't be in F1 after the two collided during practice for the 1998 Monaco Grand Prix

'The man is a millionaire but always looks like an unmade bed.' – Melbourne's *Herald Sun* newspaper, 1998

'It's all the same to me whether he has violet hair or is bald or wears a nose ring. The main point is that he is fast.' – BAR team chief Craig Pollock, 1998

Derek Warwick

'It hacks me off when Nigel gets all the headlines for not finishing and I get a passing mention for finishing fourth.' – Warwick living in the shadow of Mansell as far as the British press were concerned, 1988

'I can remember finishing fourth at Imola in the Renault and nearly strangling the whole team, I was so disappointed. But after the last three years, a fourth would be like a win.' – Warwick looking for an improvement in his fortunes, 1988

John Watson

'I think too much about my problems. I tend to analyse too deeply. Others go to the root of a problem – I get affected by the foliage.' – Watson, 1981

'I am the least macho racing driver.' – Watson, 1982

Chapter Two

The Best Job in the World

'It can be the world's most exhilarating sport, but it can also be the most cruel.' – Jackie Stewart, 1974

'When driving a racing car, I became another person. I forgot everything. I was in a different world, with only the car and the race.' – Juan Manuel Fangio

'Like my father, like all those who embrace this career, I only obey my instinct. Without it, I would not know how to live, I would not succeed in making any sense of my days.' – Alberto Ascari

'I'm not racing because my father left too early and I have to carry the name and the tradition. I don't really care about tradition. I'm racing because I have fun and I enjoy it.' – Jacques Villeneuve on the legacy of father Gilles, 1996

'I live in a closed world, but the profession of driver is the only one for which I am suited and for which I have fought.' – Elio de Angelis, 1985

'I figure I was put on this earth to drive race cars.' – Mario Andretti

'Race driving can be an addiction, so that one needs it like morphine, and one can't give up.' – Peter Collins, 1958

'Motor racing is infectious, like a disease that creeps through you with such a strength that you're in a coma and won't let go.' – Jackie Stewart

'It's like taming a wild beast. If you're good at the game, then you control the beast.' – John Watson with too much horsepower, 1981

'Grand Prix racing is like balancing an egg on a spoon while shooting the rapids.' – Graham Hill

'It is a chess game played at 180 mph, only each piece has a mind of its own.' – James Hunt, 1989

'The noise is constant and tremendous – like a woman's knitting club.' – Keke Rosberg

'I can't learn to play tennis well. You can only do one thing well in life. This is all I care about. I don't have the time or the inclination to be interested in anything else.' – Keke Rosberg, single-minded about motor racing, 1982

'The most beautiful moment is the moment when the light turns red. Everything in me is programmed, then everything is discharged, bang, bang, bang, the tension, the waiting for hours, minutes, it all disappears.' – *Ayrton Senna, from Ayrton Senna: The Hard Edge of Genius* by Christopher Hilton (Corgi, 1997)

'The start of a race is a totally unreal moment. It is like a dream, like entering another world.' – Ayrton Senna

'The most nervous time for me is two minutes before the start. You're sat there in the car with a little bit of a wobble going, invariably wanting a pee, and wishing you'd had one ten, and not fifteen, minutes ago.' – Derek Warwick

'The wonderful thing about being a Grand Prix driver is that you are presented sixteen times in a season with a challenge that you can focus on, and it's something that's never more than a fortnight away. It's a tangible goal each time and it's very appealing to live like that. The trouble is your life goes up and down each time!' – Damon Hill, 1995

'When you've been out there and had a good thrash, you feel better.' – Damon Hill, 1999

'I never raced for fun, although it was fun to race.' – Stirling Moss

'People think that to be a racing driver you need to be brave. This isn't true. There are occasions you have to call upon bravery, but the main requisite for being a racing driver is not bravery because bravery is too close to stupidity.' – Stirling Moss, 1969

'We are all racers, we love our activity, we take chances, we take risks, we go through pain, we sacrifice lots of things in life just to be in position one.' – Ayrton Senna, 1992

'I run all the time at the limit. I like to run at the limit, to push things as far as I can. I am the same at everything. If I decide to do something, I give it everything. All the time.' – Patrick Depailler, 1978. He was killed while testing at Hockenheim in 1980

'Just driving fast is a thrilling experience, for you feel every nerve, muscle and fibre of your body is alive and alert, ready to react to the slightest movement of the car, to make it do exactly what you want it to do. There is the thrill of being on the limit of the capability of the car and yourself, knowing that you can get round a corner just so fast but no faster.' – Innes Ireland, from *All Arms and Elbows* (Pelham Books, 1967)

'I love this sport because I like being on the edge. I like speed – speed when you feel the limits and when, if you go over the limit, you're going to crash.' – Jacques Villeneuve, 1995

'When you are riding on that edge you are in a different world. Nothing else exists at all.' – Jacques Villeneuve, 1997

'I love driving and I enjoy being recognised as a spectacular driver. In football, you have Paul Gascoigne who loves to play and doesn't seem to be happy doing anything else. It is like that for me. Racing makes me happy.' – Jean Alesi, 1996

'It is like tying both ends of your tie so that they are exactly the same length. Experience tells you that you can do it, practice tells you that you can do it, but you can't.' – Ayrton Senna contemplating the mystique of the perfect lap, from *Ayrton Senna: The Hard Edge of Genius* by Christopher Hilton (Corgi, 1997)

'Making a driver error probably stays longer with me than a win, because you have to remember a mistake to be able to learn from it.' – Jacques Villeneuve, from *Villeneuve: My First Season in Formula 1* (CollinsWillow, 1996)

'It is my expression of art to drive a car perfectly on a circuit, to be in complete control.' – Jochen Rindt, 1970

'A racing driver is an artist, and driving is an expression of myself. It is not a job, but a definition of who I am.' – John Watson, 1981

'Like painters, we racing drivers have an artistic inclination and are individualists. Our task is to have a free head, come to the race and do more than normal people can manage. If you haven't got a clear head, you can't give of your best.' – Niki Lauda eschewing outside distractions, 1977

'Driving well is all about confidence. With it you can do anything, without it you are nothing.' – Alan Jones, 1980

'You always see gaps in racing. The trick is to make sure they are wider than your car.' – Mario Andretti

'The most immediate and most dangerous competitor in Formula 1 is your own team-mate.' – Alain Prost, 1988

'I think motor racing is very much like boxing. You end up with two people out there, focusing on trying to beat each other. It's usually your team-mate because your team-mate is always the first man you've got to beat.' – Damon Hill, 1995

'Damon tends to be quite evasive. I find that normal. Why should he reveal his secrets to me? I would not reveal mine to him and I certainly have more to learn from him than he does from me. Even if I needed his help, he probably wouldn't give it. That's not what he's paid for. He is paid to win. Me too.' – Jacques Villeneuve on his working relationship with Williams team-mate Damon Hill, 1996

'Half the trick in racing is knowing how to mess up the other guy. You have to know the safe ways of doing it, but basically you have to intimidate him, harass him.' – Mario Andretti, from *Grand Prix Greats* by Nigel Roebuck (Patrick Stephens Ltd, 1986)

'You do not need to hate someone on the track. The best battles happen when there is no hate. All you will be thinking about is destroying the other guy instead of thinking about what you should be doing. You waste a lot of energy doing that.' – Jacques Villeneuve, 1996

'I'm not there to beat a guy off the track. I'm there to beat him on it.' – Jacques Villeneuve, 1997

'Formula 1 is a very unfriendly environment. Certainly you find some hostility in qualifying, things get heated, you have rivalries that go on all the time between certain drivers. If you screw somebody's lap they're going to get you, screw you on one of your quick laps.' – Johnny Dumfries, from *Gerhard Berger* by Christopher Hilton (Patrick Stephens Ltd, 1993)

'There's very little morality in Formula 1 and there are no prisoners taken.' – Nigel Mansell, 1990

'I don't think there is very much respect in this business. When I came into Formula 1 in '78, it was something where the top people in the sport were battling it out in Grands Prix – the top of the tree – and the behaviour was to that standard. Now it seems it's kids coming straight in from Formula 3 and bringing Formula 3 behaviour with them.' – Keke Rosberg, 1984

'So much happens in Formula 1 that it is often better to look away and think about real life.' – Mika Hakkinen, 1998

'There's nothing natural about Formula 1. I can't stand the artificiality.' – Alain Prost, 1984

'I never believe anything in Formula 1.' – Benetton boss Flavio Briatore, 1996

'When you climb the steep hill of fame, difficulties and misunderstandings begin.' – Ayrton Senna contemplating his unpopularity with some of his fellow drivers, 1990

'It's not up to me to make people outside the team like me. My job is to be as competitive as I can within the rules and to do what is best for the team. Being a nice guy is not part of that.' – Ayrton Senna, 1986

'It's no good to be nice, to take it easy. You might as well do something else or stay at home. Being in a competitive environment, and a very tough one, you have to be tough. You have to be hard, sometimes you can be a little too hard, but better to be on the harder side than on the easy one.' – Ayrton Senna, 1993

'I am in the fortunate position that I can make my own choices. Some lead to problems. But at least you are your own man and you can follow a steady direction. If you don't do that, you become a nobody, you get sucked in by the team and you are not yourself.' – Ayrton Senna, 1991

'For anybody to survive and be successful in modern Formula 1, you have to be a leader. I am a leader.' – Ayrton Senna, 1991

'You keep your emotions under lock and key. When the race stops or I've retired from the race, as soon as I get out of the car the pent-up emotions are ready to leap out. In the car they're kept under control. I think it's a normal and human way to behave, and if it upsets anyone, that's unfortunate.' – James Hunt, 1976

'Don't go near a racing driver for at least five minutes after he's out of a race. You pump yourself up for a Grand Prix weekend and all that aggression should go into the race. If it doesn't, it's got to go somewhere.' – Damon Hill, 1999

'When I was at McLaren, Teddy Mayer used to say to me, "I don't think you'll make it. You're not hard enough. You're too nice a guy." But I don't think it's necessary to be a bastard through your life to succeed.' – Patrick Tambay, 1982

'Show me a good loser and I'll show you a loser. Period.' – Keke Rosberg

'They're attracted by fast cars, which have always been considered sexy. But most of all I think it's because racing drivers are nasty. Women always prefer nasty men. You have to be nasty to be competitive. Of course, I actively try not to be a bastard, but I probably am.' – James Hunt on why he attracts so many female fans, 1974

'Formula 1 is tough. Out of 30 drivers, only six or seven are tops: and I am one of them. But we are not normal people. We are in an environment where we are constantly being told that we are the best, the most handsome, that we deserve the most money, the most beautiful girls and so on.' – Jean Alesi, 1990

'It's a sport for big egos.' – Niki Lauda, 1984

'There's a lot of people in Formula 1 who are complete arseholes.' – Derek Warwick, from *Grand Prix People* by Gerald Donaldson (MRP, 1990)

'There is no trickery and no fraud, whatever people think. Sure, there are sharks, but in Formula 1 they swim out in the open.' – Alain Prost, 1985

'If you're never over eight-tenths, or whatever, because you're thinking about a shunt, you're not going as quick as you can. And if you're not doing that, you're not a racing driver. Some of the guys in Formula 1 – to me, they're not racing drivers. They drive racing cars, that's all. They're doing half a job. And in that case, I can't figure why they do it at all.' – Gilles Villeneuve, starting out on his F1 career, 1978

'You know your limits and you try to keep within them, but on the other hand you must always try to push the limit a bit further.' – Ronnie Peterson, 1973

'If you're happy to be second, to stay in just because the money is good, better you should stop racing.' – Nelson Piquet, 1987

'Driving an F1 car is painful. For me it is sheer physical strain. I can think of no other sport in the world which is so punishing. But I love to push myself to the extreme. I love to see how far I can push my body, how much it will take.' – Keke Rosberg, from *Keke* by Keke Rosberg and Keith Botsford (Stanley Paul, 1985)

'Many times, I find myself in a comfortable position and I don't feel happy about it. I feel it is right to slow down, but something inside of me, something very strong, pushes me on, makes me try to beat myself.' – Ayrton Senna, 1989

'The harder I push, the more I find within myself. I am always looking for the next step, a different world to go into, areas where I have not been before. It's lonely driving a Grand Prix car, but very absorbing. I have experienced new sensations and I want more. That is my excitement, my motivation.' – Ayrton Senna, 1990

'When everything is smooth, I get bored.' – Alain Prost, 1984

'I'm best when I'm angry. I don't like easy drives.' – James Hunt, 1977

'My father would ask me why I did things the hard way. The answer is, difficulty sharpens desire.' – Elio de Angelis, 1985

'Qualifying is the peak of the driving experience because you rarely reach that level of commitment during a race.' – Damon Hill, 1994

'My principle of racing was always, "I would rather lose a race driving fast enough to win it than win one driving slow enough to lose it."' – Stirling Moss

'The really good drivers win races in the slowest times, not the quickest.' – Alan Jones

'The best drivers are those with the most finesse. If you have two drivers with nearly identical machines, you don't judge them by races won, or laps won, or fast laps, but by how they use up brake and fuel and rubber. You judge sheer talent by seeing how two men interpret the same machine to achieve the same end.' – Jackie Stewart, 1983

'In my view, the real sportsman is one who regards racing not as a means to an end, but as an end in itself. It is not the easy victory, it is worthwhile results that count – doing the best with the car at your disposal. It is not the title that makes the champion, but what he has got in him.' – Italian driver Piero Taruffi, from *The Technique of Motor Racing* (Motor Racing Publications, 1959)

'Races are won not merely by going fast, but often by nursing one's strength and saving one's car better than the opposition.' – Piero Taruffi, 1958

'Races are not won and lost on the first lap. They are won by consistent and coherent driving and by the careful conservation of resources.' – Alan Jones, 1981

'You come in with this youthful exuberance, driving by the seat of your pants, and it seems the easiest thing to do at the time, harnessing all that inherent talent. But you cannot maintain that flow of adrenalin through the system to keep up that kind of performance. You can't keep putting in Oscar-winning performances in every picture!' – Jackie Stewart, from *Jackie Stewart's Principles of Performance Racing* (Hazleton Publishing, 1986)

'My job is to keep it all together. Anyone can score a few points, like in tennis, when you make a couple of great shots. But it takes more than that to win Wimbledon.' – Jody Scheckter, 1977

'If you are quick for one lap only, you do not win anything.' – Nelson Piquet, 1988

'There are lots of drivers who are very quick. But for every twenty like that, there is probably only one who has a good head.' – Frank Williams

'A crazy driver finishes in the cemetery. You need a good brain to race.' – Juan Manuel Fangio

'Driving is more a state of mind than the use of intelligence. The driver's problems are moral and psychological rather than intellectual.' – Didier Pironi, 1983

'The first time is the most important because you know you can do it again. You go to every race after that thinking about winning it, not just taking part.' – Alain Prost remembering his first Grand Prix victory, at Dijon in 1981

'Once you start winning, you know you can win again, you know you can be quick consistently. Every time you go out, you're immediately in the ballpark.' – Nigel Mansell, 1986

'Winning your first Grand Prix is a passport to the future. Once you have won a Grand Prix, you are free from all the inhibitions and complexes that have held you back. You know that you are every bit as good as those around you, and Formula 1 takes on an entirely new aspect. You have climbed a mountain which, only the night before, appeared insurmountable.' – Alain Prost, from *Life in the Fast Lane* (Stanley Paul, 1988)

'I don't think many people understand just how competitive Formula 1 really is. To find that last half second which puts you ahead of the rest of the field is really very difficult, and to go half a second per lap slower than your best time is easy.' – Emerson Fittipaldi, 1972

'F1 is a tremendous sport. It's like running the four-minute mile. You break it and then someone comes along and is even faster. Everyone has to really work to get faster and it is marvellous to be part of that.' – Frank Williams, from *Damon Hill's Championship Year* by Bob McKenzie (Headline, 1996)

'Getting to the top is hard, but staying there is much harder.' – Frank Williams, 1990

'This is a sport of one per cent margins. In Formula 1, you can come down to earth with an almighty thump.' – Ron Dennis, 1999

'Nobody is going to give you any credit if you don't deliver results on the day. It's no good saying, "Well, I wasn't quick today, but I won a few Grands Prix – I was quick last year." That's history!' – Damon Hill, 1995

'It's a tough world at the top. That only makes you want to climb Everest that little bit more.' – Keke Rosberg, 1985

'The air is thin at the top. It's so much easier down below, where getting from tenth to ninth is an improvement.' – Niki Lauda, 1978

'Racing is an interesting job; it's adventurous at best. But the glamour lies in the people who come to watch. The glamour is in the crowds, not behind the scenes. Behind the scenes, the pressure to win is too great.' – Peter Revson, from *Speed With Style* by Peter Revson and Leon Mandel (William Kimber, 1974)

'It's all pressure, constant pressure. I don't react to pressure on the circuit because that's a closed world, but when I get out of the car the pressure is all over me again.' – Nelson Piquet, 1981

'There are pressures that derive from the extreme competitiveness of the sport. I am constitutionally incapable of getting into a car and being jovial and relaxed. I cannot take it easy or say it doesn't matter that there are a dozen things wrong with the car. Perhaps my ego won't allow me to do that. I have to be the quickest, I have to be the best. If I'm not, I blow my cool.' – Alan Jones, from *Driving Ambition* by Alan Jones and Keith Botsford (Stanley Paul, 1981)

'The pressure gets at you. You lead, you're on top, and you say to yourself, "I'd rather come from behind – just blow through on the last race to do it."' – Nigel Mansell feeling the championship heat ahead of the 1986 Portuguese Grand Prix. He won in Estoril, only to be cruelly denied the title two races later at Adelaide when a rear tyre shredded at 200 mph.

'Driving an F1 car is a joy for some, a pain for others, but for all it must be a very stressful experience.' – Ayrton Senna, 1991

'Motor racing is a very serious occupation. If you want to survive you have to be a professional to your fingertips. If my drivers don't understand this, it's my job to convince them.' – Ken Tyrrell, 1974

'You have to be pretty streetwise to get into Formula 1 and stay in. Fifty per cent of it is out of the car. There are lots of pressures – people pulling you one way, then the other. Formula 1 is big international business. And you have to be part of it, play the game.' – Martin Brundle, from *Behind the Scenes In Motor Racing* by Anthony Howard (Transworld, 1992)

'In one year Formula 1 can be so filled and so intensive it is more than the equivalent of five years for normal people.' – Michael Schumacher, trying to explain what hard work F1 racing is, 1992

'When I go to the race meeting I am there to race. I am not there for fun, for jokes, for enjoying myself.' – Niki Lauda, 1977

'A driver is a big motivator. Teams must have not just fast drivers, or cheap drivers, but drivers who can drive a team. I work very close to my people. I feel I am sitting in *their* car, and that they live the sport through me. It's up to me to make them feel part of me. Engineers keep thinking if they are motivated: maybe they come

up with that little bit extra if *you* show you work harder at it.' –
Ayrton Senna, 1986

'I go to a race to work my ass off and give 100 per cent effort.' –
Mario Andretti, 1978

'To be a top F1 driver you need quick reactions and cool
concentration. Mistakes are just over-reactions.' – Mario
Andretti, 1978

'What people don't realise is that winning is easy. Losing is the
thing that's bloody hard work!' – James Hunt struggling to defend
his title, 1977

'There is always something to learn. One never stops learning,
particularly when one is losing. When one loses, one knows what has
to be done. When one wins, one is never sure.' – Enzo Ferrari, 1959

'There is nothing worse than having a race going on around you
– and you're not in it.' – Damon Hill on the misery of retiring in
a Grand Prix

'Deep down the desire to win is very great because when you see
and feel the applause of thousands it moves you. No matter how
cold and calculating you are, it does get to you. But you must be
careful for when the heart and emotion take over, reason suffers.'
– Ayrton Senna driving in front of his adoring Brazilian fans at
Interlagos, 1992

'Emotions are the most dangerous things in a racing car.' – Jackie
Stewart, 1999

'The most dangerous moment is after winning one's first race; one
feels obliged to press on even harder and win again.' – Piero
Taruffi, 1958

'There's nothing quite like standing on the threshold of winning a
world championship. It makes you feel like there's nowhere else to
be, and nowhere else you'd want to be.' – Damon Hill

'The only thing that interests me in F1 is the world championship. If I began to think I couldn't win it, I would stop. I don't want to spend my life in F1 for the sake of it.' – Didier Pironi, 1980

'It's just the desire to win that keeps you in it. All those plateaux to climb up. You go in business, you look at the chairman and you say, "Some day I'm going to sit in that big leather chair." My chairman is the world championship.' – Mario Andretti, 1977

'Driving the car in the race is only a small part of winning a championship – perhaps twenty per cent, or even less.' – Jack Brabham, clinching his third title, 1966

'When you win the championship, it's like a balloon. You let the air out and all there is left is a pile of rubber.' – Keke Rosberg, 1985

'Whatever happens, life will stay the same afterwards. The sun will come up in the east and go down in the west. There are more things than just motor racing and world championships.' – Carlos Reutemann on his title bid, 1978

'Becoming world champion is important, but not a matter of life and death.' – Alain Prost, 1983

'It would have been a lot easier to rise from the shadows than to have been already in the limelight. The sunrise is not half so interesting, or so easy to accept.' – Alain Prost waxing lyrical after winning the 1985 world championship

'I think it's crazy: all the time the team owners complain about the cost of F1 in this Turbo era. So why do they waste money at these stupid tests at each track? It's like having 30 Grands Prix instead of sixteen! What difference would it make if we didn't test everywhere? There are two days of practice before the race, which should be enough. It would make no difference: the same guys would still be at the front. Maybe everyone's times would be a second slower. So what?' – Elio de Angelis, later killed while testing at Paul Ricard in 1986

'When I was eighteen, I was 28. Knowledge is the same in whatever aspect of the sport. Every test, every practice, every race, is competition. Learning, learning, learning.' – Ayrton Senna, 1985

'Being a professional is looking after your own bloody future. No one else is going to look after it for you.' – Keke Rosberg

'Sure, there are negative days when you are down and tell yourself, "I don't need this any more." The ankle hurts when it rains but you cannot allow it to beat you into submission. The desire to better yourself must drive you.' – Johnny Herbert, 1999

'When you're on the first row or the first three rows it's not too bad, but when you're farther back all you can see is wheels. Wheels everywhere. So many wheels...' – Carlos Reutemann, 1974

'There are two sides to motor racing. First of all, about 95 per cent of the time, you have the lows. And the remaining five per cent of the time you have the highs. But that five per cent of highs outweighs the lows.' – Derek Warwick, from *Grand Prix People* by Gerald Donaldson (MRP, 1990)

'The moments of joy in our sport are very intense but very short.' – Ayrton Senna after winning his first Grand Prix, at Estoril in 1985

'There are moments of joy, but there is also 75 per cent of frustration.' – Keke Rosberg, 1984

'Frustration is the biggest thing you have to fight in racing. Frustration takes you to the grave.' – Mario Andretti, 1981

'I have felt for a long time that I would have got on much better if I'd had an "i" or an "o" at the end of my name – Marco Blundelli. Because it seems to me that all the way through racing, there is this attachment to the idea of "We've got this new Italian or Brazilian and he's a great guy" – even down to the language issue. Because maybe his English is fragmented and the explanations are not quite as clear-cut, he's got this little magical mystery to him unlike the Brit who speaks his mind clearly.' – Mark Blundell, 1998

'Grand Prix racing is a roundabout, the speed of which one has no control over.' – McLaren team chief Ron Dennis, 1991

'I was no longer getting any pleasure from driving round and round in circles. I feel I have better things to do with my life.' – Niki Lauda quitting motor racing during practice for the 1979 Canadian Grand Prix. He was back three years later.

'Everyone is now half-smart and does things half-well. The sport is run by jumped-up upstarts.' – Niki Lauda, retiring for good, 1985

'It's a nice round figure, and there are lots of other things I want to do.' – Damon Hill announcing his intention to retire at 40 in three years' time, 1998

'I'll know when to walk away. It's very simple. It hurts too much to get beaten, basically. That is the bottom line. I'm up for it as long as I can be competitive.' – Damon Hill, 1999

'I've been at the top and I'm finding it difficult to get back up there. I don't want to be seen plodding around at the back.' – Damon Hill announcing his retirement, 1999

'I first had doubts at Melbourne this year. We all raced to the first corner and I thought, "What's the hurry?"' – Damon Hill, 1999

'The thought of quitting grows on a driver little by little. He finds himself thinking about it more and more. It seems ever more desirable. He sleeps a little less after each race. He enjoys driving a little less. His edge goes off, his appetite diminishes. Courage comes when a driver recognises that moment and quits.' – Alan Jones, from *Driving Ambition* by Alan Jones and Keith Botsford (Stanley Paul, 1981)

'Ten years is more than enough to satisfy anybody with the desire to win, and you must always be on the front row of the grid. If I hurt myself now, my friends would say I was stupid. Perhaps there was a god who said: "Fangio, stop!"' – Juan Manuel Fangio opting to retire in 1958

'Just being competitive, racing against others, seemed to me to be childishly immature. There was more, I thought, to racing than that.' – Jackie Stewart on the reasons for his retirement in 1973

'I'll know I've grown up when I quit racing.' – John Watson, 1983

'I always have to win. After you become champion once, what is there to do but win again? When you don't want that, you should get out.' – James Hunt, 1977

'I see myself doing the one thing I like doing until I don't like it. At the moment I'm racing to win races and I'm not doing it very well. If I don't get the right cars and the right money, I'll simply retire.' – James Hunt, 1978

'If you haven't got an absolutely competitive car these days you can forget it. And, quite frankly, it's not worth the risk to life and limb to continue under those circumstances.' – James Hunt retiring from motor racing part-way through a miserable season in the Wolf, 1979

'I no longer want to be a human honey pot.' – James Hunt citing additional reasons for his retirement, 1979

I think I will climb Everest just as long as there's a nice bar at the top.' – Gerhard Berger on his plans for retirement, 1997

'On particular occasions I wasn't driving the same way as before. If you had a wet race and you couldn't see anything, I was starting to lift off and think about what could go wrong. I needed a season off – a season to relax. But you don't get that luxury in Formula 1. It was time to stop.' – Gerhard Berger reflecting on his retirement

'If I have to do something, I could help Bernie Ecclestone run the traffic of pretty girls in the pit lane.' – Gerhard Berger at a loose end, 1998

'I've dreamed about it for so long that all I can do is think about driving...and maybe one day being able to afford a house with an indoor swimming pool.' – Nigel Mansell on his first full season in F1, 1981

'I drive for pleasure, not money.' – Nigel Mansell, 1986

'The money side is only what you get for doing the job, it is not the motivation. There is no other sport where you risk the ultimate every time you go out.' – Nigel Mansell, 1992

'All the drivers earn good money but, apart from Lauda and Pironi, are apparently not willing to do more for it than get into a racing car and push the accelerator.' – Jackie Stewart bemoaning the lack of personalities in motor racing, 1982

'I thought I could go back to Australia and race just for fun; but you don't race just for fun. It's work and if I'm going to work, I might as well be back making the money for it.' – Alan Jones returning to F1, 1983

'Let's face it, we're just whores, aren't we? We'll turn up and do our stuff for anyone if the money's right.' – Keke Rosberg, 1985

'I race for money. I try to get the top dollar in this business. Still, I'd race for nothing, but I wouldn't say that to Colin.' – Mario Andretti reaping the rewards of driving for Colin Chapman and Lotus, 1977

'I would still race even if nobody had ever paid me anything.' – Jim Clark

'With the first shilling you take from the public you throw away the right to complain about public criticism.' – Stirling Moss

'Some drivers have lost their way. Money has become more important than results.' – McLaren's Ron Dennis, 1999

'I'm not motivated by money, but equally that is one of the ways drivers are ranked in the sport, and if you offer to drive for nothing then that is your perceived worth as a Formula 1 driver.' – Damon Hill, from *F1 Through the Eyes of Damon Hill* (Little, Brown, 1998)

'I don't rush out and buy a jet or spend like it is going out of fashion to keep up with the big boys. I try to keep a real position. If you are not careful, F1 can go to your head.' – Damon Hill, 1996

'I had a new red pair but when it came to getting suited up for a race, I could only find one boot. So I raced with one red and one blue boot. I scored my first victory that afternoon and the team told me not to change anything. I've worn odd boots ever since!' – Alexander Wurz, 1998

'I like big challenges. If you overcome them, the pleasure is great, and you need the pleasure to compensate for the style of life which any driver will tell you is not that good.' – Ayrton Senna, 1987

'I feel I am cheating my children presently. It is very hurtful when you have a nineteenth-month-old son who is only speaking a few words and crying and saying, "Don't go, don't go." I think that is one of the hardest parts for me because the children don't really understand the job of work I do.' – Nigel Mansell, 1988

'When you have a mortgage and children, the world championship doesn't seem so important.' – Damon Hill, 1994

'Drivers who have children are invariably a second slower each lap.' – Enzo Ferrari

'I can switch off at home, but it doesn't take long before I am thinking about the next race.' – Damon Hill, 1995

'Motivation is the key. Formula 1 is a hard slog. Even if you have all the toys in the world, it gets to you in the end. You get very little time to yourself. That's why I don't do any more of the peripheral stuff than I need. I don't open supermarkets for lots of cash.' – Damon Hill, 1999

'It is a matter of money, fame and, if you like, a bit of an ego trip.' – James Hunt on why he became a racing driver

'I'm just beginning to wonder if I want to be world champion. There will be so much fuss and drama. Farming is really my occupation, and racing just a hobby.' – Jim Clark, 1963

'I know the people I really have to know – which is about three – but I don't like small talk and I haven't time for people who just sit down and talk about nothing, putting on as big a front as they can.' – Denny Hulme, the sponsor's nightmare, 1968

'I didn't like the press putting their noses into my office on race day and my office was my car. If someone came up and thrust a microphone at me, I'd crunch it. If someone thrust a camera at me, they'd end up with the maker's name imprinted on their forehead where I'd rammed it back at them.' – Denny Hulme, from *Grand Prix Showdown* by Christopher Hilton (Patrick Stephens Ltd, 1992)

'All the pomp and ceremony leaves me cold.' – John Surtees, 1966

'In Montreal once, at a hockey game, the crowd gave me a bigger round of applause than the players. It was embarrassing.' – Jacques Villeneuve, 1997

'I don't worry about adulation. I'm uncomfortable with it.' – Eddie Irvine, aware that he is not yet as popular with British fans as Damon Hill, 1999

'Before it was enough to be just a racing driver and concentrate in the car, and that was it. Now you have really to be also a public relations man because the sponsors require you a lot, and you must also be a public man for this reason.' – Riccardo Patrese, from *Grand Prix People* by Gerald Donaldson (MRP, 1990)

'I wanted to do my job as a Formula 1 driver, not a PR man. Of course I realise you need to do a certain amount of that, but it should be 80 per cent driver and 20 per cent PR, not 50-50. Or 20-80.' – Alain Prost on his split from Renault, 1984

'Whatever they say, whatever their protests, show them a green light and they'll go for it.' – John Watson dismissing the complaints of his fellow drivers, 1984

'Lay off for a while, and try coming back without getting back into physical shape, and you'll find yourself with your tongue wrapped around your front axle.' – Mario Andretti emphasizing the importance of fitness, 1978

'A ball, a group of friends, a goal, all afternoon in the sun. That was my pre-season training.' – Juan Manuel Fangio revving up for the season on the beach

'The days of Grand Prix drivers lying on the beach between races is long gone.' – David Coulthard, 1997

'I dream about biscuits sometimes.' – Alex Wurz, watching his weight, 1999

'Our attitude was that one fought hard and one played hard. You did your best to win on the track and you did your best to have as much fun as possible off it.' – Stirling Moss, from *Racing and All That* by Stirling Moss and Mike Hailwood (Pelham Books, 1980)

'It was quite a simple rationalization. The chances were pretty high that we'd both get killed. So we decided, then and there, that we'd celebrate as we went along.' – James Hunt making a pact with fellow Formula 3 driver Niki Lauda after a particularly hairy race in Sweden in 1971, from *Hunt: The Biography* by Gerald Donaldson (CollinsWillow, 1994)

'One night a crowd led by Luigi had somehow manhandled Harry Schell's car, a little four-wheeled Vespa, through the main door of the hotel and up the stairs to the first floor. Unfortunately Harry was on the fourth floor. They couldn't get into the lift and so the plot, which was to drive it along the corridor to Harry's room and blow the horn, misfired. They left it outside the manager's office on the first floor and put a few flowers around it.' – Mike Hawthorn recalling a Luigi Musso-led prank before the 1958 French Grand Prix. Tragically Musso was killed in the actual race. From *Champion Year* by Mike Hawthorn (Aston Publications, 1959)

'Boozing, clubbing, women – you name it. I really lived it up. I went bananas. Then I realised that the only thing you get out of doing that are headaches.' – Eddie Irvine remembering his big bender at the end of the 1996 season

'I go out with birds and my mates, so what's the big problem?' – Eddie Irvine, 1999

'James lived it up to the full on the way back. I was on the same aeroplane and I don't think he slept a wink. He drank all night and then in the morning he grabbed the microphone from a stewardess and announced his presence to everybody in Japanese.' – Team-mate Jochen Mass after James Hunt became world champion in 1976, from *James Hunt: Portrait of a Champion* by Christopher Hilton (Patrick Stephens Ltd, 1993)

'Jim Clark and Innes Ireland arrived wearing kilts but Innes being Innes had elected to wear nothing underneath. As the evening progressed Innes became more and more enthusiastic and eventually decided to dance on the table. All the girls became very excited, but it was just too much for Graham Hill who dashed outside and returned with a nice prickly cactus. Poor old Innes and his girlfriend spent the next week occupied with a pair of tweezers and a magnifying glass, pulling out the spines!' – Mike Hailwood remembering high jinks at a post-race party at the 1964 Austrian Grand Prix, from *Racing and All That* by Stirling Moss and Mike Hailwood (Pelham Books, 1980)

'I know some people may have good reasons for not bringing their wives to races, but I want mine to be with me.' – Emerson Fittipaldi, 1972

'I want to live to be 105 years old so I can have enough time to hear all the music I'd like to hear, read all the books that interest me, and have all the women I want.' – Wolfgang von Trips, 1950s

'The only reason I ever walked up and down the pit road when I was a driver was to look at the crumpet.' – James Hunt in his role as a journalist, from *Grand Prix People* by Gerald Donaldson (MRP, 1990)

'Fewer girls, more technology.' – Jody Scheckter, asked about the changes in F1 in the eighteen years since he won the title, 1997

Chapter Three

Only As Good As Your Car

'A driver is nothing without a good car.' – Niki Lauda, 1977

'A driver knows that the easiest thing to change about a car, if it is not going well, is the driver.' – Damon Hill, from *Grand Prix Year* (Macmillan, 1995)

'Racing cars are like beautiful but temperamental women in that quite small things make big differences to their behaviour.' – Stirling Moss, 1963

'I have no qualms about saying that I could win a Grand Prix. Give me a decent car and I know I could do it.' – Mark Blundell, 1998

'In my day it was 75 per cent car and mechanic, 25 per cent driver and luck. Today it's 95 per cent car.' – Juan Manuel Fangio

'It's quite easy to delude yourself. When you've got the best car and you're winning races and you feel very confident, you *believe* you're driving better than others.' – James Hunt, 1981

'Maybe all we will do is just guide the car. I think that changing the gear is part of the skill of driving a race car. You might change gear 3000 times in one race and it is the skill of the driver in being able to change on a bend or in a tight situation that can make the difference between winning and losing. If we keep on going along the road of technology then drivers will not have much to do.' – Ayrton Senna campaigning against proposals for automatic gearboxes in Formula 1 cars, 1992

'Formula 1 cars are the easiest of all to drive, but the rest is difficult. Anyone with the necessary talent can drive one, but getting the car right is an art.' – Nelson Piquet, who learnt the art of preparing a car for a race from Niki Lauda at Brabham in 1979

'There is something passionate about fighting a car gone mad.' – Jacky Ickx, 1970

'The old front-engined cars really did everything wrong: you had the weight of the mass of the engine in the front, the driver in the middle, and the fuel in the back. As the fuel load changed, it produced tremendous variations in the weight distribution which made it virtually impossible to balance the car for full as well as empty tanks.' – Colin Chapman on the virtues of rear-engined cars, from *Colin Chapman: The Man and His Cars* by Gerard 'Jabby' Crombac (Patrick Stephens Ltd, 1986)

'A great deal of nonsense has been said and written about this innovation, most of it, as far as I can see, by people who have never driven a racing car so fitted. All I can say is that a car with an aerofoil is very nice to drive and – which is the object of the exercise – faster on most circuits with the possible exception of Monza.' – Graham Hill entering the great aerofoil debate, 1968

'Sometimes it feels the same; sometimes it's not quite as good; and other times it's diabolical. And you get all three within a space of about 100 yards.' – Alan Jones comparing the 1981 cars to the previous year's following the abolition of sliding skirts

'I had to learn a completely different set of techniques, a different approach, with vastly varying mechanical hazards to master. I was almost dizzy trying to unravel the mysteries.' – Former world motorcycle champion Mike Hailwood making the switch from two wheels to four

'A new motor comes into the world with the cry of a newborn child; raw material is transformed into a living being with a voice of its own.' – Enzo Ferrari, 1977

'You are in an endless corridor, along which every door is closed. You want to get out but you can't. You have to find a solution. I find it sometimes in the night, sometimes as if in a dream. When I see a possibility, it is like a blinding light, like lightning.' – Enzo Ferrari on the process of thinking up new designs, 1977

'Designing is an immense puzzle, made up of simple ideas and complex variables, of surprising successes and inexplicable failures.' – Brabham's Gordon Murray, 1983

'Any fool can build a bridge that won't fall down, but it's up to an engineer to build one that just won't fall down.' – Lotus chief Colin Chapman outlining his philosophy to building racing cars, 1978

Alfa Romeo

'Everything about the car is fine, except we're getting absolutely blown away in a straight line.' – Eddie Cheever after the 1984 Dutch Grand Prix

Arrows

'It was undriveable and had no brakes.' – Derek Warwick finding fault with his Arrows at the 1988 Brazilian Grand Prix. Nevertheless he finished a creditable fourth

BAR

'We've been very competitive, but we just haven't finished races.' – Jacques Villeneuve enduring a traumatic start to his career at British American Racing, 1999

Benetton

'I want to be a racing driver, not a taxi driver. With this car I lose all possibility of showing what I can do. The car has a lot of problems.' – Jean Alesi, 1996

'He would be better off watching Berger's times and shutting up.' – Benetton chief Flavio Briatore, pointing out that Alesi's team-mate, Gerhard Berger, was consistently faster, 1996

'I learned something today: do not get excited in free practice, however good the car feels. Bring it safely to qualifying, because if you have a good set-up you want to keep it. Not stuff it in the wall.' – Alex Wurz after crashing the Benetton into a wall during free practice for the 1999 Australian Grand Prix

Brabham

'Here was a man, potentially a world beater, having to trundle round circuits with an engine that could have been in a museum.' – Louis T. Stanley on the Brabham BT11 driven by Dan Gurney in 1965

'We looked at the existing cars from end to end, slimmed and pruned everything to the minimum, used our own cast uprights all round and generally spent a lot of time designing just enough car to do the job. The amount of thought and time that went into producing a car as simple and light as that was tremendous.' – Ron Tauranac remembering the Brabham Repco BT24 in which Denny Hulme became world champion in 1967

'I'd forgotten how much easier they were to drive. You could really chuck those cars about. It isn't half as easy to get out of trouble today as it was.' – Denny Hulme driving a 1966 Brabham Repco in a pre-race parade before stepping back into his McLaren M23 for the 1974 French Grand Prix

BRM

'I tried it on a wet day and found it very frightening indeed. It snaked at high speed and one had to hold it very firmly to keep it going in a straight line.' – Mike Hawthorn recalling his first test drive in a BRM, 1956

'A terrible, not to say terrifying, piece of machinery. It was without doubt the worst car I ever drove.' – Stirling Moss with less than fond memories of the BRM V-16 of 1952

'The car is as rough as a bear's arse.' – Innes Ireland to the BRP pit crew following an unscheduled stop in his BRM at the 1964 Mexican Grand Prix

'The H16 was a heavy, cumbersome car; it didn't matter who you were, it would just lap at a certain speed. The car just bogged you down. It wasn't an exciting car to drive at all.' – Jackie Stewart on the BRM H16 which he drove in 1967

'I've never come across a harder car to handle. That 1500cc 16-cylinder engine with its centrifugal supercharger had scarcely any power in the lower range of rpm. But when it did start to accelerate, it was as if something had struck you a sudden blow. On the straight it was like a wild beast. 12,000 revs! You should have heard the way it buzzed along. Anyone who drove it got out of it half deaf.' – Juan Manuel Fangio, from *Fangio: My Racing Life* (Patrick Stephens Ltd, 1986)

'I said they would have to fit air vents to ventilate the cockpit, otherwise the driver's legs would roast.' – Juan Manuel Fangio, 1951

'On paper, that car was a flier. A good development team would have sorted out its problems, but they didn't have a good development team. That car was lethal. You had to corner it geometrically. If you tried to drift it, it would just fly off the road.' – Tony Brooks on the 1956 P25, from *British Grand Prix* by Maurice Hamilton (Crowood Press, 1990)

'Being that car, it just went completely out of control, spun into the bank, somersaulted and threw me out. Finally it landed upside down on the track again, and set itself on fire, which was the only thing it could reasonably do.' – Tony Brooks losing the P25 at the 1956 British Grand Prix, from *British Grand Prix*

'If you made the slightest mistake in a BRM in those days you lost it.' – Tony Brooks

'Their unreliability was almost legendary.' – Tony Brooks

'In the Centro-Sud car he would have been just as quick by taxi.' – BRM's Louis T. Stanley deriding the Centro-Sud BRM driven by Masten Gregory in 1965

'The V12 engine simply hadn't got the necessary power. It was ludicrous. We were just left standing on the straights when it came to acceleration and top speed.' – Niki Lauda recalling the slow and unreliable BRM P160 which he drove in 1973

'His car came to be known as the Stanley Steamer because on the track it behaved just like an old-fashioned tea kettle.' – Alan Jones on the BRM and company chief Louis T. Stanley

Connaught

'The all-enveloping body made access to the car for running adjustments very difficult: it was intended that the entire body should be lifted clear for this sort of work, and indeed it was very quickly detachable; but the space required and the time involved were nevertheless a severe handicap in the frenzy of a hurried pit stop.' – Author L.J.K. Setright revealing why the British Connaught cars of the 1950s failed to enjoy much success in Formula 1, from *The Grand Prix Car* (George Allen & Unwin, 1968)

Cooper

'It was what the Americans call a son of a bitch to drive. Despite the designer's intention of giving it marked understeer characteristics, it was in fact terribly twitchy and almost impossible to drive really fast round a corner without losing control...' – Stirling Moss on the prototype Cooper Alta Special-4 which he raced in Grands Prix in 1953

'Built on a shoestring with a hacksaw, the Formula 1 Cooper encompassed a revolution greater than any that had ever been brought about by any of the great and famous organisations engaged in motor racing... In 1958 the presence of a few Coopers in the major Grands Prix had been little more than a source of amusement or irritation; but in 1959, with a Coventry Climax engine that had at last been enlarged to a full 2 ½ litres, the Cooper leaped into prominence, to become a source of amazement and confusion.' – Author L.J.K. Setright on the revolutionary, rear-engined Cooper, from *The Grand Prix* (Thomas Nelson & Sons, 1973)

'The Cooper was a car that gave one enormous confidence and instilled the belief that if you did misjudge things a bit and began to lose it, you could just tweak it a bit more on the steering, lose a bit more speed and the whole situation would resolve itself without too much trouble. However, it felt very small and at first a little strange to be sitting so close to the front wheels.' – Stirling Moss remembering his first outing in a Cooper-Climax back in 1957

'It really did go round corners at an absolutely astonishing speed and because it was highly sensitive to the helm, you really could dictate to it and throw it about as you wished.' – Stirling Moss on the 1959 Cooper-Climax

'The Cooper is fantastic. You can do anything with it and still recover. It doesn't penalise Brabham's mistakes.' – Phil Hill, 1960

'The car was pretty badly designed from the cockpit point of view. The pedals were immediately behind the radiator. The brake pedal, clutch pedal and accelerator pedal were that hot I could barely keep a foot on them.' – Jack Brabham enduring an uncomfortable ride to the world drivers' championship in the 1959 Cooper-Climax

'Although the Lotus was smaller and lighter, the Cooper was always quicker in a straight line, much to Colin Chapman's amazement and disappointment.' – Jack Brabham

Ensign

'I don't know what we've done wrong, but the car feels really good here!' – Colombian driver Roberto Guerrero puzzled by the sudden improvement of the Ensign which qualified a highly respectable sixteenth in the 1982 Austrian Grand Prix. Normal service was resumed in the race, however, with Guerrero being forced to retire with a broken drive-shaft

'It's incredibly light to drive – in fact, it's almost too light. You have to drive it on tippy-toe.' – Derek Daly, 1978

ERA

'It was a car which made a big fuss about doing little.' – Stirling Moss

Ferrari

'Those bloody red cars.' – Vanwall boss Tony Vandervell slugging it out with Maserati and Ferrari in the 1950s

'Big, hairy monsters which made a noise like a banshee wail.' – Innes Ireland on the front-engined Ferrari Dino 246 of 1959

'Racing the Ferrari against the Lotus at Monaco was like trying to see which is quicker round your living room – a dog or a racehorse.' – Phil Hill, 1960s

'Derek, I want you to know that if you damage this car at all, you will never drive a red car again.' – Ferrari chief engineer Mauro Forghieri's warning to Derek Bell before Bell's first test drive for Ferrari in 1968

'Another year I've got to wait. It is as if you were writing your novel on a typewriter with five letters missing – all vowels.' – Michele Alboreto selecting a literary metaphor to explain his struggles with the Ferrari in the early part of 1986

'This is the greatest distance this car has ever done!' – Nigel Mansell pulling off a shock victory in the 1989 Brazilian Grand Prix in his first drive for Ferrari. It was to prove a false dawn as the car's anticipated lack of reliability quickly manifested itself with four successive retirements

'I still remember that first day I tested the car, at Estoril. In the evening I sat in my hotel room and thought, "What have I done?" I'd driven flat out that day, as hard as I knew, and we were seven seconds away from a competitive lap time.' – Gerhard Berger recalling his initial misgivings about rejoining Ferrari in 1993

'Same expletive, different place.' – Gerhard Berger after another retirement, this time in the 1993 European Grand Prix at Donington

'You can't grab hold of it and wring its neck.' – Eddie Irvine explaining that the Ferrari needs delicate handling, 1997

'I think Ferrari can still win some more races this year – so long as the McLarens retire!' – Eddie Irvine after the 1999 Monaco Grand Prix

'The car was understeering like a pig.' – Eddie Irvine battling to victory in the 1999 Austrian Grand Prix

'We're just not there on fast circuits.' – A disillusioned Eddie Irvine at the 1999 Belgian Grand Prix

'Ferrari are missing technical development because the car is simply not as good as the McLaren. I can't say how much better the car would have been if I had still been there, but it is very clear that if they do not make good developments for the last few races, they are going to find it very difficult.' – Michael Schumacher, sidelined after his crash at Silverstone, casting doubts over Ferrari's chances of winning the championship without him, 1999

'Michael obviously has less faith in Ferrari than I do.' – Eddie Irvine's reply to Schumacher's pessimistic comments

Fittipaldi

'Just about everything is wrong. It's slow in the straight, the handling is unpredictable.' – Emerson Fittipaldi, less than thrilled with the car which bore his name, 1977

Hesketh

'I just can't tell you how bad that car is. And all its faults are the same as they were at the beginning of the season. We've made no progress at all.' – Rupert Keegan, 1977

Jordan

'We're not a car manufacturer. We design high-technology promotional items to give the world of commerce an advertising platform. Grand Prix cars are high-speed billboards.' – Eddie Jordan in cynical mood, 1998

'My mother, God bless her, could have walked round the track faster than our cars.' – Eddie Jordan after a poor show in qualifying at Monaco, 1998, from *Against the Odds: Jordan's Drive to Win* by Jon Nicholson and Maurice Hamilton (Macmillan, 1999)

'I feel like I've gone from Roadrunner to Wile E. Coyote. Nothing I do seems to work.' – Damon Hill despairing after being off the pace in the Jordan during practice for the 1999 Hungarian Grand Prix

Ligier

'I have no doubt that the JS17 would have been better here, but then again *anything* else would have been better.' – Jacques Laffite struggling in the new JS19 at the 1982 Dutch Grand Prix

'The big problem is that these cars are simply too heavy to compete.

The turbos? Ha! I wish we could keep up with some of the Cosworths...' – Jacques Laffite still struggling with the JS19, 1982

'Absolutely hopeless. Even when the sun's out, you feel as though you're driving in the wet. The thing has so little grip. In the slow corners especially, it's a joke.' – Stefan Johansson, 1988

'When you've changed everything and nothing makes any difference to the feel of the thing, it's difficult to know what to do next.' – Stefan Johansson, 1988

Lola

'About as useful as an ashtray on a motorcycle.' – A disgruntled Alan Jones, 1986

Lotus

'I think Colin Chapman was a brilliant designer but in my view he did not give sufficient consideration to the problems which could arise if the car was driven very hard. If you drove a Lotus very hard, as was often necessary, then a wheel would fall off. This happened with me several times.' – Stirling Moss, from *Colin Chapman: The Man and His Cars* by Gerard 'Jabby' Crombac (Patrick Stephens Ltd, 1986)

'I liked Colin but he didn't have much of a sense of humour. I remember after I had won the 1960 United States Grand Prix in Rob Walker's Lotus, they bought me a cake with the shape of the car modelled in the icing. The first piece I cut off was a wheel, so I said, "Please pass this to Mr Chapman." He didn't think it was at all funny!' – Stirling Moss, from *Colin Chapman: The Man and His Cars*

'You never knew what was going to fall off next.' – Phil Hill vowing never to drive a Lotus after a spate of accidents plagued the car in the early 1960s

'Build a car that is going to hang together, and I'll drive it. But if

I think it is going to fall to bits, I am going to be two seconds a lap slower.' – Jim Clark's instructions to Lotus boss Colin Chapman

'I always felt that the Lotus was the most fragile of Grand Prix cars. I thought at one time there were rather too many mechanical failures; that I would rather drive a car that was a little more robust and would finish a race, than a car that would be faster and not finish.' – Jackie Stewart

'They were very pretty, but I was always rather disturbed at the awkward and cramped cockpit. It had the propeller shaft housing running diagonally across the cockpit, so that you sat half on it with your left leg cocked across it in order to reach the clutch. I always remember feeling distinctly nervous about that sitting position in case the prop shaft ever came loose and did me a terrible mischief.' – Innes Ireland recalling the Lotus 16 which he drove in 1959, from *All Arms and Elbows* (Pelham Books, 1967)

'One of the problems at first with the Lotus 25 was the very reclined seating position, which made visibility difficult, particularly on sharp corners. It was like a bed on wheels.' – Jim Clark adopting the horizontal position, 1962

'The tyres were holding a tenuous grip on the road with the body and chassis leaning and pulling at the suspension, like a lizard trying to avoid being prised off a rock by a small boy.' – Bruce McLaren describing Jim Clark's struggle to control the Lotus 25 on his way to victory at the 1963 British Grand Prix

'I tell him what is wanted with the car and he works out how to do it.' – Jim Clark on his working relationship with Colin Chapman

'It was quite alarming. I was going down the straight swinging the steering from one side to the other, trying to keep the car on the road.' – Jim Clark on the Lotus 49 in which he won the 1967 Dutch Grand Prix at Zandvoort

'I am probably still a little suspicious of it. I can't say that I expect anything in particular to fall off, but I'm not 100 per cent happy with the handling and I'm always a little doubtful about the brakes.' – Jim Clark expressing certain misgivings about the Lotus 49, 1967

'A monkey could have won today in this car. Thank you!' – Jochen Rindt expressing his gratitude to Colin Chapman after winning the 1970 German Grand Prix at Hockenheim in a Lotus 72. It was to be Rindt's last Grand Prix victory as a month later he was killed at Monza

'My feeling is that he could build stronger and safer cars than he does. Colin's idea of a perfect car might be one that falls to pieces the moment it crosses the finish line. Not my idea of what racing cars are about.' – Alan Jones on Chapman and Lotus, from *Driving Ambition* by Alan Jones and Keith Botsford (Stanley Paul, 1981)

'Colin was usually way ahead of all the other constructors. His designs and innovations were generally those followed by other people. I suppose that when we were successful against Colin, it was probably not because we were ahead in design but because we made our cars that much more reliable than his. Because he wanted to build cars which were as light as possible, he was often on the ragged edge, while we always tended to play safe.' – Ken Tyrrell, from *Colin Chapman: The Man and His Cars* by Gerard 'Jabby' Crombac (Patrick Stephens Ltd, 1986)

'I built cars that were too light, I just had too little input information. You can only get that information from experience. It's suck-it-and-see engineering.' – Colin Chapman discussing his unwanted tag of 'Killer Chapman', following the succession of 1960s crashes, 1978

'That Lotus was really frightening. I don't think I scare easily, but I sure as hell scared myself that weekend. It was twitchy like a go-kart.' – Mario Andretti after the 1976 Brazilian Grand Prix, his first drive in a Lotus

'This car's making an old man out of me.' – Mario Andretti in practice for the 1978 German Grand Prix. The ageing process was halted as Andretti went on to take pole and win the race

'A race car is like a woman. You think you know her, but sometimes you have to speculate and change your tactics.' – Mario Andretti courting the Lotus 79 at the 1978 Dutch Grand Prix

'We used to talk about it, Colin and I, and I realised just how many people had won titles in his cars. I didn't want to be the one who didn't.' – Mario Andretti, world champion in Colin Chapman's Lotus 79, 1978

'His personal contribution to the development of the 79 was immense. Without him it would have been a different car.' – Colin Chapman in praise of Andretti

'I guess everyone's gonna say that suddenly Andretti's a racer again, but it's nothing to do with that. For the first time this season I had the car to do the job.' – Mario Andretti showing improved form at the 1980 Dutch Grand Prix

'This car gave me back my inspiration.' – Ronnie Peterson on the Lotus 78, 1978

'I can't find words to express my utter misery, humiliation and blazing anger at the bloody fiasco of the past few days.' – Nigel Mansell after failing to make the grid for the 1981 British Grand Prix. Following protests from rival teams, his new 'twin-chassis' Lotus had been hurriedly converted back to single chassis before the final qualifying session

'It would probably have been OK for the Safari Rally, but not too good here.' – Lotus team manager Peter Warr unhappy with the set-up of the Lotus 99T for the 1987 Brazilian Grand Prix

'All we can do now is to say: "We're sorry, Nelson, but this heap of shit happens to be the best we can do. You are one of the best, and one of the best-paid, drivers in the world. Please do the best you can with it."' – Lotus team manager Peter Warr contemplating how to deal with a disgruntled Nelson Piquet before the 1989 Hungarian Grand Prix. Piquet finished sixth to continue his disappointing run of results

March

'A pretty awful car. I didn't talk to it and it didn't talk back to me.' – Mario Andretti on the March 701 which he drove in 1970

'It wasn't a very good car at all. It was too heavy – it was like a truck.' – Ken Tyrrell sharing the low opinion of the March 701

'An unpredictable handful which was tiring to drive and could never be tuned into any semblance of consistently competitive form.' – Jackie Stewart venting his frustration on the March 701

'The bloody car's useless. It's just a heap of shit!' – Chris Amon adding a few carefully chosen words to the general appraisal of the March 701

'The Formula 1 March was a colossal mechanical fiasco. The car was incredibly aggressive; the rear end especially vicious. I just could not come to terms with it at all.' – Niki Lauda unhappy in the March 721 which he drove in 1972, from *To Hell and Back* (Stanley Paul, 1986)

'This car was not fast. I always push this car very hard. Too hard. It was my feeling and I could not stop myself. I wanted to show I was the best driver. But the car could not say that.' – Vittorio Brambilla ('the Monza Gorilla') remembering his three seasons at the wheel of a March in the mid 1970s

'I tell you what, it's a good rentacar – like a Simca 1000 or something!' – Ian Scheckter, elder brother of Jody, appalled by the lack of speed of the March 771, 1977

Maserati

'Apart from being far more powerful, and far faster, than anything

I had had before, it really was a very nice car to drive with a slight but definite tendency to oversteer. I must say I prefer a car to oversteer.' – Stirling Moss on the Maserati 250F he drove in 1954

McLaren

'It seems that every time we build a new car we find something new that can happen in the first few laps.' – Bruce McLaren bemoaning the McLaren-Ford's disappointing display at Monaco, 1966

'It was a right royal handful. Its handling characteristics were completely different to a conventional car. Under braking it was pretty frightening. It had a mind of its own, so I quickly learned to keep about two feet away from the edge of the circuit when I went on the brakes because I felt it would just disappear off the track and I wanted to leave myself a bit of a margin.' – Derek Bell on the four-wheel drive McLaren M9A which he piloted at the 1969 British Grand Prix at Silverstone

'It's like hanging a man for a parking offence.' – McLaren team boss Teddy Mayer fuming at the decision to disqualify James Hunt's victory in the 1976 Spanish Grand Prix because the McLaren M23 was too wide. Hunt was subsequently reinstated

'If your car loses a wheel in every race, that's not good.' – Alain Prost succinctly pinpointing the problems which beset the McLaren M29 in 1980

'It is on another planet.' – Ferrari driver Michele Alboreto casting envious glances at the McLaren, 1985

'If you ask me what my memory of my McLaren year was, it is understeer with capital letters.' – Keke Rosberg recalling the 1986 season

'Without the McLarens, that would have been a pretty good race.' – Benetton designer Rory Byrne as the McLarens swept all before them at the 1988 San Marino Grand Prix

'It could be boring for spectators, yes, and I'm sorry for that. But on the other hand we can't be less competitive just to make people happy!' – Alain Prost on the McLaren dominance, 1988

'There's nothing tricky: it's just nicely designed and nicely built and doesn't have any vices.' – Designer Gordon Murray debunking the mystery surrounding the success of the McLaren, 1988

'This year Senna does not have the world-beating machinery and for the first time he does not look like the bullet-proof superman any more.' – Jackie Stewart as Senna's McLaren was forced to play second fiddle to the all-conquering Williams through 1992

'When you've won 31 Grands Prix, and two world titles, your tolerance threshold is that bit lower. You know straight away when you're in a bad car and you have a pretty good idea how much work needs to be done to make it competitive. I realised it was a bad car the first day I drove it in testing.' – Nigel Mansell on the new McLaren MP4/10B, from *Mansell: My Autobiography* (CollinsWillow, 1995)

Mercedes-Benz

'The 1954/55 Type W 196 Mercedes-Benz embodied half a century's experience in racing car design and has possibly never been equalled as a combination of performance and reliability.' – Stirling Moss, 1963

Minardi

'Fantastic chassis, fantastic driver... or maybe an error, I think.' – Giancarlo Minardi at a loss to explain the fact that the official timers at the 1998 San Marino Grand Prix clocked Esteban Tuero's Minardi as the fastest car of all over the start-finish line. Tuero finished a respectable eighth

Renault

'The problem was that Renault were too conservative last year.

They decided that we must play the reliability card, not change many things on the car. We went to Rio, the first race, with the old RE30C – though I knew from testing that the RE40 was a second and a half a lap quicker!' – Alain Prost, 1984

'I'm not in racing to pussyfoot around the track.' – Derek Warwick on the problems of having to conserve fuel in the Renault, 1984

Sauber

'Building an F1 car is like walking a tightrope – if you are too conservative, or if you risk too much, it will fail.' – Sauber designer Leo Ress, 1999

'It is a very driveable, forgiving car and has never performed badly. It's just that we haven't gone forward.' – Johnny Herbert, acknowledging that going forward is an essential attribute for any racing car, 1997

Scarab

'They really were the most beautiful motor cars. The trouble with them was that by the time they had been designed, developed and built, they were two years out of date.' – Innes Ireland recalling Lance Reventlow's spectacularly unsuccessful Scarabs which hit Formula 1 in 1960

Shadow

'It had diabolical understeer and a pathetic engine.' – Forthright Alan Jones at the 1977 Canadian Grand Prix

'I think I was rated at Shadow by what I could do within the limitations of the machinery at my disposal. "Look at old Jonesie," someone would say. "He's doing well in that old shit-box of his!"' – Alan Jones, who drove for Shadow in 1977, from *Driving Ambition* by Alan Jones and Keith Botsford (Stanley Paul, 1981)

Surtees

'The car rarely held together for more than five minutes at a time.'
– Mike Hailwood on the Surtees TS14A of 1973

Toleman

'The car was not very good. The "flying pig", as it was well known, was a bit of a dog.' – Derek Warwick

Tyrrell

'I was attached to it as if it was my own child in spite of its faults, in spite of its caprices – because it was the expression of a big idea.' – Patrick Depailler on the infamous six-wheel Tyrrell

'Everything they do is right. It's a really good team, it's just the fact that the car is too slow.' – Mika Salo, 1997

'I've said to the drivers on a number of occasions: "I think you both drove a spanking race. We did everything right with the strategy, the boys got the fuel in and changed the tyres as fast as anyone else – and you were racing for tenth and eleventh places!" It's mortifying.' – Tyrrell's technical director Harvey Postlethwaite as Salo and Jos Verstappen struggled through 1997

Vanwall

'Vandervell, a robust personality if ever there was one, decided to build an engine in his own image. That is to say a four-cylinder which might be a bit rough in running but would be certain to give lots of power.' – Stirling Moss on Tony Vandervell's Vanwall

'It was never an easy car to drive. You couldn't chuck it into a corner and steer it on the throttle. You had to be very precise with it. And the gear-box was terrible.' – Tony Brooks, from *Grand Prix Greats* by Nigel Roebuck (Patrick Stephens Ltd, 1986)

'Tony turned his right hand into something resembling a plate of raw meat on the Vanwall's agricultural gear-change.' – Stirling Moss as team-mate Tony Brooks finished second in a Vanwall at the 1957 Monaco Grand Prix, from *Stirling Moss: My Cars, My Career* by Stirling Moss with Doug Nye (Patrick Stephens Ltd, 1987)

'I had to climb up on to a rear wheel in order to drop into the large cockpit.' – John Surtees, from *John Surtees: World Champion* (Hazleton Publishing, 1991)

Williams

'It's like driving up to a blank wall. The wall stops you and you can't go any faster.' – Keke Rosberg considering the disadvantages of driving the non-turbo Williams in 1983

'I'm just a happy passenger.' – Nigel Mansell practising for the 1988 Brazilian Grand Prix. He was less happy after retiring from that and the next six races

'In Formula 1, 50 per cent of winning is the car. You have to treat the car very well to finish the race. Nigel is a little bit heavy on the car. The Williams car is very strong, but he has sometimes done things in a race and has had to stop. I am much easier with the car. Much easier.' – Nelson Piquet comparing his own treatment of the Williams to Nigel Mansell's, 1988

'We can't beat McLaren by making a more reliable car, or by operating it better – that's something they do superbly. We need to beat them by producing a faster car. That's all there is to it.' – Patrick Head unveiling the all-conquering FW14B for 1992

'Are you serious? Are you on the same planet? If you are, you should see a psychiatrist. You must be on drugs or something.' – Nigel Mansell to an Australian journalist who appeared to be denigrating Mansell's driving ability following his victory in the 1992 Spanish Grand Prix. The journalist had the temerity to suggest that Mansell's lead in the world championship was down to the fact that he had easily the best car

'If you're going to win the Derby you've got to have a bloody good horse. Nigel had Nijinsky and it seems unfair Williams haven't been thanked for that.' – Stirling Moss on Mansell's decision to quit Williams for IndyCar, 1992

'The first time I drove the FW14 I was like a kid in Santa's grotto.' – Damon Hill given the chance to test drive the Williams-Renault F1 car while he was still in Formula 3000, from *Williams: Triumph Out of Tragedy* by Alan Henry (Patrick Stephens Ltd, 1995)

'When I first drove the Williams I must admit that I was completely stuffed.' – Damon Hill

'The car was far too nervous.' – Damon Hill after his Williams aquaplaned out of control in the wet at the 1996 Spanish Grand Prix

'The aerodynamics and engineering on the FW18 are superb. It is a tremendous piece of equipment and every time I drive the car I enjoy playing with it.' – Damon Hill in praise of the Williams he drove to the title in 1996

'Any of the top dozen guys would have been world champion in a Williams in 1996 or 1997. That's a pretty much accepted fact. So to win a race in a Williams wouldn't be that satisfying, personally. When you have to fight for something, then it's worth winning.' – Eddie Irvine alienating Damon Hill fans, 1999

'As for my car, the less said the better. I was not pleased that my FW20 sounded like one of the new guitar pieces that I am learning.' – Jacques Villeneuve, 1998

'A very unadventurous year with a very unadventurous car. It was a bit like going motor racing with a Ford Popular.' – Technical director Patrick Head reflecting on Williams' 1998 season

Wolf

'Everything's wrong. The handling, the traction, the brake

balance, absolutely everything. It's hopeless.' – Jody Scheckter
having a good old moan before the 1977 Dutch Grand Prix. He
subsequently defied the odds to finish third

'I was ashamed. Imagine the despair when all you can do is sit in
the car and watch the other cars go by.' – Keke Rosberg driving
the big slow Wolf in 1979

Chapter Four

F1 Circuits

'The people who approve the layout of circuits don't drive round them at 150mph.' – Damon Hill, 1994

A-1 Ring

'It's got no Spa sparkle. There's not a lot of magic in it. When I drove it, it only took me about two laps to learn. It's not what the old one used to be.' – Johnny Herbert on Austria's A-1 Ring, built on the same site as, but shorter than, its predecessor, the Osterreichring

'You expect Julie Andrews and the entire Von Trapp family to come over the hills around the track.' – Murray Walker

Adelaide

'Without any doubt, this track takes more out of you physically than any other.' – Gerhard Berger, 1987

Aida

'The second corner did not have an adequate gravel run-off area.

If you left the road at that point, then you would hit the wall at almost 90 degrees.' – Damon Hill on the hazards of Aida, venue for the 1994 Pacific Grand Prix

Aintree

'It is so utterly devoid of the hazards of normal road driving that it reduces motor racing to the emotional level of a track meet. There is not even any sensation of speed...The Aintree circuit is lapped at about 90 mph, but it is speed in a vacuum, speed on a great green table. When the cars race down the back stretch along the white rails of the steeplechase course, they seem to be travelling no faster than horses.' – Author Robert Daley slamming the Aintree circuit which staged the British Grand Prix in 1955, 1957, 1959, 1961 and 1962, from *Cars at Speed* (Foulis, 1961)

Avus

'The place is a dump.' – Stirling Moss, 1963

'That was a shocking circuit; it was just an autobahn with a hairpin at one end and a banking at the other end. Every time you went round the banking you were glad to get to the other end of it. None of the drivers wanted to go back to Avus – well, none of the sane ones, anyway.' – Jack Brabham recalling the infamous Avus circuit near Berlin, venue for the 1959 German Grand Prix, from *When the Flag Drops* (William Kimber, 1971)

'Two long straights joined at one end by a sort of wall-of-death banking.' – Innes Ireland

'It was an awful place. The track itself was ridiculous, just two long straights, a hairpin and that absurd banking.' – BRM chief Raymond Mays

'If something goes wrong mechanically, you have more or less had it.' – British driver Cliff Allison, 1959

Barcelona

'That was man's stuff. I wish every circuit had somewhere like that.' – Frank Williams after Nigel Mansell and Ayrton Senna had gone wheel to wheel down the long straight at Barcelona in the 1991 Spanish Grand Prix. Mansell refused to yield at the corner at the end of the straight and Senna was forced to concede

Brands Hatch

'I like Brands Hatch but Formula 1 cars don't. All cars are pigs round this circuit.' – James Hunt, 1974

'They have spent nearly £40,000 on improving the circuit, but I must say that it is not well done. I can show you places where, if you have trouble, you can hit the guard rail at a bad angle, some places where you can hit the beginning of the guard rail. So I think it is still very bad for safety. Very bad! They have done a lot of work, but very bad work.' – Jean-Pierre Beltoise, 1972

'We are going at fantastic speeds now, but the tracks stay the same. Places like Brands Hatch – with no run-off areas – are a joke.' – Carlos Reutemann, 1981

'If you're going to have an accident, for sure you don't want to have it at Brands, but it's a very satisfying circuit to drive round. It is a real drivers' circuit.' – Patrick Tambay, 1982

'I loved racing at Brands Hatch. It's special because, being a natural amphitheatre, it's very intimate; the crowd are very close to you. You can feel the presence of the crowd, sense the emotion and the movement all the time even though you are not necessarily looking at them. It's there – and you respond to it.' – James Hunt, from *British Grand Prix* by Maurice Hamilton (Crowood Press, 1990)

'For me, the best circuit in the world is Brands Hatch. But it's a bit dangerous now for Formula 1.' – Gerhard Berger, 1989

'For us, this circuit is a mystery. We've never been competitive here.' – Renault team manager Jean Sage, 1982

'If you're on pole at Brands Hatch, you don't put your car straight; you put it three-fifths into the wall and look as odd as hell. But if you've put your car straight, your tail comes out immediately as you drop down the hill.' – Keke Rosberg, from *Keke* by Keke Rosberg and Keith Botsford (Stanley Paul, 1985)

Buenos Aires

'A very fine circuit, I think the best in the world. It is difficult, it is varied, it has a little bit of everything: slow corners, fast straights, enough room to pass and safety to spare.' – James Hunt, happy in Argentina, 1977

'There is a bump on the back straight and I am worried about the crowns in my teeth.' – Damon Hill, 1996

'It's tight and twisty, but fun.' – Damon Hill, 1996

'It's more like a go-kart track with many slow corners and hardly any straights between them. And in a racing car the severe bumps feel like an electric shock up your backside.' – Jacques Villeneuve, 1996

Dallas

'Things like this just degrade Grand Prix racing. But we have to bite the bullet, don't we? I also think that doing the race will be the best way to show the decision makers what kind of idiots they are.' – Keke Rosberg before the 1984 United States Grand Prix at the untried Dallas circuit

'For me, it's crazy to be racing at a place like this or Detroit. I like nothing about it.' – Elio de Angelis, 1984

'The only good thing here is that suddenly Detroit is not so bad.' – Alain Prost, 1984

Detroit

'It's dull. Most of the stuff is 90 degrees around the block, 50 yards and then another 90 degrees. I just can't get excited about it.' – Keke Rosberg, 1985

'Detroit is very dangerous. I hate it for two reasons: first, the track itself is a joke; second, the whole principle of racing there is wrong. We race there purely because it's in America, nothing else. Everyone says we must race in the United States because it's good for the image of Formula 1. I agree, but there's no way it's good for the image of F1 to race at a track like that. There are several circuits in the US which are considerably better than this one.' – Alain Prost, 1987

'I tell you this, if I had to race every Sunday on a track like Detroit, I would stop immediately. What I want is fun – to enjoy motor racing.' – Alain Prost, 1987

Dijon

'A track for playing it smooth and steady. The harder you try, the less well you do.' – John Watson on the venue for the 1977 French Grand Prix

Estoril

'It is one of the most dangerous circuits on the calendar. There is not enough run-off area at some corners and it is bumpy, difficult to drive. But I like it. It is very physical and to do a quick lap, you need a blend of finesse and aggression.' – Damon Hill, 1996

Hockenheim

'Anyone who goes off into the trees hasn't got a chance.' – Jim Clark to Graham Hill over dinner before a Formula 2 race at Hockenheim in 1968. Clark was killed in the race when his car ploughed into trees

'I'd much rather race at the Ring, but I'd rather survive at Hockenheim.' – John Watson as the Nürburgring was deemed too dangerous to stage the German Grand Prix after 1976

'There is a certain crazy thrill about travelling at more than 200 mph down a narrow road with trees either side. You do feel you are riding a bullet.' – Damon Hill, 1993

'There is nowhere else like Hockenheim. It's incredible. You come out of the forest and into this wall of humanity before returning to the woods for a minute and a half, back on your own amid calm.' – David Coulthard, 1998

'What next? Turnstiles? Toll booths? Where lies the point of all this phenomenal cornering ability when there are no corners?' – Journalist Nigel Roebuck complaining about the insertion of a new chicane before the Ostkurve, 1982

'It's bloody ridiculous – and dangerous. I tell you, on the first lap I'm going to keep out of the way. For sure, four cars written off there. At least.' – Keke Rosberg deploring the new chicane, 1982. Rosberg managed to avoid any trouble to finish third

'It's an unimaginative circuit and the chicanes are an artificial obstacle which I detest.' – Keke Rosberg, 1984

'Hockenheim is probably one of the most boring circuits around. It's just straight-chicane-straight-chicane.' – Johnny Herbert, 1997

Hungaroring

'Once you get off line, it's unbelievably slippery. It's like a moving target, this track. And the worst of it is, if you have to go off line, your tyres pick up dust and dirt – and you're off the pace for another couple of laps before they're clean again. You can't avoid it, either. Most of the circuit is so tight that overtaking's very difficult. Sooner or later you're going to have to go off line to get by someone.' – Nigel Mansell, 1987

'This is not a proper race circuit. It is Mickey Mouse. I can hit a one-iron further than the straight.' – Nigel Mansell, 1992

'It's like a giant kart track and it's difficult to pass because there are no straights of any consequence.' – Damon Hill, 1997

'The track is tiny and short, making it difficult to have a real race on.' – Alex Zanardi, 1999

Imola

'Imola is now one of the worst circuits, a disgusting track. They just put chicanes everywhere. It's safer, but it's not fun to drive. It's no good for racing.' – Jacques Villeneuve, 1997

Interlagos

'It is fiercely punishing physically. It is one of the very few circuits around the world laid out counter-clockwise, and this makes it very, very hard on the neck.' – Alan Jones, 1980

'The Interlagos circuit is very difficult, very dangerous and very, very unpleasant because large sections of it are so unpredictably bumpy that there is no way of knowing how the car will react.' – Alain Prost, from *Life in the Fast Lane* (Stanley Paul, 1988)

'It is a great circuit which has been imaginatively designed, making good use of the rolling terrain.' – Nigel Mansell in estate agent mode, 1992

Jarama

'It's all these bloody S-bends, short straights and hairpins. Overtaking is out of the question when circuits are like that. When new tracks are built in the future, I reckon it should be mandatory to have a right-angled corner every 200 yards or so. Circuit designers should keep in mind that the public comes to see racing – and that means overtaking.' – Alan Jones, critical of the venue for the 1981 Spanish Grand Prix

Kyalami

'It's a nice track, but personally I don't find it very exciting. I would have preferred some more high-speed corners.' – Gerhard Berger on the new-look Kyalami, home of the 1992 South African Grand Prix

'It is very demanding and I wish there was a good long straight for overtaking, but they have done a fantastic job on it.' – Nigel Mansell, 1992

Las Vegas

'A concrete maze, a Hampton Court of ten-ton blocks set out in a parking lot.' – Journalist Keith Botsford, 1981

Magny-Cours

'The trouble with this place is there's no crumpet; no anything, really.' – James Hunt underwhelmed by the new venue for the French Grand Prix

'The Mickey Mouse configuration, while testing and demanding and quite hard work for the drivers, makes it nearly impossible to overtake. It fails miserably as a suitable Grand Prix venue.' – James Hunt, 1990

'The last corner before the pits is ridiculous compared to the rest of the track. It is far too tight and twisty and that sort of corner should be outlawed.' – David Coulthard

Melbourne

'I like the circuit. It is a fun track, a mixture of Adelaide and Canada. It has a nice straight, good quick corners, plenty of overtaking areas and is quite fast.' – Damon Hill, 1996

Mexico City

'It makes Detroit look like Silverstone.' – Jonathan Palmer, 1987

'So the bumps are no problem, huh? Well, he'd know, wouldn't he? What did he use to inspect it – a Cadillac?' – Eddie Cheever after FISA chief Jean-Marie Balestre toured the Mexico City track and pronounced it a great circuit, 1987

'I do not think we should be coming here until the track is resurfaced and run-off areas are improved. We go to street circuits with better surfaces.' – Ayrton Senna speaking out against the Autodromo Hermanos Rodriguez, setting for the 1992 Mexican Grand Prix

Monsanto

'It is so twisty that if someone so much as spits on it there will be a skid and an accident. If one of us doesn't kill himself on this course, it will be a miracle.' – Phil Hill on the Lisbon venue for the 1959 Portuguese Grand Prix. Hill himself retired from the race after ploughing into his spinning namesake Graham

Monte Carlo

'It's like trying to ride a bicycle around your living room.' – Nelson Piquet

'If you suggested running a race there for the first time, you would be considered to be mad and out of touch with reality.' – Phil Hill, 1966

'The tunnel was tricky, especially on sunny days. Though it was shorter than it is today, it had no lighting, so you went from sunlight into deep shade.' – Juan Manuel Fangio

'Since the circuit has so many bends, I always looked for the shortest line so that I could corner more quickly.' – Juan Manuel Fangio

'In Monaco when you are in the lead there is no need to race to the limit. As long as you are making no mistakes, no one can overtake you.' – Jackie Stewart

'Unless you're in the lead, the important thing during the first lap is to keep out of trouble. If you charge off, flat out, on the narrow course, you're almost certain to end in a concertina.' – Graham Hill ('Mr Monaco'), from *Graham* (Stanley Paul, 1976)

'Never a year went by without somebody getting their front or back end stuffed in, and if you got round the first corner at Monaco you were doing well.' – Innes Ireland

'If you don't crash and your car doesn't give up the ghost, you're going to finish in the points.' – Ken Tyrrell pointing out that invariably there are few finishers in Monaco

'I've raced at Monte Carlo so often I'm almost part of the furniture and the invitations flood in. The hospitality makes it very hard to concentrate on the racing.' – Graham Hill, from *Graham*

'I have always considered Monte Carlo the most enjoyable race of the year. Nowhere else on the circuit do we find better accommodation, better food or better wine. The women are probably better-looking in Monte Carlo as well.' – Peter Revson, from *Speed With Style* by Revson and Leon Mandel (William Kimber, 1974)

'There is nothing like the lap of honour at Monaco – really close to that wonderful crowd who really want to communicate with you.' – Jackie Stewart

'It's not just the poseurs and their yachts, though they're bad enough. It's the race itself, which is just a bloody procession. The truth is that the cars have outgrown the circuit. And it is exceedingly boring to drive. I'm not alone in thinking it were better it died a natural death.' – Alan Jones, 1980

'I don't find it all that marvellous for someone to be standing outside the Hotel de Paris with a champagne flute in his hand when I'm screaming past through the corner a scant three yards away. I am too much of a purist to enjoy racing in Monaco.' – Niki Lauda, from *To Hell and Back* (Stanley Paul, 1986)

'I was in the wrong place and in the wrong job. This had to be ridiculous, zooming round here like so many trained monkeys, 1000 hp on this circuit. Madness. For the first time in my career, I was assailed by doubt.' – Niki Lauda after the 1985 Monaco Grand Prix. He retired from motor racing at the end of the season

'This bizarre and winding circuit really gave me the willies.' – François Cevert, 1973

'This place is nothing but an age test.' – Keke Rosberg, 1985

'It's madness to have so many cars on this circuit. Should there be an accident like the one I had, the dominoes would all fall.' – Michele Alboreto recovering from a crash in the Thursday practice session, 1987

'This really is a bloody stupid race, isn't it? Scary.' – Ferrari chief engineer John Barnard, 1987

'Monaco is a silly event, not a proper Grand Prix at all.' – James Hunt, 1990

'That's the trouble with Monaco. It's no fun any more. The fun at least allowed you to put up with the aggravation. Now it's just aggro. Nothing else.' – Jordan's technical director Gary Anderson on the cramped working conditions at Monte Carlo, from *Race Without End* by Maurice Hamilton (Patrick Stephens Ltd, 1994)

'When things are going against you there, it can be very depressing and claustrophobic.' – Damon Hill

'Monte Carlo is very hard physically because it's bumpy and it hurts a lot – your shoulders, your neck and so on.' – Ayrton Senna, 1991

'The track never goes very far in any one direction, so you're always turning, you're on the brakes as much as you're on the accelerator, and you change gear about three dozen times on every lap.' – Jacques Villeneuve, from *Villeneuve: My First Season in Formula 1* (CollinsWillow, 1996)

'If you are impulsive at Monaco, you are likely to end up in the barrier.' – Alain Prost, 1998

'To be quick means that you have to drive just inches away from the barriers. There is absolutely no room for error.' – Rubens Barrichello, 1999

'I like Monte Carlo but the track does not like me.' – Nigel Mansell before the 1992 Monaco Grand Prix. He went on to finish second, his first defeat of the season

'If you are not impressed by Formula 1 cars in Monaco, you will not be impressed with them anywhere.' – Damon Hill

'It is the jewel in the crown of the championship and it means you are a racing driver of extremely high calibre to win here.' – Damon Hill, 1996

'Drivers are challenged here in a completely different way. You do a ridiculous speed through a dark tunnel. It is exciting, terrifying, a big thrill for everyone. A unique experience.' – Damon Hill, 1996

'It might be a faintly absurd place in which to stage a race, but Monaco is crucial to the health of Formula 1.' – Damon Hill, from *F1 Through the Eyes of Damon Hill* (Little, Brown, 1998)

Monza

'A sensational speed bowl.' – Juan Manuel Fangio, 1955

'In my time, there was one curve that showed up any imperfection in a driver's technique: the Parabolica at Monza. I couldn't take it twice in succession on the same trajectory. Any variation of speed of entry, and you didn't go round it the way you'd planned.' – Juan Manuel Fangio, from *My Racing Life* (Patrick Stephens Ltd, 1990)

'A difficult circuit to make up time because it is *not* a difficult circuit to drive.' – Jackie Stewart

'I didn't like the place. It was like a scene from *Ben Hur*.' – Lotus driver John Miles who raced at Monza in 1969

'The Italian crowd is the most raucous and bullying crowd in the world. When they get near enough for an autograph, they push and shove – they will just tear any driver apart.' – Peter Revson, 1973

'The best thing about Italy is the border.' – Denny Hulme, angered by the Monza crowds, 1973

'Anyone who's out to conquer the world at the first chicane at Monza is someone you're going to bang wheels with.' – Keke Rosberg, 1984

'I had enough problems passing a Minardi!' – Michael Schumacher pointing out the difficulties of overtaking at Monza, 1998

Mosport Park

'The track itself is superb – as long as you can stay on it. The trouble is, the safety facilities are hopelessly inadequate and the organisation amateur to say the least. The people at Mosport are patently ill-equipped to handle a Grand Prix.' – James Hunt leading drivers' protests against the venue for the Canadian Grand Prix, 1977

Nürburgring

'Getting to know the Nürburgring was like getting to know a woman. You can't memorise 176 curves over more than fourteen miles, just as you can't memorise 176 feminine wiles after a short acquaintance.' – Juan Manuel Fangio, from *My Racing Life* (Patrick Stephens Ltd, 1987)

'It's one of those tracks where you lose touch with things. You think you're going fast and you're not going fast at all.' – Fangio

'The Nürburgring was always my favourite track from the first day I drove on it in an Alfetta in 1951. I fell totally in love with it and I believe that on that day in 1957 I finally managed to master it. It was as if I had screwed all the secrets out of it. I think that day I conquered it. On another day, it might have conquered me. Who knows?' – Fangio recounting his epic drive in the 1957 German Grand Prix

'I'm told there are 176 corners. I didn't stop to count them.' – Mike Hawthorn

'My favourite circuit – you don't find yourself coming up to the same corner every three miles.' – Tony Brooks

'The supreme test of the car plus the physical endurance and mental aptitude of the driver.' – Stirling Moss

'I never did a single lap more at the N(rburgring than I had to, never. I never enjoyed it when I was there; I enjoyed it in January or February in front of a log fire, or talking about how I did it. But no, I didn't enjoy the place when I was there.' – Jackie Stewart

'It gave you amazing satisfaction, but anyone who says he loved it is either a liar or wasn't going fast enough.' – Jackie Stewart

'Had I not won a Grand Prix at the Nürburgring, there would have been something missing from my career.' – Jackie Stewart, triumphant in 1968, 1971 and 1973

'When I left home to race in the German Grand Prix I always used to pause at the end of the driveway and take a long look back. I was never sure that I would come home again.' – Jackie Stewart on the dangers of the Ring

'Going round it you'd see a lot of holes in the hedge and you'd think, "That is where so-and-so got killed, this is where so-and-so went off."' – Stirling Moss, from *Stirling Moss's Motor Racing Masterpieces* (Sidgwick & Jackson, 1994)

'My personal opinion is that the Nürburgring is just too

dangerous to drive on nowadays. On any of the modern circuits if something breaks on my car I have a 70-30 chance that I will be all right. Here, if you have any failure on the car, 100 per cent death!' – Niki Lauda before practice for the 1976 German Grand Prix, the race in which he sustained near-fatal injuries

'The antithesis between the modern-day racing car and the Stone Age circuit was such that I knew every driver was taking his life in his hands in the most ludicrous degree.' – Niki Lauda in the wake of his terrible accident

'It's so exciting, each corner is like a blue movie!' – Swedish driver Gunnar Nilsson experiencing his first drive at the Nürburgring, 1976

'They ruined the Nürburgring in 1970 when they opened up the corners and knocked all the trees down. That took most of the challenge away.' – Chris Amon, 1976

Paul Ricard

'I hate this circuit. It is bullshit for me.' – Gerhard Berger on Magny-Cours' predecessor as venue for the French Grand Prix, 1990

Phoenix

'Disaster lurks around every corner.' – Nigel Mansell, 1990

'These town circuits are funny, they are so unpredictable. Many of the guys are ready to take a chance here. This is where you can make your name.' – Italian driver Stefano Modena before the 1991 United States Grand Prix. Modena finished a gallant fourth in a Tyrrell

Reims

'As slipstreaming is everything, the first man out of the corner is beaten by the man behind him, for the latter gains from the wake of the leading car. So no one wants to lead out of Thillois. One has to come out of Thillois in second place.' – François Cevert discussing Thillois, the final hairpin at Reims in France, from *François Cevert: A Contract With Death* by Jean-Claude Halle (William Kimber, 1975)

Sebring

'It was dull for both spectators and drivers and had the appearance of being set up for a driving test in a rally.' – Jack Brabham unimpressed by the Sebring circuit in Florida, venue for the 1959 United States Grand Prix. Brabham had ample opportunity to study the tarmac at close quarters since, having run out of fuel on the final lap, he had to push his car over the line to clinch the world championship

Sepang

'I have been learning the circuit on PlayStation. From what I have seen it looks quite difficult – a lot of hairpins.' – Rubens Barrichello's appraisal of the venue for the Malaysian Grand Prix, 1999

'It has some very demanding corners where it's difficult to find the braking points.' – Jacques Villeneuve, 1999

'There are some ridiculously slow corners which you think you could walk faster through!' – David Coulthard, 1999

Silverstone

'Silverstone is as dull as ditch water from a driver's point of view. OK, it is reasonably challenging because of the quick corners, but it has no character, no atmosphere.' – James Hunt

'It is difficult to enthuse about an airfield circuit. Silverstone is no exception. It is featureless and characterless with amenities, such as they are, housed under canvas.' – BRM chief Louis T. Stanley, 1965

'The key to Silverstone is to enter corners accurately and fast.' – James Hunt, 1989

'No one goes fast there except Englishmen and Froilan Gonzales.' – Phil Hill, 1960

'You have to be really, really smooth if you want to find that extra tenth of a second in those quick corners. You have got to have a lot of commitment through the likes of Stowe and Club.' – Alan Jones

'People talk about watching Jochen [Rindt], Ronnie [Peterson] and myself through Woodcote. That was great fun. But at the back of everyone's mind was the thought that if something went wrong we'd end up in the tenth row of the grandstand. The good guys didn't brake for Woodcote, and it was simply getting too fast. Nothing was done about the cars, so in came the Woodcote chicane. A great pity.' – Jackie Stewart, 1982

'The new layout is the best in the world. It's hairy all the way round. You have to commit yourself in the corners and hang on.' – Nigel Mansell, 1991

'This is the meanest, most physical circuit in the world.' – Mansell, 1992

'I feel I own this place. It is my special place, my comfort zone.' – Mansell, 1992

'It is a very exposed circuit because it is so flat and that means you have to take into account the wind.' – Jordan technical director Gary Anderson, 1996

'Luffield is probably the most frustrating complex of corners in the world.' – David Coulthard, 1996

Spa-Francorchamps

'It is a circuit for men.' – Niki Lauda, 1983

'It's one of the fastest tracks in the world and during the practice I was so scared I returned to the pits. Then I remembered my early struggles to get even this far up the motor racing ladder. I got back into the car and set off round the track a little more slowly at first to play myself back in – and then increased the speed up to the point where I had been scared before. Then I pushed it beyond that. I felt better and at the end of the practice session I had no problem.' – Graham Hill on his first experience of Spa in 1958, from *Graham* (Stanley Paul, 1976)

'Personally I don't feel it necessary for me to prove my bravery by driving in shirt sleeves on a circuit which is unnecessarily dangerous to myself, the other drivers, spectators and the racing fraternity.' – Jackie Stewart, 1969

'I reckon if you are going to get scared anywhere, it would be there.' – Chris Amon, 1970

'If you go off the road at Spa, the chances are that you will not get away with it.' – Innes Ireland, from *All Arms and Elbows* (Pelham Books, 1967)

'I prefer somewhere like Spa. There you cannot make a mistake and be safe. You have to race really precise.' – Pedro Rodriguez, 1968

'Sure, I'd like to race. I'm on pole. But if I kill someone? Is that worth it?' – Michele Alboreto before the 1985 Belgian Grand Prix. Drivers were concerned about the state of the surface at Spa

'The trouble is on the line we all take. There the track is worse than ice; you can't control the car. If we move to another line, the track isn't set up for it. The protection is planned to a specific line, and there are places where, if you go outside that line and go off, then you've had it.' – Martin Brundle voicing his fears over the state of Spa, 1985

'Spa is an amazing place to go racing, like a really wild rollercoaster ride that takes your breath away.' – Jacques Villeneuve, 1996

'The pleasure you get from driving at places like this is why you became a racing driver in the first place.' – Jacques Villeneuve, 1996

'It's a great track, more like the old-fashioned circuits. We don't have enough of these. Because it is so long, by the time you get to the end of a lap, you have almost forgotten what it was like when you started. But when you do complete a lap, you feel like you've travelled somewhere, like you've really achieved something.' – Jacques Villeneuve, 1997

'Anything can happen here. A marvellous challenge can be transformed into a harrowing experience in a matter of minutes.' – Damon Hill, 1999

'It's so demanding and presents such a challenge. Every aspect of a driver's expertise is tested.' – Johnny Herbert

'When you arrive there in sixth gear, you know you have the chance to do it flat. You just see the first turn, you don't see the exit out of the corner. You go in, your foot still on the throttle, and if you can keep it there you feel so good when you know you have done it. It is a fantastic feeling. You block out the fear. It is more sensational than frightening. I would say it is the greatest corner in Formula 1.' – Michael Schumacher on the buzz of Eau Rouge, from *Designs On Victory: On the Grand Prix Trail With Benetton* by Derick Allsop (Stanley Paul, 1993)

'Eau Rouge is a difficult corner even if you have a good, strong and reliable car. If you don't, then it can be a nightmare.' – Mika Hakkinen after BAR drivers Jacques Villeneuve and Ricardo Zonta crashed separately at Eau Rouge during qualifying for the 1999 Belgian Grand Prix

'I went back there recently and it was unreal, unbelievable that we ever raced there. I couldn't believe that bit of banking at Stavelot. Sure, it was nice to drive, really high speed; but dangerous, so dangerous.' – Denny Hulme, from *The World Atlas of Motor Racing* by Joe Saward (Hamlyn, 1989)

Alberto Ascari in a Ferrari at the British Grand Prix, Silverstone, 1953. He won.
(The Allsport Historical Collection)

Above: Mike Hawthorn in action at Gasworks Hairpin in a Ferrari, at the Monaco Grand Prix, 1957. (The Allsport Historical Collection)

Right: Juan Manuel Fangio, winner of the British Grand Prix at Silverstone in 1956. (Hulton Getty)

BRITISH
GRAND PRIX
1956

Above: Jack Brabham, in a Lotus, at Silverstone in 1964. (The Allsport Historical Collection)

Below: Graham Hill at the wheel of his Lotus, 1967. (The Allsport Historical Collection)

Right: Ayrton Senna celebrates his fourth Belgian Gran Prix win in 1991. (Allsport)

Above: Nigel Mansell after spinning out of the Spanish Grand Prix, Jerez, in 1994. (Allsport)

Above, right: The Schumacher brothers, Ralf and Michael, in Jerez, Spain, 1997. (Allsport)

Right: Michael Schumacher wins the 1993 San Marino Grand Prix. (Allsport)

Damon Hill, at Silverstone, 1999. (Allsport)

Suzuka

'Very narrow, very bumpy and very quick.' – Nelson Piquet's view of the Japanese track, 1987

'It's a great circuit, but for traffic it's disastrous because it's narrow.' – Stefan Johansson, 1987

'What I really like about it is that your times improve as you try harder. At some tracks it's the other way round. But here you can see some reward for effort.' – Jonathan Palmer, 1987

'Suzuka gives you a terrific sense of accomplishment. After you really attack a lap – throwing everything you have into it – you feel really complete as a driver. The only thing that spoils the lap somewhat is a silly slow chicane. I don't like slow corners.' – Jacques Villeneuve, 1996

'Suzuka is my favourite circuit. It is like my home Grand Prix because I raced in Japan for three years and had a lot of fun there. I always get a real buzz from the place.' – Eddie Irvine, 1999

Watkins Glen

'The old Glen was a nothing circuit. We all went to play golf. The trees looked lovely in the autumn. When they modified the track, it became a good circuit.' – Denny Hulme on the one-time setting for the United States Grand Prix, before and after its 1971 facelift

Zandvoort

'The wind is something else. The North Sea, so black and cold in late May or early June, often sends in brisk gusts. Racing drivers, like bullfighters, dread wind. Race cars are light, considering their power, and they are driven so fast that there is very little road adhesion. Every time they top a rise – and there are many at Zandvoort – they are momentarily airborne. At such speeds the shock of smacking a wall of wind is capable of deflecting the car; the driver does not know until the car lands again just how much it has been deflected, and he may not then have time enough to make corrections.' – Author Robert Daley on the hazards of Zandvoort, one-time venue for the Dutch Grand Prix, from *Cars at Speed* (Foulis, 1961)

'There is little attractive about the setting. It lacks the glamour of Monte Carlo, the grandeur of Spa and Nürburgring, the atmosphere of Monza and the Gallic excitement of the French event. Instead the fare is solid, homely and enthusiastic.' – Louis T. Stanley, from *Grand Prix* (Macdonald, 1965)

Chapter Five
Memorable Races

'I was very tense, very anxious. I had to rush to the toilet about five minutes before the start and I remember I was talking to myself all the time! There were some people there from Argentina trying to calm me, but I couldn't talk to them. I was thinking about nothing but this race and I didn't even hear what they were saying. Of course, I didn't speak English, so I didn't understand anything else that was going on all round me. I seem to have been in a trance.' – Argentine driver Froilan Gonzales (known as 'the Bull of the Pampas') before the start of the 1951 British Grand Prix

'On the winner's podium I was embraced warmly by Fangio. That meant a lot to me. Then they played the Argentine national anthem. I had never experienced anything like this before. When I saw my country's flag being hoisted, it was just too much for me and I cried.' – Froilan Gonzales winning the 1951 British Grand Prix

'I still remember that instant of terror. I knew where there was an extremely steep drop, just beyond the corner where my car began to skid, and came on to it as though leaping from a spring-board. By chance, a tree trunk stopped the machine as I managed to swing across the road. No damage to the car and not even a scratch on me. All alone, I put the car back on the road. Thirty feet from me, a spectator standing behind the tree trunk drank half a bottle of brandy to recover from his fright.' – Juan Manuel Fangio recounting his spin at Adenau during practice for the 1951 German Grand Prix at the Nürburgring, from *My Twenty Years of Racing* (Temple Press Ltd, 1961)

'He finished the race with a fountain of fuel streaking along the road behind him – rather like driving a hand grenade with the pin out.' – *The Motor* describes Giuseppe 'Nino' Farina's third place in the 1951 Italian Grand Prix

'I had a habit of humming as well as chewing gum during a race. This time I spat out my gum and began to pray, silently. My prayer was answered.' – Juan Manuel Fangio on his way to clinching the first of his five world championships at the 1951 Spanish Grand Prix

'The voices of 300,000 yelling fans accompanied me on the lap of honour. I was deeply thrilled at the sound of a crowd shouting in Spanish. It seemed as though I were in Buenos Aires.' – Juan Manuel Fangio victorious at the 1951 Spanish Grand Prix at Pedralbes

'When I regained consciousness, Farina was there by my bed, holding a laurel wreath. I thought he must be dead also! Eventually I began to believe I was still alive and realised that he had won and brought the laurels to me in tribute.' – Juan Manuel Fangio following a serious crash at Monza in 1952

'We would go screaming down the straight side by side absolutely flat out, grinning at each other, with me crouching down in the cockpit, trying to save every ounce of wind resistance. We were only inches apart and I could clearly see the rev counter in Fangio's cockpit.' – Mike Hawthorn recalling his duel with Fangio at the 1953 French Grand Prix, a race which Hawthorn won by a second, from *Challenge Me the Race* (Aston Publications, 1957)

'The rest of that lap was a nightmare. I was braking late, over-shooting the corners, driving like a drunk.' – Mike Hawthorn overcome by exhaust fumes at the 1954 Belgian Grand Prix. He somehow managed to bring the Ferrari to a halt near the pits before passing out

'I saw Fangio's amazing stamina in the Argentine Grand Prix. He drove the 96 laps to win in terrible heat when every other car that finished was shared between two or even three drivers just to make it to the line.' – Stirling Moss on Fangio's courageous drive at the 1955 Argentine Grand Prix

'When I finished, the car was junk.' – Juan Manuel Fangio following a hair-raising drive at the 1956 Monaco Grand Prix during which he bounced off walls, skimmed kerbs and succeeded in denting both the nose and tail of his Lancia-Ferrari

'My anxiety and misery gave way to joy, so much so that I threw my arms around him and kissed him and got into his car.' – Juan Manuel Fangio after Peter Collins had generously handed over his car to Fangio during the 1956 Italian Grand Prix. Fangio went on to finish second and clinch the world championship for the fourth time

'All I could think of out there was that if I won the race and the championship I would become an instant celebrity. I would have a position to live up to. People would make demands of me. I would be expected at all times to act like "the champion". Driving would not be fun any more. I wanted things to go on just as they were, and so I handed my car over to Fangio.' – Peter Collins explaining his gesture at the 1956 Italian Grand Prix

'After the race the officials came to me and said I was disqualified because I'd been given a push. "But," I said, "Piotti is my team-mate, he is entitled to give me a push." Strictly speaking, Piotti wasn't my team-mate, he was a privateer although we were both in Maseratis. The officials said, "Oh, well, OK."' – Stirling Moss on how he managed to keep the 1956 Italian Grand Prix despite being given an illegal push by Luigi Piotti who used his own car to nudge Moss back to the pits after Moss had run out of fuel

'Only Hawthorn in a Ferrari and Behra in the Maserati were ahead of me. Then fate, which I think at times dealt me unnecessarily hard blows, stepped in with a masterstroke from the Moss viewpoint and eliminated my two rivals at the same moment. The Maserati engine blew up and with exceptional adroitness scattered parts over the track so as to puncture Hawthorn's left-hand tyre.' – Stirling Moss recounting his famous victory in a Vanwall at the 1957 British Grand Prix – the first Englishman to win the British Grand Prix in a British car, from *Design and Behaviour of the Racing Car* by Moss and Laurence Pomeroy (William Kimber, 1963)

'Even now I can feel fear when I think of that race. I believe I was inspired that day. I knew what I had done, the chances I had taken. I'd driven my car to the limit, and perhaps a little more. I'd never driven like that before, and I knew I never would again.' – Juan Manuel Fangio who pushed his Maserati to the limit to catch and overhaul the Ferraris of Peter Collins and Mike Hawthorn and win the 1957 German Grand Prix

'If I hadn't moved over, I'm sure the old devil would have driven right over me.' – Mike Hawthorn in awe of Fangio's determination at the 1957 German Grand Prix

'It was remarkable to see anybody get past two such great drivers as Collins and Hawthorn in a single move and with such relative ease. I already had great admiration for him, but to see him do that underlined my knowledge of his greatness.' – Stirling Moss paying tribute to Fangio's drive at the 1957 German Grand Prix

'Fangio threw that Maserati round the Nürburgring like no one I've seen before or since.' – Jack Brabham's view of Fangio's epic drive at the 1957 German Grand Prix

'The course was heavy on tyres and my problem was that we just didn't have any, so that it was not merely a matter of avoiding the time loss involved in changing a wheel but simply that if we ran out of tyres that, no kidding, was the end. By scrounging I managed to get enough tyres and I drove at a pace which I thought was as slow as would get me home. With no tread on the tyres, the last fifteen laps were pretty nerve-racking. So then I had to start going really very slowly round the hairpins, without provoking wheelspin; when I could see an oily or rubbery part of the track I would let the car go wide on to it, and perhaps over it on to the grass.' – Stirling Moss taking it steadily for once to win the 1958 Argentine Grand Prix in a Cooper, from *Design and Behaviour of the Racing Car* by Moss and Laurence Pomeroy (William Kimber, 1963)

'I pulled over to the right-hand side of the road thinking that maybe it would work if it was pushed. There was a *Motor Sport* photographer there, Michael Tee, and a French photographer, and I yelled to them to give me a push. Michael rushed up straightaway, but this Frenchman stood back to photograph it; he just wouldn't help. I was livid with anger and leaped out of the car with the idea of making him, but he refused to do a thing. I was almost on the point of giving him one, I was so angry.' – Mike Hawthorn spluttering to a halt on lap 46 of the 1958 Monaco Grand Prix, from *Champion Year* (Aston Publications, 1959)

'I was terribly lucky. The shaft had snapped close to the rear wheels. The rear part of it was thus short; if it had been longer it would have dropped into the road, dug in probably, and turned the car over.' – Jo Bonnier who was doing 165 mph in a Maserati at the 1958 Belgian Grand Prix when the drive-shaft snapped directly beneath his seat. The steel shaft rose up and whacked Bonnier's bottom with such force that it nearly catapulted him from the car

'I took one 160 mph corner half standing in the cockpit. The crowd thought I had gone mad – but the gearbox had got so hot it melted the solder holding the oil-filler cap in place and boiling oil was splashing over my legs.' – Graham Hill having fun and games in the Lotus 16 at the 1958 French Grand Prix, from *Graham* (Stanley Paul, 1976)

'Peter and I had talked over our plan for the race. Pete, in his typically generous way, had said that he was going to do everything he could to help me win the title. The general idea was that he went out in front and forced the pace in an effort to blow the Vanwalls up; if he blew himself up it would be too bad.' – Mike Hawthorn revealing the Ferrari team plans for the 1958 British Grand Prix. In fact, Collins didn't blow up and went on to win – his last Grand Prix victory

'I coveted that championship. After Fangio's retirement I felt I was his natural heir. Only his presence had kept it from me the previous three seasons.' – Stirling Moss, about to be denied again, before the decisive 1958 Moroccan Grand Prix

'I was coasting. If I had gone any slower I would have been a menace out there. Also it would have been dangerous for me because I would have lost my concentration. That's how accidents happen.' – Stirling Moss defending himself against accusations that he was hard on cars after retiring near the end of the 1959 Monaco Grand Prix while in the lead

'I was almost at the stage of collapsing at the wheel, so I broke all the windscreen away with my hand to try to get some air. Every car I got near showered me with bricks and stones. I was coasting into the corners rather than braking, because my feet were so badly burnt that I could hardly put any pressure on the pedals. When the race was over I had to be lifted out of the cockpit.' – Jack Brabham struggling to finish third in the 1959 French Grand Prix at Reims, a race run on such a hot day that the road was breaking up

'It wasn't until I'd stopped rolling that I realised where I was. I sat up in the middle of the track – and found myself looking straight into the radiator of Masten Gregory's car! He came belting out of the corner straight for me and this made me wake up. I was off that circuit pretty damn quick.' – Jack Brabham as he was thrown out of his Cooper when it hit a telegraph pole and rebounded on to the circuit at the 1959 Portuguese Grand Prix in Lisbon, from *When the Flag Drops* (William Kimber, 1971)

'At the hairpin just before the main straight, Jo Bonnier, whose

BRM had quit earlier, now set up a "refreshment bar" for the tired drivers. As they came past, crash helmets filled with water were thrown over them to cool them down.' – John Cooper recalling a bizarre scene from the 1959 Portuguese Grand Prix, from *John Cooper: Carpetbagger* (Foulis, 1977)

'They changed the clutch for the race without telling me! It wasn't bedded in, so when I let it out at the start it slipped and burnt itself out. My race lasted 100 yards.' – Tony Brooks remembering his short drive for Ferrari at the 1959 Italian Grand Prix, from *Grand Prix Greats* by Nigel Roebuck (Patrick Stephens Ltd, 1986)

'It must have been the first time the new world champion was escorted to the line by a motorcycle escort.' – Jack Brabham running out of fuel on the last lap and pushing his Cooper across the line in the 1959 United States Grand Prix at Sebring

'Graham had a wrist watch with an expanding metal bracelet which he did not remove when driving the racing car. He did not allow for the BRM vibration; the watch strap broke, and the watch fell on to the track about four feet from the edge of the kerb. This happened right opposite our pit. Graham saw his watch lying in the road and hoped no one would run over it. We saw it all, but no one dare try to pick it up as there was not enough warning of a car coming round the slight curve from the Gasworks hairpin. Eventually Graham ran it over himself, much to his disgust!' – BRM chief engineer Tony Rudd recalling Graham Hill's mishap at the 1960 Monaco Grand Prix, from *It Was Fun!* (Patrick Stephens Ltd, 1993)

'The car spun five times through 360 degrees, all the way down the middle of the track. I left great black marks on the road like some gigantic doodle which were still there the following year, I think.' – Innes Ireland crashing his Lotus at the double left-hander before La Source in the 1960 Belgian Grand Prix at Spa, from *All Arms and Elbows* (Pelham Books, 1967)

'I thought, "I'll have to stay in the tramlines all the way to the depot, wherever that is."' – Jack Brabham, his car caught up in the tramlines on the second lap of the 1960 Portuguese Grand Prix at Oporto. He managed to extricate himself after his unscheduled detour and recovered to win the race and clinch the title for the second successive year

'I was very nervous at the start, thinking, "After you, Mr Moss, after you, Mr Gurney", but when the flag dropped they became just drivers, men I had to beat.' – Giancarlo Baghetti in awe of his elders on his F1 debut, the non-championship 1961 Syracuse Grand Prix. The young Italian won and repeated the feat in his first championship event a few weeks later, steering his Ferrari to victory in blistering heat in the French Grand Prix at Reims

'Going down the Masta straight – the quickest section of this very quick circuit – I found that the rush of air was getting under the peak of my helmet and threatening to force it up. I decided that the only thing to do was to throw the peak away, so I caught hold of a strap at the back and gave it a yank. I'd got hold of the wrong strap though and I pulled off my goggles by mistake! Fortunately I had another pair round my neck and managed to get them in place. Then I tugged at the peak and eventually, after a lot of effort, it ripped off. I suppose it has something to do with the air flow round the cockpit of the Lotus 25, but since then I have never worn a peak on my helmet.' – Jim Clark recounting his victory in the 1962 Belgian Grand Prix at Spa

'I had to steel myself to drive fast enough to win, but no faster. The Ring is no place for pressing on regardless, particularly when it is damp.' – Graham Hill winning the 1962 German Grand Prix in difficult conditions at the Nürburgring

'Nürburgring still makes me shudder to think of it! I suppose I was reacting from being annoyed with myself, but that day I attempted things with the Lotus I didn't think were possible before.' – Jim Clark on his drive from last to fourth at the 1962 German Grand Prix. He had been left on the grid at the start when his engine died after he had inexplicably forgotten to switch on the fuel

'Jimmy came in so quick and left his braking so late that I leapt back four feet, convinced that he wouldn't make the corner.' – Bruce McLaren, as a trackside spectator following his retirement in the race, watching Jim Clark go through Club Corner on his way to victory in the 1963 British Grand Prix at Silverstone

'We came up behind Innes Ireland and his car was much quicker than ours down the straights but we had him on the corners. I tried on one bend to get past on the inside but Innes blocked me, then I tried again and the same thing happened. The next time I thought I would play it craftily so I waited until Gurney had come up close behind me and I made a pass at Innes. But I eased off slightly and let Gurney go through. Innes thought that the car coming inside him was me and he moved over again but he found out it was Dan and no one did that sort of thing to Dan. In the ensuing battle of wits Dan eased Innes out and while he was doing that I passed both of them.' – The wily Jim Clark en route to becoming world champion by virtue of victory in the 1963 Italian Grand Prix

'Myself, Bonnier, Siffert, Gurney, Brabham, Ginther and Bandini – we all streamed along in close company like a pack of dogs after a bitch on heat.' – Innes Ireland leading the chasing pack at the 1964 Italian Grand Prix

'When I arrived back at the pits after the slowing-down lap I looked at all the faces to see whether or not I was champion and I could tell from their expressions I hadn't won it.' – Graham Hill coming home eleventh in the decisive 1964 Mexican Grand Prix. John Surtees had pipped him for the title by finishing second

'It was enormously satisfying to have won a race in which I'd had to stop and get out and push. What made it even more satisfying was that both Stirling Moss and Fangio were there to see me pull off my third win in three consecutive years.' – Graham Hill on the 1965 Monaco Grand Prix, during which he had stalled the BRM on an escape road and been forced to push the car backwards on to the track, from *Graham* (Stanley Paul, 1976)

'He had driven a race in the style of the grand old days when men were men and racing cars were monsters.' – Bruce McLaren in praise of Graham Hill's victory at Monaco, 1965

'Hush Puppies don't seem to have been developed with Formula 1 racing in mind.' – Bruce McLaren following practice at Monaco in 1966. He had accidentally left his racing boots at the hotel and been forced to drive in ordinary shoes after first hacking off the toes (of the shoes)

'I must have been doing 165 mph when the car began aquaplaning and I lost control. First I hit a telegraph pole, then a woodcutter's cottage and finished up in the outside basement of a farm building. The car ended up shaped like a banana and I was still trapped inside it.' – Jackie Stewart recalling a hairy crash in the 1966 Belgian Grand Prix at Spa

'I guarantee we drove every lap under a different set of circumstances because of rain showers on different parts of the circuit. You would come to rivers running across the road. We were sliding all over in mud and water.' – Jack Brabham winning in the wet in the 1966 German Grand Prix at the Nürburgring

'It was by no means a funny situation rushing down the straight at over 160 mph and trying to slow down by slipping down through the gears. It was a terrifying ride.' – Denny Hulme finishing fourth in the 1967 South African Grand Prix at Kyalami despite driving the last quarter of the race without brakes in his Brabham

'It was a real old-fashioned dice I had with Jack. He was throwing everything in the bloody book at me – stones, grass, dirt, *everything*.' – Chris Amon recalling his battle with Jack Brabham at the 1967 British Grand Prix. Amon finished third, one place ahead of the Australian whose cause was not helped when both of his wing mirrors fell off

'In all my years of motor racing, I can only think of a couple of times when I mastered the machine as at the Nürburgring in 1968. It was foggy, rainy and aquaplany: that day, the machine was my passenger. Otherwise, I was always doing my best to reconcile a difficult marriage.' – Jackie Stewart, from *The Champions of Formula 1* by Keith Botsford (Stanley Paul, 1988)

'On the third lap, as I came into the straight, I pushed the pedal to flatten the wing – and the pedal went light. Crumbs, I thought, we're in trouble. I turned my mirror – I always have them mounted fairly loose – and had a look: there was the old Bungee rubber band waving in the breeze. I had a look in the other mirror, slightly despairing, because if that one was gone, I was sunk. Without the rubber bands to pull the wing into the maximum downward load position, the car oversteers like a pig, but it was all right and it held all through the race. With only one rubber Bungee, it couldn't come back to the maximum download position for braking at the end of the straight when I let off the pedal, but, as the speed dropped, it came into the right position of its own accord and stayed there. It was all a bit hairy under braking, but it held.' – Graham Hill overcoming wing problems on the Lotus to become 1968 world champion thanks to victory in the final race of the season, the Mexican Grand Prix

'It sprinted right into my path. My right front tyre hit it; there was no question of me deviating even a fraction to avoid it. I would have had an accident and taken half the starters in the Italian Grand Prix off the road with me . . . I went through agonies for the next few laps thinking a bone had lodged in the tyre. I could hardly take my eyes off the front tyre, or the rear which I watched through the mirror. The shape of the tyre is often the first warning you get of a puncture.' – Jackie Stewart triumphant despite running over a hare at the 1969 Italian Grand Prix, from *Jackie Stewart: World Champion* (Pelham Books, 1970)

'I never drove quicker than I did on that day, but I couldn't have won if Jack hadn't made that small mistake. He braked too late, thinking that I was actually closer than I was, and he lost it because he was on the right-hand side of the road to stop me going through on the inside and he found himself on the "marbles".' – Jochen Rindt snatching victory in the 1970 Monaco Grand Prix. Jack Brabham had been leading into the final corner on the last lap but he made a mistake while lapping Piers Courage and slid into the straw bales, allowing Rindt through to win

'I was happy. Everybody was happy. It was like a love story film.' – Emerson Fittipaldi clinching the title at the 1972 Italian Grand Prix, from *Grand Prix Showdown* by Christopher Hilton (Patrick Stephens Ltd, 1992)

'Before I got into the car I was puking all over the place and on the grid. I was just a shaking wreck.' – James Hunt making his Grand Prix debut, at Monaco in 1973, from *Hunt: The Biography* by Gerald Donaldson (CollinsWillow, 1994)

'When I looked to my right, there were cars hitting each other before they hit me. I put my head down and felt a lot of banging. Then it went quiet for a bit and I thought, "Time to get out of here." I looked up, only to see another load of cars heading towards me so I put my head down again. I jumped out and ran across to the pit wall. Phil Kerr [the McLaren team manager] said: "I'd better hide you." You see, John Surtees had just seen his team wiped out before his very eyes and he was soon round at our pit demanding Scheckter's head.' – Jody Scheckter recounting his spin at the start of the 1973 British Grand Prix which caused a multiple accident and wiped out a sizeable proportion of the field, from *British Grand Prix* by Maurice Hamilton (Crowood Press, 1990)

'I stopped playing tennis and took ridiculous precautions when I walked upstairs or around the house. I was ready to shoot myself if I threw the title away because of a strained ankle or a broken bone.' – Jody Scheckter leaving nothing to chance in the build-up to the 1974 Canadian Grand Prix. In the event, brake failure proved Scheckter's downfall

'It was the most wonderful attack; Clay at his best. He just did not appear to brake at all and then he assaulted Niki. For a brief moment I thought I had the pleasure of watching the two Ferrari drivers take each other off the road – and then I realised I was in their accident as well.' – James Hunt remembering the 1976 British Grand Prix. After being eliminated in that first-corner collision, Hunt won the restarted race in the spare car, only to be disqualified following an objection from Ferrari

'Niki had just climbed out of his deathbed and they wheeled him in, all wrapped in bandages, more for dramatic effect than anything else. Really, at that point I knew we didn't have a chance.' – McLaren team manager Teddy Mayer as the team's appeal against disqualification from the 1976 British Grand Prix fell on stony ground

'James had quite a temper and he was hot, yelling and screaming. I realised he thought he'd blown it from the expression on his face. We were telling him it had all come right but he couldn't hear because of his helmet. Then he dragged it off and paused for breath and I just said: "You've won it, you were third, you've done it."' – McLaren boss Teddy Mayer as James Hunt became 1976 world champion after finishing third in the Japanese Grand Prix

'I stayed so close to him I could read the labels on his collar.' – Mario Andretti tailing Jody Scheckter at the 1977 United States West Grand Prix at Long Beach

'I never felt so much like crying in my life. Mario was climbing up my backside the first half of the race, but in the second half I thought I had him.' – Jody Scheckter overhauled by Andretti three laps from the end of the 1977 United States West Grand Prix

'He already put me on the grass twice trying to get by and in the end I tried so hard I lost it myself.' – Alan Jones going out of the 1977 United States East Grand Prix at Watkins Glen following a set-to with Ronnie Peterson

'He passed car after car. I remember turning to Patrick [Head] and saying, "I don't mind if we don't finish; I've had my money's worth, because he's not just a good driver, he's an exciting driver." And I hadn't been excited by a driver's performance in many years.' – Frank Williams enthusing over Alan Jones's drive at the 1978 United States West Grand Prix at Long Beach

'For three hours I knew I was in the crap. The car wouldn't work, we tried this, we tried that; we just came up with the lucky number.' – Mario Andretti conjuring victory out of nothing for Lotus at the 1978 French Grand Prix

'I spent the race fighting understeer, oversteer and no steer.' – Riccardo Patrese enduring a nightmare drive in the Arrows at the 1978 French Grand Prix

'No, nothing broke. I wish I could tell you that something had! I just made a mistake, I'm afraid.' – Mario Andretti blundering out of the 1978 British Grand Prix

'I went into the corner behind Jones. I think something must have happened in front of him, because he just stopped dead right in front of me. I went straight over him, the car went up in the air and crashed down. I don't know whether the accident went on behind me, whether he was avoiding the accident, or whether they were avoiding me!' – Derek Daly at the 1978 Dutch Grand Prix

'Every time I looked in my mirrors, there was Nelson. So I tried hard for a couple of laps, looked again and he was still there, right behind.' – Niki Lauda, impressed by his new young Brabham team-mate Nelson Piquet at the 1979 South African Grand Prix

'I felt the year's pressure fall from my shoulders. It hadn't been like a race's pressure, it was a year's pressure. It was tremendous pressure.' – Jody Scheckter finally securing the world drivers' championship at the 1979 Italian Grand Prix

'I had reached the point, the very minute I had worked towards all my life – and there I was getting my arse burned!' – Nigel Mansell enduring a painful F1 debut on the grid for the 1980 Austrian Grand Prix. His problems were caused by fuel being spilt over him when his tank was being topped up

'The decision to race was the right one: it showed I wasn't a quitter. But the problems started when I got out of the car and discovered that my hamstrings had shrunk where they'd been immersed in petrol for so long. Afterwards I had to have them stretched.' – Nigel Mansell after the 1980 Austrian Grand Prix

'The pits didn't really keep me well enough informed of the progress I was making against Jabouille. I was catching up – not spectacularly, but slowly – and eventually he beat me to the finish by less than a second. If I'd been told a bit earlier, I might have launched an attack and quite possibly won.' – Alan Jones finishing a close second in the Williams to Jean-Pierre Jabouille's Renault at the 1980 Austrian Grand Prix

'On the end of the straight the front end was literally jumping off the ground. It was porpoising so badly that my knees were being thumped at the top of the bulkhead and I had no control whatsoever over the pedals.' – Nigel Mansell struggling with the Lotus at the 1980 Italian Grand Prix

'I took up my line, Piquet didn't back off and the result was a multiple-car, spectacular shunt. Piquet did exactly the same thing to Pironi after the restart, but Pironi had the common sense to back off and live to fight another day.' – Alan Jones on his first-lap collision with Nelson Piquet which forced a restart to the crucial 1980 Canadian Grand Prix. Jones went on to win and Piquet's retirement handed him the world championship

'The championship? You take it any way it comes.' – Alan Jones reacting to suggestions that he had won the 1980 title by default

'Oh, absolutely. You see, they keep the wheels from touching the ground.' – Alan Jones's answer to NBC 'interviewer' Mark Thatcher who asked him after his victory in the 1981 United States West Grand Prix: 'Did tyres play an important part today?'

'I don't often piss myself laughing in a racing car, but I did when I saw that.' – Alan Jones after rival Nelson Piquet ran into a barrier at the 1981 Monaco Grand Prix

'It was one of the most tiring races of my life. The go-kart ride we all have now is hard on the driver because he gets pitched around a lot. My helmet kept smashing into the roll-over bar, and I ache all over.' – Gilles Villeneuve fighting the pain barrier to win the 1981 Monaco Grand Prix

'It was like taking a plane into a cloud.' – Alan Jones ploughing into Gilles Villeneuve at the 1981 British Grand Prix. Villeneuve had spun right in front of Jones, obscuring the Australian's vision and leaving him with nowhere to go

'When I took the flag I was totally embarrassed. The spectators were behaving in a very un-British manner. There was an incredible free flow of emotion and I kept wondering what I had done to deserve it. I didn't know how to cope with it. I almost wanted to hide.' – The unassuming John Watson, awkward in victory at the 1981 British Grand Prix

'I was dead. I was destroyed. I couldn't even stand up on the podium, but it was really fantastic.' – Nelson Piquet after winning a gruelling 1982 Brazilian Grand Prix at Rio. His joy subsequently turned to dismay when his Brabham was disqualified over water-tank irregularities

'I had a go at catching him because he was there. He wasn't in my way, but he was the man who was either going to allow me to win my first race or wasn't. He was the last little bit of the package. He was my rabbit; I was just about to shoot him. Instead, it all went wrong.' – Keke Rosberg making a mistake while trying to lap Marc Surer on the penultimate lap of the 1982 Belgian Grand Prix. Rosberg's error allowed John Watson through for victory. From *Keke* by Keke Rosberg and Keith Botsford (Stanley Paul, 1985)

'I was blocking everyone a little bit and I can't really blame them if they were upset. But, on the other hand, they couldn't pass me. I was happy enough with what I was doing. Getting past me was their problem!' – Patrick Tambay holding up the field at the 1982 Dutch Grand Prix

'It was terribly disappointing but you don't know how good it felt to be part of a *race* again.' – Derek Warwick, after failing to qualify in three of the first six races of the season, at least getting to taste a slice of the action before being forced to retire at the 1982 Dutch Grand Prix

'Now we're equal. I blew Monaco and you've blown this race for me.' – Keke Rosberg to the Williams team after his car, already badly understeering, finally gave up the ghost at the 1982 British Grand Prix. Four races earlier, Rosberg had been forced to retire at Monaco after hitting the kerb and breaking the car's suspension while trying to pass his old friend Andrea de Cesaris

'I saw him almost crying, he was so happy, and I was happy too. It was my first victory and for me a victory with Colin Chapman meant more than one with anybody else.' – Elio de Angelis winning the 1982 Austrian Grand Prix in a Lotus

'One race does not a season make.' – Nelson Piquet after winning the first race of the 1983 season, the Brazilian Grand Prix

'I was so nervous during the last few laps that I started getting pains in my stomach. You know, so many times have I been in this position and something has gone wrong.' – Alain Prost, triumphant on home soil in the 1983 French Grand Prix

'If Bruno wanted the place badly, he was welcome to it.' – Nigel Mansell, criticised by Lotus team chiefs for easing up in the finish straight and allowing Bruno Giacomelli to steal seventh place in the 1983 Italian Grand Prix

'It was a bore, wasn't it? Rewarding for me because I got some points out of it. But I'm glad that I wasn't watching.' – Derek Warwick finishing third to Alain Prost at the 1984 German Grand Prix

'I tell you, if the engine had lasted the lap, the time would have been incredible!' – Patrick Tambay after the engine on his Renault blew during a fast qualifying lap for the 1984 Austrian Grand Prix

'I heard a big bang in my gear-box, and suddenly there were no more gears.' – Niki Lauda overcoming a considerable handicap to win the 1984 Austrian Grand Prix

'There was no signal, nothing. Suddenly his rear wing was right there in front of me.' – Thierry Boutsen after René Arnoux made a sudden tyre stop at the 1984 Dutch Grand Prix. Boutsen's Arrows hit the rear tyre of Arnoux's Ferrari and was catapulted into the air

'We made a mistake, a team mistake. First we didn't get our ballast right, and second we didn't stick to our usual back-up system. We took the car to be weighed Sunday morning, and hung around three-quarters of an hour, and there was no one there to weigh it. So we thought we'd weight it up after warm-up. It was raining, we had a few jobs to do, so we said bugger it. I have no complaints. We were wrong, we lost, we've learned a lesson.' – McLaren's Ron Dennis after Alain Prost was disqualified from first place in the 1985 San Marino Grand Prix because his car was found to be underweight

'I did my job. I'm punished for something which can't be put at my door.' – Alain Prost, smarting after the 1985 San Marino Grand Prix

'I won it. I was fastest on the circuit. I did 99 per cent of everything right. Morally, I should have won. I thought I had won.' – Nigel Mansell finishing second in the 1986 Spanish Grand Prix

'Obviously, I'll make sure I find first gear.' – Nigel Mansell asked whether he had any special plans for the decisive 1986 Australian Grand Prix. In the previous race at Mexico City he had been last away after failing to put the Williams into gear on the grid and could only finish fifth

'Hmm. Mansell, Piquet, Senna, then me. Three people ahead of me on the grid – and they all hate each other. I will have a very quiet first lap, I think.' – Alain Prost's softly-softly approach to the 1986 Australian Grand Prix

'The car started to dance all over the road. I was out of control at

200 mph. I can't believe it. I can't believe it. I can't believe it.' –
Nigel Mansell after waving goodbye to the title when his left-rear
tyre blew out during the 1986 Australian Grand Prix

'I can't remember a more miserable race. All that for a single
point. The whole afternoon was a complete joke.' – Nigel
Mansell, a disappointing sixth in the 1987 Brazilian Grand Prix

'I was in so much pain that it drastically affected my driving.
Every time I came towards the pits, I was tempted to come in and
quit.' – Nigel Mansell, stricken by cramp at the 1987 United
States Grand Prix at Detroit

'If I score points at Detroit, I feel as if I have won.' – Alain Prost
happy with third in the 1987 United States Grand Prix at his least
favourite track

'It was an extraordinary feeling. I drove maybe the last twenty
laps at ten-tenths, right on the limit, and I don't really like to do
that on such a quick circuit. But I knew that was what it was
going to take to beat Nelson, and support like that really inspires
you.' – Nigel Mansell winning the 1987 British Grand Prix in
front of his adoring Silverstone fans

'The tyre began to go down immediately after the first corner,
would you believe? So I had to do virtually a whole lap like that.
It finally went in a big way on the approach to the first chicane,
but I had to keep going. The car was all over the place! And I had
to drive as hard as possible because I didn't know how far ahead
I was of the next guy. The suspension was gone, and everything.'
– Stefan Johansson finishing second in the McLaren at the 1987
German Grand Prix despite doing the last lap on three wheels
after the front right-hand tyre disintegrated

'The car was shaking like a hot banana.' – Nelson Piquet as his
Williams suffered from tyre vibration at the 1987 Hungarian
Grand Prix

'Everything in the car got tired, including me.' – Ayrton Senna finishing a distant second to Piquet at the 1987 Hungarian Grand Prix

'I just spent too much time watching my mirrors – and not enough watching the road.' – Gerhard Berger spinning out of the lead in the 1987 Portuguese Grand Prix while under pressure from Alain Prost

'Actually, I feel very pleased with myself today. I can honestly say that I drove flat out the whole way. The steering on that thing's unbelievably heavy, and I'm absolutely spent. But I finished nowhere, so who's going to notice?' – Martin Brundle coming home eleventh in the Zakspeed at the 1987 Spanish Grand Prix

'When someone has worked all year to beat you and then you see them go up in the air and get hurt, it is not very pleasant.' – Nelson Piquet after Nigel Mansell's crash in qualifying for the 1987 Japanese Grand Prix at Suzuka handed the world title to the Brazilian

'The two McLarens stop, the Ferraris spin off and I win the race.' – Derek Warwick's masterplan for the 1988 British Grand Prix. It didn't quite go according to plan but the Arrows driver still managed to finish a respectable sixth

'There was no chance of winning the race and no chance of gaining any points, so there was no point in taking risks, in breaking my legs for nothing. Everyone does what they want with their car and with their life. Today I decided to stop and fly back home. It is the privilege of a champion and of being ahead in the championship.' – Alain Prost who, after a poor start, quit the rain-soaked 1988 British Grand Prix on lap 24

'Senna chopped across twice to make me back off but he shouldn't try that with me. Never in my life will I back off in that situation.' – Gerhard Berger after an altercation at the 1989 Brazilian Grand Prix

'The only way out of the problem would have been to go straight up in the air. Patrese and Berger trapped me and I lost the nose section. That's all there is to it.' – Senna's view of the same incident

'I wasn't tense or scared. I just felt great, it was exhilarating. I was laughing when I did it.' – Jean Alesi having the nerve to overtake Ayrton Senna on the inside at the 1990 United States Grand Prix

'You can never relax with Ayrton. I showed him up on Friday and he will not like that. At this rate I will age ten years in one season.' – Gerhard Berger after pipping his McLaren team-mate in practice for the 1990 San Marino Grand Prix

'Gerhard moved over on me. He's a friend of mine and my team-mate only last year. I can't believe what he did. There was nowhere for me to go.' – Nigel Mansell irked by Berger at the 1990 San Marino Grand Prix

'It feels good to give the red-and-whites a good thrashing.' – Frank Williams as Riccardo Patrese defeats the McLarens at the 1990 San Marino Grand Prix

'I was crying all round the last lap.' – Riccardo Patrese overcome with emotion at Imola, 1990

'Obviously I'm very happy for Ferrari, but I'm bound to wonder why these problems don't seem to happen to the other guy.' – Nigel Mansell retiring when his Ferrari was in the lead at the 1990 British Grand Prix. Team-mate Alain Prost won the race – his fourth of the season – while Mansell had been plagued by mechanical trouble.

'You can say your car is two seconds quicker than someone else's but proving it is something else. Here I had the opportunity.' – Alain Prost winning the 1990 Spanish Grand Prix for Ferrari

'I was so excited during the race I felt like jumping out of my skin.' – Jean Alesi, finding himself second in his first drive for Ferrari before being forced to retire at the 1991 United States Grand Prix

'We had a bit of a problem on one of the bends but at the end of the race we looked each other in the eye and decided that it was every man for himself on the track.' – Riccardo Patrese following a set-to with Williams team-mate Nigel Mansell at the 1991 United States Grand Prix at Phoenix

'It was pass or crash. I was surprised, I must say.' – Alain Prost, muscled out by Ferrari team-mate Jean Alesi at the 1991 British Grand Prix

'In the end I was just relieved to make the finish. I was missing gears, not getting any gears, getting stuck in gears – you name it.' – Nigel Mansell overcoming gear-box problems to win the 1991 British Grand Prix at Silverstone

'Being fourth at the start means two things for me. Either I run a conservative race and benefit from other people's mishaps, or I go to bed tonight and take something to become ten years younger.' – Alain Prost before the 1991 Hungarian Grand Prix. His race ended in retirement

'I was on the edge of fear, and that is when a driver really starts enjoying himself.' – Nigel Mansell snatching second place on the grid to Ayrton Senna at the 1991 Italian Grand Prix

'I got wheel spin over a puddle and went sideways. It didn't seem like a problem, but Alesi tried to pass me and hit my right front wheel.' – Michael Schumacher explaining his crash at the 1991 Australian Grand Prix

'I must say I was surprised to see Alesi alongside me with the light still red!' – Gerhard Berger as Jean Alesi got a flyer from the fourth row of the grid at the start of the 1992 Spanish Grand Prix

'Michael must have found a short cut.' – Nigel Mansell stunned to find Schumacher right behind him at the 1992 Spanish Grand Prix

'I tried to pass, he came in and I just couldn't stop.' – Michael

Schumacher explaining his collision with Ayrton Senna at the 1992 French Grand Prix

'I actually ran one person over, but I was only going a few miles an hour and he loved it.' – Nigel Mansell, mobbed after winning the 1992 British Grand Prix

'I don't think a result like this does my P45 chances any harm at all.' – Martin Brundle, looking for a drive for 1993, in optimistic mood after finishing third in a Benetton at the 1992 Japanese Grand Prix. Sure enough, he was snapped up by Ligier

'I will never forget that lap. He'd psyched them out, demoralised the whole lot of them. He won the whole race on that first lap.' – McLaren team co-ordinator Jo Ramirez as Ayrton Senna moved from fifth to first by the end of the first lap of the 1993 European Grand Prix at Donington Park, from *Ayrton Senna:The Second Coming* by Christopher Hilton (Patrick Stephens Ltd, 1994)

'I like a good fight but perhaps it was a little too close on this occasion. I was lucky to get through and lucky not to hit the wall. Maybe he didn't see me. He appeared to slow down as I was catching, so maybe he was just tired and wanted to stop for a rest!' – Michael Schumacher after his battle with Ayrton Senna at the 1993 Canadian Grand Prix. Schumacher finished second as Senna cruised to a halt with alternator failure

'That's what it should all be about – two guys getting really stuck in and giving each other a bit of stick.' – Patrick Head after a duel between Williams team-mates Alain Prost and Damon Hill for pole position at the 1993 British Grand Prix. A late surge earned Prost pole and he went on to win the race – his 50th Grand Prix success

'Perhaps after the big fight I had there, people will stop asking me if I am ready to retire.' – Riccardo Patrese after a battling third in the 1993 British Grand Prix

'I don't think these people are capable of judging these things properly. I think they really called me in to make the race more interesting.' – Alain Prost, hit with a controversial ten-second stop-go penalty for cutting the corners at the Ostkurve chicane at Hockenheim during the 1993 German Grand Prix. Prost recovered to win and protested that he had been forced to go straight at the chicane in order to avoid Martin Brundle's Ligier

'My dad once said you meet a much nicer class of person there, but I'm not so sure.' – Damon Hill finding himself at the back of the grid for the 1993 Portuguese Grand Prix

'I was trying to stay close to Gerhard Berger to stop Hill from moving inside, but he did and I hit his wheel.' – Michael Schumacher explaining his shunt with Damon Hill at the 1993 Japanese Grand Prix

'I've never heard such a lot of bollocks in all my life.' – Damon Hill smarting from media criticism before the 1994 British Grand Prix that he wasn't up to the job

'I had a lot of motivation to win, not least because my father never did. It's funny, but I almost feel it was my destiny to win this race. I feel everything in my life has come together to this point.' – Damon Hill after confounding his critics by winning the 1994 British Grand Prix

'I missed a golden opportunity today. I touched Katayama trying to pass him at the third chicane. Perhaps if I had been more patient then I could have won this race. I had seen him make room for Michael and I thought he was going to do the same for me. I guess it's one of those things when you have someone you are not used to racing against – you don't know what they are going to do.' – Damon Hill following his collision with Ukyo Katayama's Tyrrell which put him out of contention for the 1994 German Grand Prix. Hill had been challenging for third place at the time but dropped back to finish eighth

'I won't tell you what he said, but it wasn't complimentary.' – Mika Hakkinen, berated by Ayrton Senna for over-aggressive driving at the 1994 Pacific Grand Prix at Aida, Japan

'I drove on a completely different level that day. I was in what I call a twilight zone of driving where I just offered myself up completely to my instincts.' – Damon Hill on his victory in torrential rain in the 1994 Japanese Grand Prix

'When I went to go on the brake, I couldn't get my foot off the throttle.' – Roberto Moreno suffering in a Forti at the 1995 French Grand Prix. The sole of his right shoe was coated in glue as a result of contact with a faulty piece of equipment and it became stuck to the accelerator. Not surprisingly he finished last

'I had heard a lot about this winning of a Grand Prix and when it happened, it was all a bit of a shock.' – Johnny Herbert, triumphant in the 1995 British Grand Prix

'I am sure my car was still behind the line when the green light came on. I was told that when I put it into first gear, the car moved only seven centimetres, but I was still penalised. I think the electronic control system is too sensitive.' – Gerhard Berger after being given a ten-second stop-go penalty for jumping the start of the 1995 German Grand Prix

'He drove like God in Brazil.' – Niki Lauda, hugely impressed by Damon Hill's drive in the wet at Interlagos, 1996

'I am more Damon Hill than the son of Graham now.' – Hill feeling that he had come of age after his drive in the 1996 Brazilian Grand Prix

'DINIZ IN THE OVEN' – *Sun* headline after Pedro Diniz's car went up in flames at the 1996 Argentine Grand Prix

'For the last couple of races I have managed to send the German fans home happy.' – Damon Hill reflecting on his failure to finish on his most recent drives at the Nürburgring or Hockenheim, before the 1996 European Grand Prix at the Nürburgring. Championship leader Hill's German jinx struck again and he could finish only fourth

'The only way he was going to get past was by going over the top.' – A determined Coulthard keeping Hill at bay in the 1996 European Grand Prix

'It was like a punch in the stomach when I saw Schumacher's time.' – Damon Hill pipped for pole at the 1996 San Marino Grand Prix

'After moving over to let the car in front of me go by, Badoer then cut across in front of me and we collided. Once he moved over to let one car past, he should have stayed there.' – Jacques Villeneuve put out of the 1996 Monaco Grand Prix while trying to lap Luca Badoer's Forti

'I was amazed, stunned – but delighted.' – Damon Hill as Michael Schumacher exited the 1996 French Grand Prix

'I can offer no explanation for what happened other than I didn't concentrate hard enough. It was probably the easiest race victory I could have picked up, but I threw it away. I don't blame anybody but myself.' – Damon Hill taking the rap after hitting tyres which were guarding the kerbs at the 1996 Italian Grand Prix

'Monza proved two things: God is on the side of Ferrari and he wants me to win the championship. To knock myself out of the race and not lose my points advantage was something of a miracle.' – Damon Hill looking back on the 1996 Italian Grand Prix. Michael Schumacher won for Ferrari but Hill's nearest rival in the championship race, Jacques Villeneuve, also failed to score

'Obviously I was surprised when he overtook me. I looked in my mirror and couldn't find him – then suddenly he was beside me. It was a scary moment but we got away with it.' – Michael Schumacher after Jacques Villeneuve daringly overtook him on the outside of a corner at the 1996 Portuguese Grand Prix

'When they told me, I went into a bit of a spin in my head for a few laps because I came to the realisation that I didn't actually have to carry on driving any more!' – Damon Hill learning of the exit of Jacques Villeneuve on lap 37 of the 1996 Japanese Grand Prix, which clinched the title for Hill

'It got to the stage that it was really painful. I forgot to switch the radio off and when I was braking, I was screaming my head off I was in so much pain, and I didn't realise they were all in the pits listening to me. They must have thought I was having orgasms or something!' – Eddie Irvine enduring a painful ride at the 1997 Brazilian Grand Prix owing to an ill-fitting harness

'There was all sorts going on. Villeneuve was on the grass, and the next thing I knew I was on two wheels doing a kind of stunt-driving balancing act, trying to stop it turning over. I was just hoping it wasn't going to hurt when it came down again.' – Damon Hill following a multiple collision at the first corner of the 1997 Brazilian Grand Prix

'He knocked me out of it. My team-mate came right on top of me and bumped me off the track.' – Giancarlo Fisichella after Jordan team-mate Ralf Schumacher crashed into him at the 1997 Argentine Grand Prix

'I was never very emotional when I was driving. But here, when Rubens crossed the line, I burst into tears.' – Jackie Stewart as Rubens Barrichello picked up the first points for the fledgling Stewart team by finishing second at Monaco in 1997

'Alesi drove into the back of my car as I entered the hairpin, which spun me around and pushed me into the gravel, so my final result is very disappointing. His apologies after the race do not give the points back to the team or excuse the manoeuvre.' – David Coulthard, shunted out of fifth place by Jean Alesi on the final lap of the 1997 French Grand Prix. Coulthard could only finish seventh

'It was like driving on soap.' – Ralf Schumacher on the wet conditions at the 1997 French Grand Prix

'I made a good start but then Frentzen came flying past everyone.

Obviously he is quicker than me, but as soon as he got past he turned sharply left and just destroyed my nose. I couldn't believe it.' – Jos Verstappen's Tyrrell comes to blows with Heinz-Harald Frentzen's Williams at the 1997 British Grand Prix.

'The one point to me at the moment is just as good as a victory.' – A relieved Damon Hill finally picking up his first point of the season in the Arrows by virtue of finishing sixth in the 1997 British Grand Prix

'I knew there was a car in there somewhere and I did not want to come across it at 200 mph.' – Gerhard Berger slowing down when Jan Magnussen's Stewart blew up in a mass of smoke at the 1997 German Grand Prix

'I made a good start but the two Minardis did a kamikaze manoeuvre trying to overtake me, and put all three of us off the track at the second corner.' – A disconsolate Pedro Diniz sandwiched by Ukyo Katayama and Tarso Marques at the 1997 Hungarian Grand Prix

'It's a shame that the incident happened with my brother but I don't think anyone is to blame.' – Michael Schumacher colliding with brother Ralf at the 1997 Luxembourg Grand Prix

'I spotted him checking his mirror. Even though I was ten or fifteen metres behind him, I just went for it and braked very late. I was actually surprised that he hadn't closed the door yet. But it was just a matter of seconds before he decided to turn in on me. But he didn't do it well enough because he went off and I didn't.' – Jacques Villeneuve after Michael Schumacher's controversial move at the decisive 1997 European Grand Prix at Jerez. Schumacher came off worse, handing Villeneuve the title

'He tried a rather optimistic attack. It worked for him but not for me.' – Michael Schumacher's view of the same incident

'The driving standards need to be cleaned up. Maybe a red-card system is one way of doing it.' – Niki Lauda's verdict on the

Schumacher-Villeneuve episode. Schumacher's punishment was to be stripped of his second place in the world championship

'Being stuck in the middle of the pack in first is pretty scary. I don't recommend it!' – Alexander Wurz, whose Benetton jammed in first gear at the start of the 1998 San Marino Grand Prix

'My neck feels as if I have been sucking a Viagra pill.' – Heinz-Harald Frentzen swelling up after the 1998 French Grand Prix

'I seemed to have a different weather forecaster to Hakkinen.' – David Coulthard after aquaplaning off the road in the wet at the 1998 British Grand Prix. Coulthard had been given a set of intermediate tyres by McLaren when he came into the pits. Two laps later, team-mate Hakkinen got wets

'I felt a bit of a twit.' – Damon Hill after spinning off on lap 13 of the 1998 British Grand Prix

'While I was rotating, it passed through my head that there would be no points today.' – Mika Hakkinen's matter-of-fact description of his high-speed spin at the 1998 Italian Grand Prix

'Sometimes the playing field doesn't seem level.' – McLaren's Ron Dennis suggesting that Ferrari received preferential treatment at the 1998 Italian Grand Prix. The race was restarted after Hakkinen had beaten Schumacher off the grid first time round

'There is a tendency for your mind to start thinking about other things. I almost started whistling in the car.' – Mika Hakkinen as Michael Schumacher's retirement handed the Finn the world championship at Suzuka, 1998

'I wish I'd had a stereo in my car to keep me amused.' – Eddie Irvine after a dull Spanish Grand Prix, 1999

'To win anything you must, at times, take a calculated risk. That's what I did in the first lap. OK, I didn't intend to push my team-mate off but...' – David Coulthard following the collision with Mika Hakkinen at the 1999 Austrian Grand Prix

'When you see your team-mate in your mirror, you do not expect him to go into you.' – Hakkinen's view of the incident with Coulthard at the second corner of the 1999 Austrian Grand Prix

'It was my nightmare scenario – I crash into my team-mate and Eddie Irvine wins for Ferrari.' – A distraught Coulthard's final word on the 1999 Austrian Grand Prix

'I was just checking in my mirror that everything was still OK and suddenly, bang!' – Mika Hakkinen going off when leading the 1999 German Grand Prix

'It's very frustrating. I must have done something really bad to someone up there.' – Johnny Herbert bemoaning his misfortune after yet another retirement, this time near the end of the 1999 German Grand Prix when he was lying fifth

'To be honest I am embarrassed by my performance and feel I have let the team down.' – Michael Schumacher's temporary replacement, Mika Salo, after finishing a distant twelfth for Ferrari at the 1999 Hungarian Grand Prix

'It was an experience. Not very pleasant.' – A restrained Mika Hakkinen after his first-corner touch with McLaren team-mate David Coulthard at the 1999 Belgian Grand Prix. Hakkinen never recovered and had to settle for second place behind the Scot

'It was a simple mistake. I selected the wrong gear at the chicane, spun and stalled the engine. It was a driver's nightmare, such a waste.' – Mika Hakkinen squandering ten priceless points after spinning out of the 1999 Italian Grand Prix while holding a comfortable lead

'Mika's got to be nervous. He's gone out twice now while in the lead. A hat-trick would be nice.' – Eddie Irvine stepping up the pressure on the Finn after the 1999 Italian Grand Prix

'This is pay-back for all the bad luck I've had.' – Johnny Herbert winning an incident-packed 1999 European Grand Prix at the new Nürburgring

'I am very annoyed with myself. I had a good lead, the car was running well and I made a mistake – a huge mistake.' – David Coulthard after throwing away the chance of victory at the 1999 European Grand Prix

'Mika Salo came in before me with a damaged nose and they moved my tyres to put his on. When I came on, they had lost one of mine. It is a problem when you have one team of mechanics serving two cars – we should have two teams doing it. We screwed it up.' – Eddie Irvine after coming in for a fresh set of tyres at the 1999 European Grand Prix, only to discover that the right rear tyre had been left in the garage. The delay cost him any hope of championship points

'Ferrari's fans are rightfully very upset and we cannot tolerate it. We made a complete mess of it and it must never happen again.' – Irate Ferrari president Luca di Montezemolo on the fiasco at the European Grand Prix, 1999

'If things go wrong tomorrow, people will forget what has happened today.' – Michael Schumacher taking pole in his comeback race – the 1999 Malaysian Grand Prix

'What were conditions like? I couldn't tell you. I wasn't out there long enough.' – Damon Hill shunted out of the 1999 Malaysian Grand Prix at the second corner

'Soon after the race, the stewards told us that they had found an irregularity in our cars. It was a bolt from the blue.' – Ferrari sporting director Jean Todt, clearly so confused after the 1999 Malaysian Grand Prix that he thought the problem part was a bolt rather than a deflector

'I have complained for years that F1 rules and regulations are too tight. My view is over-simplistic – let anything go, slap in a 3.5

litre engine and let it rip.' – Bernie Ecclestone speaking out after Ferrari were initially disqualified from the 1999 Malaysian Grand Prix

'It would be a great shame if the world championship finished here because someone quite junior had made a mistake in the factory.' – Bernie Ecclestone sympathising with Ferrari, 1999

'I will be an old man before I understand any of this.' – Mika Hakkinen, proclaimed world champion for six days following the Ferrari disqualification in Sepang

'I don't really like it. It is not the way to win a title. It doesn't feel good to me.' – Mika Hakkinen after Sepang, 1999

'The real losers are those people who love the sport.' – McLaren's Ron Dennis as Ferrari win their appeal against disqualification

'Deciding the championship in the last Grand Prix is nerve-racking. I do not recommend it to anyone.' – Mika Hakkinen finally retaining his title at the 1999 Japanese Grand Prix

Chapter Six

Team Spirit

'The teams can go to hell. Some of them think they've got me by the balls, but their hands aren't big enough.' – Bernie Ecclestone showing who's the boss, 1997

'Team managers have enjoyed for some years now such unrealistic power and influence, have commanded so much attention, they have begun to think of themselves and their cars as the stars. Were a great driving talent to appear, all that sort of talk would be hushed. No team owner had the guts to belittle a Clark or a Fangio.' – Jackie Stewart, 1983

'If you want to win races, there is never a situation in which you can't overrule the team.' – James Hunt

'The team, the people, must be right. If it is only 90 per cent, then it is not enough. I give my maximum, and I want the maximum.' – Ayrton Senna, 1990

Alfa Romeo

'You've got nothing to lose. I'm an unknown and if I lose, Fangio loses. If I win, Alfa Romeo wins.' – Juan Manuel Fangio convincing Alfa Romeo to sign him, 1950

'On that day, I felt as though I had killed my mother.' – Enzo Ferrari as Froilan Gonzales steered Ferrari to their first world championship Grand Prix win – at Silverstone in 1951 – at the expense of Alfa Romeo with whom Ferrari had learned the ropes in the 1930s

'I still feel for Alfa the tenderness of first love.' – Enzo Ferrari's telegram to the Alfa team following the 1951 British Grand Prix

Arrows

'We should be going head to head for the championship by 2000.' – Optimistic Arrows boss Tom Walkinshaw signing Damon Hill, 1996

'Damon thought he was leaving the first division with Williams for the third division but after he saw the facilities we have got here, he knew we had the tools to do the job.' – Tom Walkinshaw, 1996

'Tom fulfilled every criterion I set for myself: the opportunity to make rapid progress with a team, test, develop – and the carrot of winning races at the end of it all.' – Damon Hill before his move to Arrows, 1996

'I'm under no illusions and it's going to be a very tough year for me. I don't know when I'm going to see a clear track in front of me again.' – Damon Hill starting out at Arrows, 1997

'When Damon says he lacks motivation, I am horrified. I don't believe any professional sportsman has any difficulty in motivating himself. Damon is one of the best drivers in the world. It is up to him to push the team forward and not the other way around.' – Tom Walkinshaw becoming frustrated with his new signing, 1997

'The current rumour is that Damon is leaving us for a better team. But the opposite situation could well be the truth. If he continues not to do his job properly, then he could be losing us. Up until now, I have been very friendly towards him, but now I might have to try a more direct approach. It's time to be blunt. It's time for me to remind him that he's better than he's delivered.' – Tom Walkinshaw returning to the offensive, 1997

'I had got used to seeing my name at the top of the list of times, or very close, and this year I have sometimes found myself having to scroll down to page two just to see my name. That saps a bit of your oomph.' – Damon Hill defending himself against Walkinshaw's blast, 1997

Aston Martin

'Reg persuaded me that Aston Martin had a high budget for Formula 1 and a good development track record. He appealed to my loyalty to the team – after all, they had shown faith in me in my early days and I should have faith in them now. I stayed with Aston Martin and had a rather unsuccessful 1959 season in Formula 1.' – Roy Salvadori on his decision to stay with Aston Martin rather than move to what turned out to be the all-conquering Cooper team

Benetton

'I never think of this business in terms of pleasure any more. I think of it in terms of the amount of aggravation!' – Benetton technical director John Barnard, from *Grand Prix People* by Gerald Donaldson (MRP, 1990)

'Here it is not war. I look in other garages and it is like somebody has just died. It is as if these people have such a dramatic job. My philosophy is that the way to work is with enthusiasm and humour. I guarantee I can show many sadder jobs than Formula 1.' – Benetton team managing director Flavio Briatore, from *Designs On Victory: On the Grand Prix Trail With Benetton* by Derick Allsop (Stanley Paul, 1993)

'His behaviour within the team was totally unacceptable. In fact it never was a team as far as I was concerned. I was never in it.' – Johnny Herbert hitting out at Flavio Briatore, 1996

'Johnny knew what to expect when he joined us. I don't tell Johnny how to drive a car and I don't expect him to tell me how to run the team.' – Briatore hits back in the war of words with Herbert, 1996

'He couldn't give a damn about me. All they worried about was Michael. Everybody knew Benetton was a one-car team.' – Johnny Herbert unhappy with what he saw as Briatore's concentration on team-mate Michael Schumacher, 1996

'It is always difficult when you lose the driver you have built the team around. We all knew how Michael Schumacher worked and now we have to find new ways for new drivers. It is like getting a new girlfriend – you have to find out what she likes, what makes her smile.' – Flavio Briatore on life without Schumacher, 1996

'The older you get, the more you get used to somebody and the more difficult it is to change. If you are a young boy and you get a new girlfriend, it is easy to adapt, you stay together and you feel fine. But if you get to 40 or 45 and you start something new, it is so hard to get used to it.' – Gerhard Berger choosing a similar theme to explain how he was taking time to adjust to life at Benetton following his move from Ferrari, 1997

Brabham

'If you want to get to the moon, you don't count the pennies.' – Bernie Ecclestone considering signing the expensive Niki Lauda for Brabham, 1977

'I always felt that Bernie seemed to like people with a more aggressive nature than I'd got. I was no less ambitious than Niki behind the wheel, but I certainly wasn't as aggressive as him out of the cockpit in everyday life.' – John Watson who was Lauda's team-mate at Brabham in 1978 but was then replaced by the more forceful Nelson Piquet

'I am proud to carry the name forward to Formula 1. It doesn't bring extra pressure. If my presence helps the team, either because my name attracts money or through results, then that is fine.' – Damon Hill joining Brabham in 1992. Hill managed to qualify just twice in a dismal eight races with Brabham before moving to Williams

BRM

'I thought I'd better move in case they painted me over.' – Graham Hill leaving BRM in 1967 after seven years

'There wasn't enough money, technique or organisation, not enough class.' – Niki Lauda

'It was like comparing NASA to a group of kite enthusiasts.' – Journalist Helmut Zwickl comparing Ferrari to BRM after Niki Lauda's move to Maranello in 1974

Cooper

'The heat of Grand Prix racing is something like the heat of battle – it either welds people together or breaks them apart. In the eight years I have been with Coopers I have to think very hard to remember a cross word between John and myself.' – Bruce McLaren on his excellent relationship with John Cooper, 1965

Copersucar

'It was the biggest mistake I ever made in my life. I had offers from Ferrari, from Frank [Williams]...It was extremely demoralising for me, having won the championship twice. Sometimes I didn't even qualify. It was terrible.' – Emerson Fittipaldi on his decision to join brother Wilson's Copersucar team for 1976

Embassy Racing

'There's nothing pleasant in knowing you're driving among the wankers...I don't like having the finger pointed at me and people saying, "Oh, he doesn't count for much: he only qualified fifteenth."' – Alan Jones recalling his miserable 1975 and 1976 driving for Graham Hill's Embassy Racing team and then for Surtees

Ensign

'It was a great surprise to see the car here. The team is so short of money that I thought we would miss the race. I decided to come out anyway, and then the transporter arrived!' – Roberto Guerrero pleasantly surprised to find himself with a drive at the 1982 German Grand Prix

Ferrari

'It was like a command from the Pope: how could I refuse?' – Nigel Mansell receiving an offer to drive for Enzo Ferrari, 1988

'I wanted to tell my grandchildren that I once drove for Ferrari. It is every child's dream.' – Nigel Mansell, 1990

'Mr Ferrari was happy that I won, but not so happy because all the papers talked about Baghetti, Baghetti, Baghetti – not Ferrari. He say to me: "What car are you driving at Reims, Baghetti?"' – Giancarlo Baghetti after his debut victory at the 1961 French Grand Prix

'The ambition of any motor racing driver must be to drive for the Scuderia Ferrari. If he achieved it, the driver would know that it was with the personal approval of the great man himself.' – Innes Ireland following the death of Enzo Ferrari, 1988

'The magic of Ferrari is that you're driving for the whole of Italy, not just the team.' – Jody Scheckter

'I even started wearing seat-belts when driving a road car. I never cared before, but I did now. I wanted to get into that Ferrari, wanted to have my first drive in it. I really cared.' – Jean Alesi playing it safe to make sure that he could take up the drive for Ferrari, 1991

'It's not like being with any other team. Psychologically, you have the feeling, when you drive, that you are doing it for somebody rather than something.' – Didier Pironi, from *Grand Prix Greats* by Nigel Roebuck (Patrick Stephens Ltd, 1986)

'When I met Enzo Ferrari, I discovered what it is to have a real passion in life. It is something noble. Once you find that out, you know that any singular passion – even collecting butterflies – is worthy of one's total devotion. Now I have no doubt. This is my life.' – Didier Pironi, 1982

'He is not a myth, but a man. He leads the family. He is available to all, at a human or a sporting level. I talk to him before, during and after every session at a race. When I won my first race for Ferrari, in Belgium, he said: "That was pretty good. You made two mistakes, but on the whole not bad." He was right. I knew them and he knew them.' – Michele Alboreto, impressed by the wisdom of Enzo Ferrari, 1985

'The man can be congratulatory, like a father patting his son on the head. Sometimes the tap can be pretty hard...' – Michele Alboreto on Enzo Ferrari, 1985

'I didn't speak the language, but you know he liked to speak about girls, I liked to speak about girls, so it went well.' – Gerhard Berger finding common ground with Enzo Ferrari

'People think Ferrari is a monster with many heads, but I find it very little different from the smaller teams with whom I used to drive. Just better prepared.' – Stefan Johansson, 1985

'Ferrari has something extra. It's something indefinable and unique, and every time I walked through the doors of the factory at Maranello or stepped into the car, I felt the added importance of being that unique thing – a Ferrari driver.' – Niki Lauda, from *Ferrari: The Passion and the Pain* by Jane Nottage (CollinsWillow, 1998)

'Ferrari was simply the biggest name, the most established firm, so much greater, and more important, and to be taken more seriously than the odd BRM enterprise, in which old Louis Stanley pulled motors and men like rabbits out of a hat.' – Niki Lauda on his 1974 switch to Ferrari, from *For the Record: My Years With Ferrari* (William Kimber, 1978)

'I soon twigged how things are for a foreign Ferrari driver in Italy. In part of the press you have no hope; you can drive like a god, say nothing but nice things in Italian and always eat spaghetti, it doesn't do the slightest good, you are still a swine according to them.' – Niki Lauda, from *For the Record: My Years With Ferrari*

'He has the psychological finesse of a sand viper. When the Ferrari went well and all was perfect, he considered me a very good driver, perhaps the best. When things went wrong, I was an idiot.' – Niki Lauda on Ferrari engineer Mauro Forghieri

'It became like being married to a bad woman.' – Niki Lauda on his decision to quit Ferrari, 1977

'I come in and say the car doesn't handle well. Gordon Murray, our designer, looks at the car. At Ferrari, they look to fix the driver.' – Niki Lauda comparing Brabham and Ferrari, 1978

'Ferrari's biggest problem is its past.' – Niki Lauda, 1992

'I didn't want to be in the shoes of those boys – too much competition. When you drive for Ferrari you are headed one way only: for that little box under the ground.' – Harry Schell, 1958

'It was like going into a hornet's nest at Ferrari because there were four drivers for the two Formula 1 cars.' – Chris Amon joining Ferrari for 1967

'I happened to be the guy who was beating the great Ferrari machine. They didn't like it and they've done a lot of work to make sure I didn't succeed, starting with the fuel business at Monza and now this.' – James Hunt sounding off after being stripped of his win in the 1976 British Grand Prix

'To win a championship, you have to have a driver who *wants* to win.' – Enzo Ferrari taking a pop at Carlos Reutemann, 1978

'At Ferrari I was always made to think that though I was capable of winning races, it wasn't in my temperament to be a winner.' – Carlos Reutemann, 1981

'I was extremely nervous about the politics of driving for Ferrari. He was by nature a creator of insecurities, feeling that it motivated people to prove themselves.' – Jackie Stewart on why he rejected an offer to drive for Ferrari

'I am a professional race-car driver not a politician so I shall just drive the car. If I have any problems I'll put my police uniform on.' – Special Constable Nigel Mansell asked about the legendary in-fighting at Ferrari prior to his move to Maranello in 1989

'Ferrari are very hard to get on with. There are only three drivers who managed to impose their will at Ferrari: Fangio, Lauda and Prost.' – Stirling Moss, 1990

'He was rather like a puppeteer: he liked to have all the strings in his hands, everybody dancing to his tune.' – John Surtees on Enzo Ferrari, from *John Surtees: World Champion* (Hazleton Publishing, 1991)

'There are no excuses in this team. Everything is so much more demanding. There's no margin for error.' – Jean Alesi, 1991

'Crisis is almost the normal state at Ferrari. When you win there is a crisis of optimism. The problem is that there are one or two people in the team who have slight experience of Formula 1. It's possible for them to think that if a car is competitive at the end of a season you must keep it for the start of next season. That was true ten years ago. Now things change from race to race.' – Alain Prost, 1991

'Ron Dennis is a leader of men, a catalyst of energies, he is completely respected. That's what's missing here.' – Alain Prost comparing Ferrari to McLaren, 1991

'Basically the difference between an English and Italian team is in the way they listen to their drivers. I've pointed out and underlined the defects of Ferrari throughout the season but no one really listened to a word I said. When I was at McLaren every remark was taken into account, from Ron Dennis down to the lowest mechanic.' – Alain Prost, fired by Ferrari, 1991

'There are many, many problems associated with driving for Ferrari and it demands a lot from the driver. Then there's the pressure from the Italian media, but I wouldn't understand what they were saying!' – Damon Hill vaguely contemplating a move from Williams, 1995

'Our trouble at Ferrari is that everyone is too clever by half. At Ferrari people don't like to look at reality; they like to think they have an ideal world.' – Michele Alboreto on the demise of Ferrari, 1985

'At Ferrari so many egos lie between information and results, between what I tell them about the car and what they think the car is really like, that there is no real communication.' – Michele Alboreto, 1985

'What Ferrari did is completely unacceptable. This is not my idea of how the sport should be run.' – Team boss Alain Prost after Ferrari's Eddie Irvine allegedly blocked Prost's Olivier Panis as the Frenchman tried to lap him at the 1997 Spanish Grand Prix

'Ralf fell foul of Ferrari's cynical approach, running a one-car team with a blocking tactic to protect Irvine's position. Ferrari have been doing this for a number of years.' – Williams' technical director Patrick Head after Ferrari's Mika Salo shut out the faster Williams of Ralf Schumacher at the 1999 Belgian Grand Prix

'Ferrari are proof positive that Formula 1 success is not only about money.' – Frank Williams, 1993

'All that lovely money and they haven't won the world championship for twenty years. Twenty years!' – Ken Tyrrell savouring the continuation of the Ferrari drought, 1998

'Ferrari did not win the championship for twenty years because it made too many changes.' – Ferrari sporting director Jean Todt, 1999

'I was not happy to see our car so far behind the front runners, but here it was more important for us to make the chequered flag. That was important for team morale.' – Ferrari president Luca di Montezemolo, relieved to see Michael Schumacher finish fourth in the 1996 German Grand Prix after three successive retirements

'Ferrari have a tradition of winning the *winter* world championship.' – McLaren's Ron Dennis hearing that Ferrari's winter testing programme suggested that they would be favourites for 1990

'It would be very nice if Ferrari were rewarded for their years of hard work. They deserve it. Ferrari is Formula 1.' – Bernie Ecclestone, 1998

'F1 without Ferrari is unthinkable.' – FISA boss Jean-Marie Balestre concerned about rumours that Ferrari was considering withdrawing from Formula 1 to go Indy racing instead, 1985

'If you want to make pasta, then you have to be in Parma. I want to make a sophisticated F1 project, so I want to be involved in England.' – Ferrari president Luca di Montezemolo stressing the importance of Ferrari's UK facility, 1992

'In Formula 1 you are part of a racing stable and the number one driver is the stud and he's the one you're always compared with every race. What they do is to praise the one and forget the other one. You feel wounded and resentful so between two men with the same team, ironically you get more, a lot more rivalry.' – Didier Pironi on his time at Ferrari as number two to Gilles Villeneuve

'We want to have two top guys and to have somebody who is really happy to be with Michael. We also want Michael to be happy to be with Eddie. So, before the wedding, everything is nice and everything is beautiful. But sometimes things change when you are really living together. So sometimes we will have hard days, but I'm used to that.' – Ferrari sporting director Jean Todt pairing Schumacher and Irvine for 1996

'Ferrari does not really exist. Although the team is registered under that name, it is Schumacher who controls everything.' – Jacques Villeneuve, 1998

'At Ferrari, everything is done to suit Michael Schumacher. What will these people do if Michael ever becomes ill?' – Keke Rosberg, 1998

'Being a number two at Ferrari is better than being a number one at anywhere else, other than McLaren.' – Eddie Irvine, 1998

'The only way I could get to be number one at Ferrari is if Michael breaks a leg.' – Eddie Irvine's jocular remark a few days before the 1999 British Grand Prix...the race in which his Ferrari team-mate Michael Schumacher broke a leg

'Eddie is not number two because he is faster than me but because he has been slower for the past three and a half years.' – Michael Schumacher responding to the suggestion that Irvine should no longer be content with playing a supporting role at Ferrari, 1999

'Jean Todt is visibly happier when Michael wins. You can see it in his face. With me, there's a professional relationship but there's no feeling.' – Eddie Irvine tired of being second best at Ferrari, 1999

'If he's the number one again, I'm leaving.' – Irvine demanding a new role when Schumacher regains fitness, 1999

'At Ferrari there was one man they worked for and that was Schumacher. If they had time for anything else, that was Eddie – only second.' – Jackie Stewart signing Eddie Irvine for the new Jaguar team, 1999

'I was in my dancing lesson for my wedding waltz when I got a phone call telling me to jump on a plane.' – Mika Salo getting the call to join Ferrari as mid-season replacement for Schumacher, 1999

'Winning the championship for Ferrari is the Holy Grail of motor racing.' – Eddie Irvine, 1999

'It is not the title I or the team wanted. It is just a consolation prize.' – Eddie Irvine as Ferrari win the 1999 constructors' championship but miss out on the drivers' title

Fittipaldi

'He kept fiddling about with the team and interfering with the professionals who were trying to run it in a professional way.' – Keke Rosberg on Emerson Fittipaldi, head of the Fittipaldi team with whom Rosberg spent two unsatisfactory years in 1980 and 1981

Hesketh

'Hesketh Racing showed it was still possible to have fun and yet figure competitively in modern racing.' – Graham Hill

'We did some fairly extraordinary things, like standing around in a circle and clucking, praying to the Great Chicken in the Sky for a good weekend and reliability in the race.' – Hesketh Racing's team manager Bubbles Horsley, from *Hunt: The Biography* by Gerald Donaldson (CollinsWillow, 1994)

'We were like a menagerie of kids out from school.' – Alan Jones on the Hesketh team for whom he drove at the start of 1975

'His attitude was that we were doing pretty badly in Formula 2 and for very little additional cost we could do badly in Formula 1!' – James Hunt on Lord Hesketh's decision to step up to Formula 1 in 1973, from *Hunt: The Biography*

'Entertainment is being cut to a minimum. Yachts are out and all the money available is being spent on the racing car.' – Lord

Hesketh getting serious at the start of 1975 after a disappointing 1974 season

Jordan

'Selling has always been my biggest talent. I was dealing in marbles and chestnuts before my fourth birthday.' – Eddie Jordan, 1998

'We were like the hippies of Formula 1. We went to races not knowing where we would find the money to pay for anything and I said: "Let's go, we can sort it out later." At the end of the year we would have these mountains of bills. It was very tough but incredibly enjoyable.' – Eddie Jordan recalling the team's entry into Formula 1 in 1991

'I'm at my best when my back is to the wall. Deep down, I'm perhaps basically lazy, but if I absolutely have to perform, then I'm at my best.' – Eddie Jordan, 1991

'Our biggest asset at Jordan is our relationship with drivers. With us, they play a bigger part than in many other teams.' – Eddie Jordan, 1990

'Eddie Jordan understands motor racing and he understands drivers, which makes him a very rare beast among Formula 1 team managers...' – James Hunt

'A bit of a rascal.' – Ron Dennis on Eddie Jordan

'Jordan is becoming an old people's home for ex-Williams drivers.' – Damon Hill as Heinz-Harald Frentzen joins him at Jordan, 1998

'I don't like making forecasts because reality has a brutal axe to its bow.' – Eddie Jordan mixing his metaphors while talking about the team's prospects for 1998

'When it comes to rock 'n' roll or hype or whatever you want to call it, Jordan are as good as the best. What we need now is to become the best technology-wise.' – Eddie Jordan, 1998

'Our reputation is as a confident, young, gung-ho team having fun. But in reality we're deadly serious.' – Eddie Jordan, 1998

'The way I run the team is on a fairly casual basis. Anyone can have a chat and a laugh. The Irish do play the role of the underdog beautifully. But behind this façade is a man so desperately serious, I'm just glad that I haven't blown my cover.' – Eddie Jordan, 1999

'With Jordan, you never know what might happen. Take last year: one minute we're on our knees, the next we're on top of the world. You wouldn't expect any other leading team to get into the sort of trouble we manage to find from time to time.' – Eddie Jordan, 1999

'I no longer want a kindergarten.' – Eddie Jordan signing the experienced Damon Hill and Heinz-Harald Frentzen as his drivers for 1999

'Had we said at the start of the season that we'd be fighting for the title, we'd have been laughed at. So just to be where we are is fantastic.' – Eddie Jordan as a late surge gives Heinz-Harald Frentzen a chance of lifting the championship for Jordan, 1999

Ligier

'They will turn up at a track, do a handful of laps in super-quick times and then retire for a three-hour lunch to celebrate. While they're off having their snails and Beaujolais, other teams will plod away, modifying their cars, getting on with their work and catching up.' – Alan Jones, from *Driving Ambition* by Alan Jones and Keith Botsford (Stanley Paul, 1981)

Lotus

'It takes more than six months to find out how a team works. To learn what is right, what is wrong, what to do. It takes time to know who are the liars, who are the good guys, who are the idiots.' – Nelson Piquet on life at Lotus, 1989

'Like Barnum and Bailey in two separate rings.' – Jochen Rindt's scathing assessment of Lotus's chaotic organisation at the 1969 British Grand Prix

'Lotus came along with a ten-page contract which rather frightened me and a list of "can't do this, can't do that". I didn't want to be bound by that sort of thing at such an early stage in my career.' – Jody Scheckter turning down Lotus in 1972

'They seemed to be of the opinion that their drivers shouldn't be paid.' – James Hunt in the wake of an unsatisfactory meeting with Lotus, 1975

'From the word go I always wanted to drive for Colin Chapman and Lotus. I was a fantastic fan of Jimmy Clark and basically I've never been a Ferrari man. Although one romances about it and thinks, "Wouldn't it be fantastic, an Englishman driving for Ferrari", I'd much rather be where I am now.' – Nigel Mansell, 1981, from *Nigel Mansell* by David Tremayne (Hazleton Publishing, 1989)

'In my opinion Warwick is not a number two, and I wanted a second driver in the team. In some teams you can have two competitive drivers, but at Lotus the best solution is a firm number one because in my first season I realised they could not run two competitive cars at the same time.' – Ayrton Senna blocking plans for Derek Warwick to join him at Lotus, 1986

'Every team has to have a strong man at the heart of it. Perhaps not just a strong man, but a great man. Trying to be that is what keeps the edge in racing. It is that which is missing at Ferrari and which I try to give at Lotus.' – Ayrton Senna, 1987

'One of the big things about Colin is that he will talk man to man with his drivers. There's none of the "I'm the boss and you'll do as I say" stuff. As a past driver himself, he knows how important it is for the man in the cockpit to be in the right frame of mind, and he does a very good "fatherly act" on new drivers to give them confidence. At the same time, he'll make it pretty clear to them, in a nice sort of way, that he expects to have the car back in one piece!' – Jim Clark on Colin Chapman, 1965

'He was a racer to the core. When you were part of his team you quickly came to realise that this was a guy working at redefining the cutting edge of racing technology.' – Dan Gurney on Colin Chapman

'He is a hard taskmaster but retains the knack of getting people to work near miracles for him. Many a time I've seen him talk mechanics into doing what they genuinely think is impossible. But somehow he fires them with some of his own tremendous enthusiasm, and the job gets done. The thing is, if it's really necessary, he'll always be prepared to roll up his own sleeves and lend a hand, and I think people respect him for that.' – Jim Clark on Colin Chapman, 1965

'Colin's ideal world of motor racing would be one which enabled him to do every single job himself.' – Jim Clark, 1965

'He was actually quite aloof. He was astute enough to know that any answers he got from this young driver would be of no value, so why bother to ask? That's the way he was – very hard. You had to be very tough to survive in the team after Jimmy's death.' – Jackie Oliver, who drove for Lotus in F1 in 1967 and 1968, on Colin Chapman, from *Colin Chapman: The Man and His Cars* by Gerard 'Jabby' Crombac (Patrick Stephens Ltd, 1986)

'It was very difficult for Colin to trust us because neither Reine [Wisell] nor I had much experience. When we were explaining a problem to him we had a job to convince him that it was a real one and not simply our lack of experience.' – Emerson Fittipaldi recalling his teething troubles at Lotus in 1971

'Colin was more than just a team manager. He introduced so many things to Formula 1. For me, he was like a teacher. He was a genius. He could be very difficult to work with sometimes but he knew a lot about motor racing and racing cars, more than anybody I ever worked with.' – Emerson Fittipaldi

'From Colin Chapman I learned tenacity, determination and how to question, not accept.' – Benetton team manager and ex-Lotus man Peter Collins, 1986

'He is a great engineer but he is also a very special personality and I couldn't deal with him.' – Carlos Reutemann's diplomatic appraisal of Chapman, 1981

'I find him rude and aggressive. He is a driven man, but in the wrong way: the cockiness and aggro are a cover-up for some sort of insecurity, and Colin is inconsistent. I like someone who is consistent.' – Alan Jones speaking his mind about Colin Chapman, from *Driving Ambition* by Alan Jones and Keith Botsford (Stanley Paul, 1981)

'When he was right on, Team Lotus was right on and if one looks back at the span of Lotus there are peaks and troughs which correspond with Colin's moods.' – Mario Andretti on Colin Chapman, from *Lotus* by Bruce Grant-Braham (Crowood Press, 1994)

March

'There wasn't much harmony in the March team. Everybody blamed each other.' – Derek Daly

'Because March wanted to become a top team, they didn't worry so much about all the crashes. They needed to take risks to get results.' – Accident-prone Italian driver Vittorio Brambilla

'He treated me as though I were a speck of dirt on his carpet.' – Nelson Piquet going to see Max Mosley at March in the hope of securing a Formula 1 drive

McLaren

'Teddy is really unpredictable. I won the British Grand Prix and

Teddy fired me. At Ontario I failed to finish and I wasn't out of the car ten minutes when he told me he wanted to make me an offer – and complimented me on my driving during the previous two months!' – Peter Revson confused by McLaren team boss Teddy Mayer, 1973

'There are times when I feel like punching the little white-haired guy right in the mouth.' – Peter Revson on his complex relationship with Teddy Mayer, 1973

'He has in his time fired more world champions than most people have hired.' – James Hunt on Teddy Mayer, 1981

'He got us out of bed at 4.30 in the morning to make sure we didn't get bogged down in race-day traffic. Sure enough, we were at the track by 5am, and we had to wait a good three hours before we could even have breakfast. In circumstances like those, how on earth can you be expected to develop the concentration you need to drive a Grand Prix?' – Alain Prost bemused by Teddy Mayer's orders for the 1980 Italian Grand Prix, from *Life in the Fast Lane* (Stanley Paul, 1988)

'What really made up my mind to leave was the accident. I got back to the pits to find that people in the team were talking about driver error, going too fast on cold tyres and things like that. I said, "OK, if you want things like that, it's finished. If you won't release me, I stop Formula 1, I won't drive."' – Alain Prost citing the team's response to his practice crash at the 1980 United States East Grand Prix, when the car's suspension failed, as the prime reason for him quitting McLaren for Renault

'Teddy is highly intelligent, but also arrogant, difficult and with his ideas rooted in the past.' – John Watson, 1981

'Teddy is a very competitive person, and he wants his team to be competitive, successful. At times he was just plain, out-and-out rude.' – John Watson, 1982

'Teddy Mayer makes no attempt to boost a driver psychologically, to build up his confidence. McLaren's attitude is always to put the driver down. Their way – when I was there – of trying to make you go quicker was to make jokes about you, belittle you. I don't think that's the right approach. You need to feel an aura of confidence around you, and I never felt that at McLaren.' – Patrick Tambay, 1982

'When you were really down, when you needed encouragement, they kicked you in the balls. They rubbished you to the press, the mechanics, everyone.' – John Watson recalling his experiences at McLaren in 1980

'I'm not particularly thick-skinned, but I've been with McLaren for four years – and I've *survived*, so I must be less sensitive than I was.' – John Watson, 1982

'I'm not sure it was a partnership made in heaven.' – John Watson assessing the pairing of Alain Prost and Niki Lauda at McLaren, 1984

'I have learnt so much at McLaren, learnt how to manage the race weekend better, how to pace myself, how to think, how to race, how to improve. Between this team and Ferrari there is an abyss.' – Gerhard Berger, 1990. After three years at McLaren, Berger returned to . . . Ferrari

'To me, Ron's weakness seems to reside in a sort of chip-on-the-shoulder complex. It hurts him to be reminded that he started life as a modest mechanic at Cooper and Brabham. It is for this reason that he overreacts as team boss. His arrogance can be unbearable.' – Niki Lauda on Ron Dennis, from *To Hell and Back* (Stanley Paul, 1986)

'The red and white team have been on top of the world for years and they don't like it now that Williams and Renault are doing such a magnificent job.' – Nigel Mansell responding to criticism from McLaren's Ron Dennis, 1992

'When I joined McLaren, I really believed that the team was

something special, but in fact they were no different from the other teams I had driven for – Williams, Ferrari and Lotus – in that they are not infallible and they make mistakes... What I found to my dismay was that some of the people in the McLaren team hadn't a clue what to do about the problems.' – Nigel Mansell on his short-lived stay at McLaren in 1995, from *Mansell: My Autobiography* (CollinsWillow, 1995). One of the major problems he encountered at McLaren was that he was too big to fit in the cockpit

'It is sad that he should not only put myself and this company, but many other companies he has driven for, into a position where they have to make a choice as to whether to highlight his own weaknesses or let the moment pass.' – Ron Dennis in reply to Mansell's comments, 1995

'If you pay a driver five million dollars a year it seems silly not to have a car which fits him.' – James Hunt as Gerhard Berger also struggled to squeeze into a McLaren, 1990

'If you want to drive a McLaren, earn it.' – McLaren boss Ron Dennis to Martin Brundle, 1994

'I don't get too emotional about winning – that is what I go motor racing for. I have a much stronger reaction when I lose, because that's when the whole team falls down from the pinnacle of achievement.' – Ron Dennis, 1991

'The greyness and lack of emotion that people see as the hallmarks of our team are nothing more than a desire to control our emotion and retain focus.' – Ron Dennis, 1999

'Ron's only words of advice to me have been to avoid hitting my team-mate again.' – David Coulthard receiving pearls of wisdom from Ron Dennis following the collision with Mika Hakkinen at the 1999 Austrian Grand Prix

'Our decision is right, even if you have to pay a price for it on occasions. At least you have a real Grand Prix team, not a sham.'

– Ron Dennis defending the McLaren policy of having both Hakkinen and Coulthard as number ones, 1999

'Both our drivers get the same treatment and that is not going to change. They have to earn their race wins and their world championships. We have no intention of stepping in at this stage to influence the outcome. We will not sacrifice our integrity. If you have a racing team, you must allow your drivers to race.' – Ron Dennis underlining the McLaren stance with a thinly veiled swipe at Ferrari thrown in for good measure, 1999

'Ron is a great competitor but hasn't got it in him to say "well done".' – Eddie Jordan after Ron Dennis's low-key response to Jordan's win at Monza, 1999

'Either the team or the driver have screwed up on too many occasions. It's been a litany of failure for them so far.' – Eddie Jordan as McLaren's title bid appears to be faltering, 1999

'They've tried very hard this year to lose the world championship – more than any team I've ever known.' – Jackie Stewart, 1999

Mercedes-Benz

'Better than anything I had known or even imagined up until then; better than anything I have experienced since.' – Stirling Moss, 1963

'Although they were absolutely stuffed with science they were also quite fantastically adaptable.' – Stirling Moss

'Their cars didn't break down. I never had any worries when I was driving for them because the team was so strong technically. If I asked them to make a change of any kind, they got down to work, and in no time at all I was back at the wheel with things as I wanted them to be.' – Juan Manuel Fangio, from *Fangio: My Racing Life* (Patrick Stephens Ltd, 1987)

'Although Mercedes never insisted on me being number two, Fangio, many years older than me and current world champion, was clearly the senior driver. I was the new boy in the team and no way was I going to mess things up by trying to dice with the established genius.' – Stirling Moss on the Mercedes team for whom he drove in F1 in 1955, from *Racing and All That* by Stirling Moss and Mike Hailwood (Pelham Books, 1980)

'He was the best team director that existed and Mercedes was the most complete team.' – Fangio on Mercedes team director Alfred Neubauer

'He used to fight the people away from his cars in the pits and if the police were amongst them he would fight them, too, but he never fought his drivers.' – Stirling Moss singing the praises of Alfred Neubauer

'We knew that he thought we would be better drivers if we tucked ourselves up alone and early before a race.' – Stirling Moss on Alfred Neubauer

'Neubauer virtually dominated his drivers, and they ran to his orders. This situation prevailed in a number of other teams but at Mercedes Neubauer made a fetish out of it.' – Jim Clark, from *Jim Clark at the Wheel* (Arthur Barker, 1964)

Minardi

'Since last year F1 has become a better package – and we're happy to be last in this F1. But we're still working hard to make someone else last!' – Minardi team member, 1997

'Minardi is famous because it is a family team and they put great importance on human relationships.' – Giancarlo Fisichella, 1996

'I have had two Japanese team-mates and I don't speak Japanese.' – Jarno Trulli on life at Minardi and Prost, 1997

Osella

'For a long time I have been telling them that the chassis flexes, but only when Jarier tells them do they believe it. I have spent a lot of money on driving for this team, and now all the support is for Jarier. I will not continue like this.' – Young Italian driver Beppe Gabbiani angry at playing second fiddle at Osella to Jean-Pierre Jarier during preparation for the 1981 British Grand Prix. After that first full season in F1 resulted in twelve failures to qualify and three retirements, Gabbiani wisely returned to Formula 2.

Parnell

'The Parnell equipe was not exactly renowned for its preparation. It became a standard joke on a Monday morning that Tim, just returned from the weekend on his Derbyshire pig farm, would solemnly forage through the works' dustbins, retrieving all the bits which had been discarded in his absence and returning them to the stores, "because they might come in handy one day".' – Mike Hailwood, from *Racing and All That* by Stirling Moss and Mike Hailwood (Pelham Books, 1980)

Prost

'Running a team is very tiring. It might not be noticeable from the outside but one is under enormous pressure. My heart skipped a beat when I saw the car go out on the track for the first time on Friday and it nearly stopped completely when I saw the same car go off the track a few moments later!' – Alain Prost on his team's debut at the 1997 Australian Grand Prix

'As a driver I have been four times world champion but that doesn't mean that my team will be world champions immediately.' – Alain Prost, 1999

Renault

'Teams that whine don't deserve to win a championship.' – Jackie Stewart fed up with Renault's complaints about fuel difficulties, 1984

'There is just one person I can do without, for I could have won the championship for Renault last year. But Prost was their blue-eyed boy.' – René Arnoux, 1983

'In a Formula 1 team, you must have a boss. One man. In Renault you have many bosses in the racing – and then more back at the factory. It's impossible to get anything done quickly because all the time there are too many people to convince and persuade.' – Alain Prost, 1984

'I have found Formula 1 to be full of hypocrisy and deceit. When I was with Renault, I was on my guard all the time, always wondering if that hand slapping me on the back had a dagger in it.' – Alain Prost

Sauber

'Easter and Christmas would have to fall on the same day for our drivers to appear on the podium.' – Peter Sauber predicting a difficult year ahead, 1998

Stewart

'If you wrap yourself in cotton wool, all you taste is cotton wool.' – Jackie Stewart taking the plunge into running an F1 team, 1996

Surtees

'He thought he knew everything there was to know about racing. Former drivers always think they know best – their driver is just a surrogate for themselves. His ego got in the way of the team.' – Alan Jones on John Surtees for whom he drove in 1976

Theodore

'A super bloke. He asked Eddie Cheever to drive for him before he asked me, but Eddie turned the drive down, thinking a Chinese team wasn't good enough for him. I jumped quick. There aren't many ways for a Finn to get into F1.' – Keke Rosberg on his entry into Formula 1 with Teddy Yip's Theodore team in 1978, from *Keke* by Keke Rosberg and Keith Botsford (Stanley Paul, 1985)

Toleman

'It's just sour grapes. When a team's struggling and then suddenly rises to fine form, there's always someone wanting to knock them straight back down again.' – Derek Warwick as a whispering campaign started against Toleman, 1982

'We weren't on about money, we were on about the humiliation that he'd caused us, and the embarrassment, and the fact that he'd probably put us out of motor racing for ever, breached the credibility to such an extent that Toleman could no longer continue in motor racing and get support from sponsors and suppliers. He'd accomplished that in one hit – all the credibility I'd been working flat out for years to achieve. He didn't just cost us the possibility of Formula 1, he cost us the possibility of being super-competitive with a major engine manufacturer.' – Toleman boss Alex Hawkridge bitter about Ayrton Senna's defection to Lotus for the 1985 season, from *Ayrton Senna: The Hard Edge of Genius* by Christopher Hilton (Corgi, 1997)

Tyrrell

'I wasn't interested in motor racing, I didn't know anything about it. I was about 27 and I got on a coach party to go to Silverstone. We could just as easily have gone to Bognor or Brighton. It was 1951 and BRM was racing. I sat in the grandstand at Stowe. I watched the motor racing and I was hooked.' – Ken Tyrrell

'My performances as a driver didn't satisfy me. I was always disappointed and usually angry with myself that I could not go any faster. On the day I began to run a racing team I knew that I had found my vocation.' – Ken Tyrrell

'Managing a team is well within the capacities of any good secretary.' – Ken Tyrrell, 1973

'Small teams have always blown off big teams because they don't have to hold a board meeting to agree to a change of suspension settings.' – Ken Tyrrell

'His great strength is to rely on no one but himself.' – Jackie Stewart on Ken Tyrrell, 1973

'I felt like an amateur footballer who had just been asked to play for Real Madrid.' – François Cevert on being signed up by Tyrrell in 1970

'My first driver is the fastest driver.' – Ken Tyrrell discussing number twos

'For 1979 they just copied the Lotus 79, so we were a year behind already! They were just too conservative.' – Didier Pironi

'I think the start of our problems dates back to 1973. Jackie [Stewart] had decided to retire at the end of the season and François Cevert should have replaced him. He was as quick as Jackie. When François died, we had nothing and had to start over again with two drivers who did not have enough experience. We never got back to where we were.' – Ken Tyrrell sounding the death knell for the team, 1997

Williams

'He was not a particularly good driver but that doesn't matter. Compare it with someone who can't paint masterpieces. What they can do is organise an art gallery, organise studios, create an atmosphere that allows others to paint masterpieces.' – Stirling Moss's portrait of Frank Williams, from *Stirling Moss's Motor Racing Masterpieces* (Sidgwick & Jackson, 1994)

'He is utterly unrelenting. Having been at the bottom and worked his way up, he has a very intense fear of falling back. That's the spur that keeps him going.' – Keke Rosberg on Frank Williams, 1985

'Frank's team worked like a military machine.' – Benetton team manager Peter Collins on his time with Williams, 1986

'When you've got a good picture on the TV set, why the hell change it?' – Alan Jones on the Williams decision to replace the successful Clay Regazzoni with Carlos Reutemann for the 1980 season

'Patrick Head listens 99.9 per cent only to Alan.' – Carlos Reutemann resenting what he saw as the preferential treatment given to Williams' number one driver, Alan Jones, 1981

'Frank and Patrick have never quite forgiven me for not being Alan Jones.' – Keke Rosberg, 1984

'This must be the only team in the business with more PR men than championship points.' – Keke Rosberg, 1985

'I felt very much at home at Williams with the exception of the 1984 season when I found Patrick [Head] impossible to deal with. He had been on a diet and lost about 30 lb and, frankly, was like a bear that had been shot in the backside.' – Keke Rosberg

'You can't stamp on a man's career, and in any case we would have held the sport up to ridicule.' – Frank Williams deciding against putting out a pit-board to tell Nigel Mansell to slow down and allow his number one driver, Nelson Piquet, to overtake at the 1986 British Grand Prix. Mansell went on to win with Piquet second

'At Williams, if you suggest something that could make you go faster, they don't care. No one talks to anyone. Frank wants me to re-sign for next year, so he says next year I'll have the car I want. I say, why should I have to wait until next year?' – Nelson Piquet, 1987. The car was good enough to give the Brazilian the world championship that year

'We were not quite on the floor, but the countdown had almost begun.' – Frank Williams looking back on his team's disappointing showing in 1988

'I want to be in a position where I feel I have 100 per cent backing from the team.' – Damon Hill sounding the first note of discord, 1995

'I'm pretty disgusted with some of the things which have gone on. I feel that they have not contributed to making me feel that the team is behind me to win the championship. I reckon I am a lot better than my contract says I am. I have won nine Grands Prix. This year I have had to carry the role of number one driver in only my second season in F1. I'm one point off the championship lead with one race to go.' – Damon Hill feeling aggrieved before the decisive 1994 Australian Grand Prix

'Williams is a team that wins together and loses together.' – Frank Williams laying down the law to a discontented Damon Hill, 1995

'I couldn't care less who Damon talks to. It's all perfectly healthy. I've probably talked to every driver in the pit lane 74 times this season.' – Frank Williams unconcerned about rumours that Damon Hill was talking to other teams, 1995

'I will be thrilled to bits to win the constructors' championship. That is always what has been the most important to me. It is a team business and I am not here for the benefit of the drivers. I am here to enjoy myself and keep up my living. The drivers come and go but the team is here for ever.' – Frank Williams, 1996

'It was my leaving present to Williams.' – Damon Hill clinching the 1996 title before departing for Arrows

'It seems Frank Williams does not like world champions in the team. He makes them and then gets rid of them.' – Bernie Ecclestone on Hill's departure, 1996

'Losing someone as good as Adrian is only half the story. The other half is that in future he will be working against you.' – Frank Williams on the loss of chief designer Adrian Newey to McLaren, 1997

'It's not right to go round thrashing our backs with twigs, saying, "woe, woe and thrice woe".' – Patrick Head on the team's mid-season slump, 1997

'Williams are a team that have little time for wet-nursing their drivers. They're into the engineering and it's up to the driver to look after himself.' – Johnny Herbert, 1998

'We're not very good at cuddling people here.' – Patrick Head reiterating the Williams philosophy towards drivers

'In my first two days I spoke more with Frank Williams than I did in two seasons with Eddie Jordan.' – Ralf Schumacher switching from Jordan to Williams, 1999

'I love racing. And I get very aggressive if we're not doing well.' – Frank Williams, 1990

Wolf

'People think he's an arrogant fool, but he's got a good heart.' – Niki Lauda on Canadian millionaire and team owner Walter Wolf, 1977

'They told me I could go on racing for them or retire permanently.' – James Hunt claiming that the Wolf team refused to release him from his contract when he received an offer from Ligier in 1979. So he decided to retire permanently

'Where some drivers regenerate enthusiasm in the team, I was never the man to do that. With McLaren in '78 and then with Wolf, I quite frankly saw no chance of matters improving, and I was buggered if I was going to put in a lot of effort and waste my time.' – James Hunt, 1981

Chapter Seven
Danger Ahead

'We all know, every one of us, that death is in our contract.' – François Cevert, 1970

'It is about people coming to tracks to see the likes of me killed. They will deny that but it is the truth.' – James Hunt on the appeal of Formula 1

'We are bloody mercenaries and we can't get hysterical every time someone gets killed.' – Alan Jones, 1981

'You don't go into motor racing expecting that people are going to weep if you get killed. You know the risk you're taking. One or two people would weep if I should happen to get killed, but most would just shrug and say, "He was asking for it."' – Stirling Moss, from *Cars at Speed* by Robert Daley (Foulis, 1961)

'He risks his life, yes, but it is a glamorous death he faces and all racing drivers are volunteers.' – Enzo Ferrari on the lot of the racing driver, 1977

'The essence of motor racing is to go as fast as you can without killing yourself.' – Dan Gurney, 1960

'There is no point in having a complex about losing half an ear.' – Niki Lauda following his dreadful crash at the Nürburgring, 1976

'I even capitalised on my semi-baldness by signing with Parmalat to wear a cap with their name on it!' – Niki Lauda making the most of his misfortune after Nürburgring

'After the accident I am looking worse than some people are born – but at least I can say it was an accident.' – Niki Lauda, 1977

'We racing drivers are quite a strange bunch – we love to frighten ourselves.' – Damon Hill, 1999

'I like the feeling of fear. After a while you get to be an addict and have to have it.' – Marquis de Portago, 1956

'I think it's fair to say we're a callous lot about death.' – Alan Jones, 1986

'There isn't a single driver who hasn't left his hotel room in the morning well aware that he may well not return.' – Jacky Ickx, 1970

'Perhaps we appreciate life more because we live closer to death.' – Marquis de Portago, 1956

'I wouldn't say that motor racing is too dangerous but there is danger in all sports and in all walks of life. I know a chap who broke his neck falling off a bar stool. Drinking in bars can be dangerous.' – Professor Sid Watkins, F1 flying doctor, 1997

'Safety was never discussed in my time. Nobody gave any thought to it. Obviously we took the precautions we could, like wearing the best available helmet, but we hadn't even got round to flame-proof clothing. The attitude in those days was that the spectators had to be protected at all costs, and that was it.' – Tony Brooks on Formula 1 in the 1950s, from *Grand Prix Greats* by Nigel Roebuck (Patrick Stephens Ltd, 1986)

'When I got into motor racing, the circuits had been the same since the Dark Ages. They hadn't been changed since the day they were built, some of them. All you had then were grass banks and trees, and to me such things were unnecessary hazards. Drivers were supposed to act like gladiators, not give a thought to safety – their own or anyone else's.' – Jackie Stewart, 1982

'As a driver, I was being paid for my skill. I wasn't being paid to risk my life.' – Jackie Stewart

'If you believe that mechanical failure causes all the accidents, then we drivers are not taking calculated risks, we are all playing a game of Russian roulette, waiting around for something sooner or later to kill us.' – Phil Hill, 1960

'Motor racing is a sport like any other. There'll be winners and there'll be losers. It's a game of skill, and if a man makes a mistake he shouldn't have to die for it.' – Peter Revson, 1972

'I always believe a man makes his own luck. I never thought I would die in a race. Never.' – Juan Manuel Fangio

'Motor racing is a job, like any other job. If you want to do well at it you've got to be single-minded. I can't afford to think about the risks.' – Masten Gregory, 1960

'I don't have any fear of a crash. I never think I can hurt myself. It seems impossible to me. If you believe it can happen to you, how can you possibly do the job properly?' – Gilles Villeneuve, 1978

'I never think about the danger, but it's probably unhealthy to think you are immortal.' – Jacques Villeneuve, 1996

'Once in a while you will get a freak accident where someone will get hurt, but that's racing and life. There's not much you can do about it.' – Jacques Villeneuve, 1997

'He has two broken legs and that is not so serious. You can break both legs skiing, for example, and then no one gives a damn, or says that skiing is dangerous and should be banned. This sort of accident happens to motorcyclists on the road every day. It won't be the end of his career. We're paid to take risks.' – Jacques Villeneuve on the injury to Olivier Panis at the 1997 Canadian Grand Prix

'If I died in a Grand Prix, I would not want the race to be stopped. I know the risks and I enjoy taking them.' – Jacques Villeneuve following the Panis incident at Montreal, 1997

'Safety is a good thing, but not when it destroys what racing is all about. Nobody is looking to kill themselves – that would be pure stupidity – but there needs to be that small sense of danger, that feeling that if you go one kilometre an hour quicker you are going to lose it.' – Jacques Villeneuve, 1997

'Formula 1 must not be made into a circus. If it goes on like this, then a driver who is prepared to take risks will not gain any advantage. Formula 1 is more safety-conscious than ever – too much so. I want to go even faster.' – Jacques Villeneuve opposing new safety proposals, 1997

'I thought, "Oh dear, this is going to hurt."' – Jacques Villeneuve recalling his spectacular 186 mph crash during practice for the 1998 Belgian Grand Prix

'It is the best accident I've had in Formula 1 so far.' – Jacques Villeneuve still enthusing about his 1998 crash at Spa

'When you spin off at 210 mph, you get some more grey hairs, I can tell you.' – Mika Hakkinen after the 1999 German Grand Prix

'I've never been as scared as that in a racing car, because I had such a long time before I actually hit the tyre wall. I just knew I was at least going to break my legs!' – Derek Daly on his crash at the 1980 Dutch Grand Prix

'I got to the brow and was confronted by somebody having an enormous accident. I sort of recognised it as Streiff's car, broadside across the track, about a quarter of the way from the barrier on the right. I started to pull left and Philippe's car was moving into my path. It was just fragmenting – wheels, engine, gear-box – and a huge dust cloud enveloped everything. I just drove into nothing. I kept aiming left and couldn't avoid what turned out to be the Tyrrell tub, without engine and with Streiff strapped into it. The right-hand front corner of my car came off at once, and I slid on for another 50 yards before stopping. As it did, I moved my legs around, and was very relieved to find everything was still intact.' – Jonathan Palmer following his smash with Philippe Streiff's Tyrrell at the start of the 1987 Belgian Grand Prix

'When I went up in the air I thought, "Martin, this is not good", because when you are flying, you are totally out of control.' – Martin Brundle going skywards in a Jordan at 180 mph at the 1996 Australian Grand Prix. His car flew over that of a startled Johnny Herbert

'It was like the scene from *Top Gun* where he flies upside down. I could actually see Martin in the cockpit.' – Johnny Herbert's view of Brundle's unscheduled flight at Melbourne, 1996

'I could not see how anyone could get away with a thing like that. I honestly thought he had had it and I was in no mood to go on motor racing.' – Mike Hawthorn after Luigi Musso crashed at the 1958 Belgian Grand Prix. Remarkably, Musso survived with nothing worse than a bruised back

'I got a massive fright and I was so lucky it hit the suspension. If it had been head on – just a few centimetres to the right – I reckon that would have been it for me.' – Stefan Johansson after a large deer ran into his McLaren while the car was doing 150 mph during practice for the 1987 Austrian Grand Prix. The car ploughed into a guard-rail and Johansson was carted off to hospital for X-rays

'I think I am lucky to be alive. I had no steering, no control, nothing.' – Bruno Giacomelli following a crash in practice for the 1982 British Grand Prix

'You can have a shunt and that doesn't scare you. But this was different. I saw the bodywork come off the car, and it fluttered high into the air and seemed to hover there. I was sure it was coming down on top of me but, believe it or not, it fell on a bridge – just as I went under it!' – Derek Daly counting his blessings during practice for the 1982 French Grand Prix. Daly had been following Bruno Giacomelli when the rear bodywork of Giacomelli's Alfa Romeo came adrift at high speed

'Something snapped at the front of the car and it went completely out of control. I tried to brake a little. I was heading straight for the wall. I thought, "My God, this is going to be the big one."' – Gerhard Berger on his horrendous crash at the 1989 San Marino Grand Prix, from *Gerhard Berger* by Christopher Hilton (Patrick Stephens Ltd, 1993)

'I have always raced with my heart. I lived for it. Racing is what I've done for my whole life. However, if my feelings tell me that I am unable to take the risks required, then I will quit. My big problem at the moment is that I have lost faith in technology. I have had so many accidents in which technical failure was the cause that I have lost confidence.' – Gerhard Berger, 1994

'If you're wondering if you'll get round the next bend, that is the time to go.' – Gerhard Berger, 1994

'My concentration wasn't good enough. My speed was OK but I could see that I was dangerous. I would go into a corner and think, "Christ, I should be braking by now!" I was scratching around because I had enough ability to do that but I wasn't smooth. I thought, "I can't do this, I'm going to hurt myself." So I announced my retirement. It was a mistake.' – Stirling Moss blaming the pressure which was put on him to make an instant decision about his future after his horrific crash at Goodwood on Easter Monday, 1962, as the reason for his premature retirement

'Once you sit in a racing car you know you are taking risks. We never think we are going to have an accident or get hurt but it is always at the back of the mind. It is that knowledge which determines the limit you establish for yourself. It is very important because it helps you to stay together and not go beyond your limit. You can be guided by self-preservation without losing your commitment.' – Ayrton Senna

'There's a fine line that separates commitment from risk. All drivers know about that line, just as they know the risks are there. The question is, where does judgement end and risk begin? What is normal in racing and what is dangerous? Every driver feels that point to be in an entirely different place.' – Keke Rosberg, 1986

'Every race I do is a calculated risk.' – Alan Jones, 1986

'If you're a driver and not too stupid you have to accept that machines can fall to pieces or you can make some silly mistake and then, if everything is stacked the wrong way, cop it.' – Graham Hill, 1971

'It could happen tomorrow. That's the thing about this business – you never know.' – Wolfgang 'Taffy' von Trips talking to the *New York Times* about the thin dividing line between life and death on the race track, 1961. In the following day's Italian Grand Prix, von Trips was killed when his Ferrari plunged into the crowd at Monza

'The thought of being killed is a shadow that follows you always. It's a cloud that hangs over your head, even though you don't always look up at it.' – James Hunt, 1976

'All racing drivers learn to live with fear. The challenge is controlling it.' – Ayrton Senna, 1990

'Going through a corner flat out, you know you'd be more comfortable lifting off. You can feel how much easier it would be. But, despite the fear, your mind tells you that you *can* go through that corner flat, because you've done so in the past.' – Alan Jones, from *Driving Ambition* by Alan Jones and Keith Botsford (Stanley Paul, 1981)

'I don't think anybody ideally likes the wet, because of what it can do to you. You can be in good shape one minute, and the next stick your backside in the guard-rail.' – Nigel Mansell, 1987

'I felt helpless. Didier was going much quicker than me and his car actually overtook me in the air. It landed gear-box first in front of me, then bounced away somersaulting down the road. It was terrible. Since that day I have guarded an incredible memory of what wet conditions mean.' – Alain Prost following Didier Pironi's crash in practice for the 1982 German Grand Prix

'I am quick in the wet, but that doesn't mean I like it.' – Ayrton Senna, 1987

'In the wet you have to concentrate much harder because a curve that barely merited a thought when it was dry becomes a corner, and the straights that were previously flat-out blasts become skid-pans.' – Damon Hill, from *F1 Through the Eyes of Damon Hill* (Little, Brown, 1998)

'I really did have a sense of foreboding at the start. Lightning hit the ground not far from the car. The conditions were, shall we say, risky. There were rivers on the track.' – Damon Hill on the 1996 Brazilian Grand Prix

'It was impossible to see anything. I was a little bit scared. I had to fight with a big nerve.' – Jean Alesi's view of the same race

'When a beginner is killed, people say he was mad, but it's not really true – he was only playing double or quits.' – Daredevil Swiss driver Jo Siffert, 1966

'I don't dwell on the scares. If you give them time to grow inside you, they become more important than they really are.' – Alan Jones

'I won't hang on too long once I've stopped enjoying things. It's too dangerous not to require 100 per cent effort.' – Jody Scheckter, 1979. He retired the following year

'Suddenly I realised what I was doing. I said to myself: "You fool, what are you trying to do? You might break your engine. You might crash. You might kill yourself. For what? To finish fifth instead of sixth? Slow down."' – Harry Schell, striving to catch up after being delayed in the pits with engine trouble at the 1958 Monaco Grand Prix

'There's no way I'm going to take big chances to be sixteenth instead of eighteenth.' – Nigel Mansell after qualifying for the 1988 Mexican Grand Prix

'If someone could guarantee that I would split the McLarens, I would take the risk. But I will not, because it could cost me my life.' – Gerhard Berger knowing his limits in qualifying for Ferrari at the 1988 United States Grand Prix

'I began to believe there was a jinx on me. It seemed impossible for me to get into a car without something going very wrong and me ending up sitting in a heap of wreckage.' – Innes Ireland lamenting his run of bad luck in 1964

'A crash happens and is over in an instant. You don't have time to think. But that skid lasted so long that I had plenty of time to think. Too much time.' – Jean Behra crashing at 150 mph during practice for the 1958 Belgian Grand Prix

'I've had enough. I'm tired of being banged up all the time, of always being scared. I'm getting out.' – Jean Behra before the 1958 Belgian Grand Prix. He quit the race on lap six, complaining that the BRM's oil pressure was wrong. The mechanics could find nothing amiss

'A lot of people think I'm braver than Dick Tracy, but I can be just as scared as anybody.' – Jochen Rindt

'Yes, I get scared, we all get scared, but I get scared that something will happen with the car. It's the cars that break, not the drivers.' – Jochen Rindt, 1970. Later that year, he was killed in practice at Monza

'Every driver has a place deep inside him where he's afraid.' – Wolfgang von Trips, 1960

'At Monza I was rigid with fear. Terrified. Diarrhoea. Heart pounding. Throwing up.' – Niki Lauda on his comeback race – the 1976 Italian Grand Prix – just 33 days after his horrific crash at the Nürburgring, from *To Hell and Back* (Stanley Paul, 1986)

'It's just like murder out there. I'm not going to do it. Sometimes I could not tell which direction the car was going. For me it was the limit. For me there is something more important than the world championship.' – Niki Lauda pulling out after two laps in torrential rain at his fourth comeback race, the 1976 Japanese Grand Prix. Lauda's departure effectively handed the title to James Hunt

'He's got a man under contract, not an ape. He can give the ape a kick up the arse and order him to drive, but a man must be expected to think. And if he didn't consider me an idiot before, then he must accept the result of my thoughts.' – Niki Lauda on the Ferrari reaction to his retirement at the 1976 Japanese Grand Prix, from *For the Record* (William Kimber, 1978)

'All I heard in the night were screams. Someone in the ward died. At that point I didn't know if I had internal bleeding. When you are exposed to that kind of trauma, your thoughts are vulnerable.' – Nigel Mansell after a high-speed crash while qualifying for the 1987 Japanese Grand Prix

'Normally it is noisy but everyone was a bit nervous. When I accelerated, it felt fantastic. I thought, "This is great, this is fun", and I did not feel scared any more.' – Mika Hakkinen describing his first testing since his dreadful crash in the 1995 Australian Grand Prix

'Fangio once told me that in the ten years he was racing he had known 33 drivers killed. That's three drivers a year. That made me philosophical.' – Tony Brooks on why he retired

'I will never go to a race again, even to watch. They were my brothers – Faglioli, Marimón, Collins, Musso, Levegh, Ascari, Castellotti, Portago – and now they are dead, all dead. I will not go to a race again because the association is too painful for me.' – Juan Manuel Fangio announcing his retirement, 1958

'There are too many old drivers in this sport. A few years ago a couple of drivers a year got killed and no one took any notice. It was a sort of natural culling.' – F1 supremo Bernie Ecclestone, 1993

'With me, racing is a business. I don't take chances.' – Harry Schell later killed in a practice accident at Silverstone in 1960

'My first priority is to finish above rather than below the ground.' – James Hunt

'I have never lost a single drop of blood while motor racing. I tried very hard to drive cleanly and carefully at the risk of not being very spectacular. Drivers who want to be spectacular are very often dangerous drivers.' – Jackie Stewart, 1974

'In my sport the quick are too often listed among the dead.' – Jackie Stewart

'I don't doubt that motor racing is dangerous. But it's the technique of racing that I find stimulating. I don't feel the risk factor is so important and I don't get excited by it.' – Niki Lauda, 1977

'Grand Prix racing is a calculated risk accepted by those who take part in it; no regulations could be drawn up which would guarantee safety. If you take away the normal hazards of motor racing, you take away the reasons for going motor racing.' – Mike Hawthorn, 1959

'To do something well is so worthwhile that to die trying to do it better cannot be foolhardy. Life is measured in achievement, not in years alone.' – Bruce McLaren, 1966

'If man can't look at danger and still go on, man has stopped living. If the worst ever happens, then it means simply that I have been asked to pay the bill for the happiness of my life.' – Graham Hill, 1971

'I don't think I am callous but I have been blessed with a bad memory for such things. A day later you feel a little better, three days later you start packing your bags for another race.' – Jim Clark on coping with the deaths of his fellow drivers

'You accept that motor racing is futile and stupid and you still carry on. You are able to do it because what is out there on the track is so exhilarating for the selfish man behind the wheel. It is as if someone has given you an injection that anaesthetises you against the terrible possibilities and leaves you hooked on the marvellous, irreplaceable excitement.' – Jackie Stewart

'Losing really hurts. To fail in the race is the most painful thing imaginable. The physical fear is another matter. You get shaken when certain things happen on the race course, but during a race you are protected by a certain resilience.' – Peter Revson, from *Speed With Style* by Revson and Leon Mandel (William Kimber, 1974)

'Fear is a brake. If you're scared, you're not competitive, not fast. I have never been scared while driving.' – Jean Alesi, 1990

'You don't have nerves when you're in a car – that's something you only think about when you've got out.' – James Hunt, 1979

'When you are racing you don't feel pain.' – Heinz-Harald Frentzen winning the 1999 French Grand Prix despite still limping from a crash in Canada two weeks earlier

'I know as every racing driver knows that I am living on borrowed time. The girl you marry knows it too. But the drivers have had the kick. It's the people who are left behind that suffer – the families and the children.' – John Watson, 1982

'Look at me, I'm a nervous wreck. What I need is a four-month rest – four months of not having to worry about Jack's life.' – Betty Brabham, wife of Jack, 1960

'For me, it is a relief at the end of the race. It has always been that way. A race is a long time to bite your nails. You get excited if he has gone well, disappointed if not, but there is always relief that he is fine.' – Damon Hill's wife Georgie, from *Damon Hill's Championship Year* by Bob McKenzie (Headline, 1996)

'There are times when you get out of the car and thank God that you got out of a race in one piece.' – Damon Hill, 1997

'No Formula 1 driver dwells on the bad side of the job. I don't look at my daughters and think, "I might lose my legs." I don't think, "Maybe I'll kill myself and miss them growing up." I force myself to look at the positive side, to hope that having a father as a Formula 1 driver will educate them in the ways of the world.' – Johnny Herbert, 1999

'If you went off, you were in the lap of the gods. You might get away with it, you might not.' – Tony Brooks

'We are hostages to others, to luck, to fate.' – Alain Prost, 1985

'Even when a shunt seems inevitable, you fight it right up to the end: until it really is. When that moment comes, everything is happening so quickly that a driver doesn't really have much time to do anything, nor even think very much. I go into a state that is not really a daze so much as an acceptance of the inevitable. My thought is: "It's going to happen; I've got to make sure I get out of this alive."' – Alan Jones, from *Driving Ambition* by Alan Jones and Keith Botsford (Stanley Paul, 1981)

'Everywhere the marshal looks he sees everyone having a great time while he is expected to rush into danger for a bottle of Coke, a pork pie and his bus fare home.' – Graham Hill hitting out at the over-reliance of a multi-million-pound sport on unpaid enthusiasts, 1971

'You cannot leave somebody beside the track like that with cars continuing at 180 mph. And the guys who removed my helmet need to be shown how to do it, because they just didn't have an idea. Then when I got to the hospital, there seemed to be 25 doctors pulling me this way and that. One said we need to X-ray this, the other said we need to X-ray that. The whole thing was unbelievable, a big casino!' – Gerhard Berger after his crash during the warm-up session for the 1994 Italian Grand Prix. It took officials ten minutes to wave the red flag to bring proceedings to a halt

'I glimpsed a hole in the hedge on the outside of a corner and two straight black skid marks leading up to it. I knew someone had gone over the edge and at this particular point there would not be much hope of survival.' – Mike Hawthorn recounting the demise of Argentinian driver Onofre Marimón, killed during practice for the 1954 German Grand Prix at the Nürburgring

'I have won at Reims, but the price is too high. I have lost the only Italian driver who mattered in Formula 1 racing.' – Enzo Ferrari after Hawthorn's win in the 1958 French Grand Prix was overshadowed by the death of team-mate Luigi Musso

'I was just thinking of some choice words to say to him when we climbed out of two bent Ferraris when, without the slightest warning, fantastically quickly, his car just whipped straight over. I could not believe that it had happened. There was a blur as Pete was thrown out.' – Mike Hawthorn witnessing the death of his Ferrari team-mate and close friend Peter Collins at the Nürburgring, 1958

'It was a great race. No one was killed.' – Juan Manuel Fangio after the 1958 Italian Grand Prix

'I had been given number two. No doubt it was partly due to nerves, but as Peter and Luigi had both been killed with the number two on the car, I asked to have it altered.' – A cautious Mike Hawthorn before the 1958 Moroccan Grand Prix at Casablanca. Hawthorn was given the number six instead and finished second to take the world championship

'When such a terrible accident happens through no fault of the driver, people seem to feel it more. It is one of those times when you realise that a similar thing could happen to you, and it goes quite deep down. For a time, nobody feels like having much of a go.' – Innes Ireland after Stirling Moss's crash in practice at the 1960 Belgian Grand Prix. By the end of the race two drivers (Alan Stacey and Chris Bristow) had been killed and two more (Moss and Mike Taylor) badly injured

'I saw Alan lying in the ambulance. He looked as if he was asleep, the way I'd seen him a hundred times in countless hotel rooms. I just couldn't believe my eyes. I was completely devastated. I don't think I had ever seen anyone dead before. I simply turned round in absolute horror and ran away.' – Innes Ireland on the death of Lotus team-mate Alan Stacey, killed when a bird flew into his face at the 1960 Belgian Grand Prix, from *All Arms and Elbows* (Pelham Books, 1967)

'It looked like a rag doll. It was horrible. I'll never forget the sight of his body being dragged to the side. I found afterwards that my car was spattered with blood.' – Jim Clark, first on the scene when Chris Bristow was killed at Spa in 1960. Bristow had been decapitated when his car crashed through a trackside fence at Burnenville and his body was thrown back on to the track

'If I had seen Alan Stacey's accident right after Bristow's, I would have retired from motor racing for good.' – Jim Clark

'I was still on his tail slipstreaming round the Vialone to keep up as we came down at full speed to the braking point for the North Curve. By this time I was preparing to overtake him, and my front wheel was almost level with his back wheel as he started to brake. Suddenly he began to pull over towards me and he ran right into the side of me. I honestly think that Taffy never realised that I was up with him. I am sure that when he passed me he had decided that as he was in a faster car, I would be left behind. Everything happened at lightning speed. We touched wheels, and oddly enough I had a split second to think about the accident before it actually happened. I thought: "God, he can't do this." I remember mentally trying to shout at him to look in his mirror and see me.'

– Jim Clark after his Lotus touched wheels with Taffy von Trips' Ferrari in the 1961 Italian Grand Prix at Monza. The Ferrari soared out of control and ploughed into the crowd, killing von Trips and fourteen spectators

'One minute I was racing and enjoying it, the next I was walking away from a ghastly mess. I didn't want to see a racing car again.' – Jim Clark after the fateful 1961 Italian Grand Prix

'If it could happen to him, what chance did the rest of us have? I think we all felt that. It seemed like we'd lost our leader.' – Chris Amon stunned by the death of Jim Clark, 1968

'I was terribly upset over Jimmy's death but, as a racing driver, I couldn't allow my emotions to come through. If I did, I would have been lost and unable to cope – and I'm sure all racing drivers feel the same. You may feel the loss deeply and grieve inwardly – but it must never be allowed to get on top of you.' – Graham Hill on the death of Jim Clark, from *Graham* (Stanley Paul, 1976)

'Jimmy Clark's accident affected me for many years. I had used him as my yardstick. He'd done everything, won everything, yet had never so much as broken his skin in a racing car accident. When my wife and family said, "Surely motor racing is dangerous," I would point to Jimmy as an example of somebody who got away with it. A driver simply *has* to believe he is going to get away with it. So when it happened to Jimmy, it smashed my beliefs and philosophy.' – Derek Bell, from *My Racing Life* (Patrick Stephens Ltd, 1988)

'That year of 1968 was horrific with a driver being killed on about the seventh of each month. Jim Clark on 7 April, Mike Spence on 7 May, Scarfiotti on 8 June, Jo Schlesser on 7 July. On the seventh day of the month you weren't that keen to go out in the car.' – Chris Amon, from *It Beats Working* by Eoin Young (Patrick Stephens Ltd, 1996)

'I remember I had breakfast with Jochen at the hotel on Saturday morning, and we talked about me doing a few Formula 2 races for the team he was running with Bernie Ecclestone at the time. I said: "Sure, Jochen, I accept." Two hours later he was gone.' – Emerson Fittipaldi recalling Jochen Rindt's death during qualifying for the 1970 Italian Grand Prix

'What I felt was a sense of release. I was saying to myself: you're not going to win this race any more, you're not going to be champion. If I had won, it would have given me no satisfaction – no satisfaction at all.' – Jacky Ickx finishing fourth in the 1970 United States Grand Prix, a result which meant that Jochen Rindt – killed at Monza two races earlier – became Formula 1's only posthumous world champion, from *Grand Prix Showdown* by Christopher Hilton (Patrick Stephens Ltd, 1992)

'The easiest way to escape is just to slip back into the cockpit of a racing car. Once in there and on the track, all the awkward questions are forgotten. You are anaesthetised: no more pain, no more conscience, no more guilt.' – Jackie Stewart in the wake of the deaths of Piers Courage and Jochen Rindt in 1970, from *The Champions of Formula 1* by Keith Botsford (Stanley Paul, 1988)

'At a time like this I defy anyone to find any sense in our profession.' – Jackie Stewart following the death of Jo Siffert at Brands Hatch, 1971

'I was afraid to look. I am not all that brave. I hate hospitals and refuse to look at suffering. I got into my car. I didn't know whether François was still alive. As I returned to the pits, remorse overtook me. "You should have gone on to look. You should know," I said to myself; but still my cowardice allowed me to go on hoping.' – Jean-Pierre Beltoise afraid to look at the crashed car of fellow countryman François Cevert, killed in practice for the 1973 United States Grand Prix at Watkins Glen, from *François Cevert: A Contract With Death* by Jean-Claude Hall((William Kimber, 1975)

'I was not driving the car in the race. I was just sitting there like a robot and could not think, just could not understand what I was doing in the car.' – Patrick Depailler, an unwilling participant in the 1978 Italian Grand Prix following Ronnie Peterson's fatal accident

'I wanted that title so badly but I did not want to win it like this. What the hell shall I do with it now? I don't feel anything for it.' – Mario Andretti clinching the 1978 world drivers' championship at Monza, but finding his triumph overshadowed by the death of Peterson

'For four years I had to ask myself the same question: am I a killer? All the time I knew I was not, but it was almost too much to bear. None of the drivers ever had the guts to tell me, but for many I was the killer of Ronnie Peterson.' – Riccardo Patrese, initially blamed but ultimately cleared of causing the death of Peterson

'Gilles had to make his decision before the accident too – how he could overtake me. He drove right too, to overtake me on the right. You have been a racing driver long enough yourself to know that we both had no chance of correcting our decision. There is no time for that in this decisive hundredth of a second. You know yourself it is usual for us in races and practice to let an overtaking car pass inside. That's what I did.' – Jochen Mass writing an open letter to Niki Lauda who had criticised him for his part in the death of Gilles Villeneuve, killed in practice at Zolder in 1982. Mass had moved to the right to let Villeneuve pass inside, unaware that Villeneuve was going in the same direction. The two cars touched and the Canadian's Ferrari cartwheeled across the track to destruction

'That accident with Gilles overshadowed my season, my career and my life. It still does. It made me stop racing.' – Jochen Mass on the 1982 death of Gilles Villeneuve, from *The New Villeneuve* by Timothy Collings (Bloomsbury, 1996)

'When I first met Gilles he was extremely polite, a gentleman. I remember he said, "I hope I never need you." When I identified his car as we arrived at the scene of the accident...well, I just thought of those words.' – F1 chief medical officer Professor Sid Watkins at Zolder, 1982

'Villeneuve dies and we come to North America a few weeks later and nobody talks about him. I think that's bloody sad. Life moves too quickly.' – Niki Lauda spotlighting the uncaring face of Formula 1, 1982

'I was first on the scene. I watched him burn. I found it difficult to get close to other drivers after that.' – Nigel Mansell on the death of the popular Elio de Angelis during testing at Paul Ricard in 1986

'After the race at Imola, I went to the hospital because I wanted to see Ayrton again. I did see him, and then Monday morning back home was very, very difficult, a strange day. Very empty. I felt nothing. I felt very far away from myself.' – Gerhard Berger after viewing Senna's body at the hospital, 1994

'When you are young, obviously you want to race a lot. It is your life. You have accidents, or you see accidents, maybe you see people die. It doesn't affect you so much. But when you're older, you've had your own accidents, your own experiences. You feel completely different.' – Gerhard Berger struggling to come to terms with the death of Ayrton Senna, 1994

'To learn that Ayrton was dead was like having someone turn off your power supply. I was totally shattered.' – Damon Hill, 1994

'God has had his hand over Formula 1 for a long time. This weekend, he took it away.' – Niki Lauda following the deaths of Roland Ratzenburger and Ayrton Senna at Imola, 1994

Chapter Eight

Starting Out

'I started out driving my father's hearse – he is the local undertaker.' – Heinz-Harald Frentzen

'When I was about fourteen I got my first race – on a motorbike – because I had this priest who was a really good friend. He knew this burning desire I had to race and so he fixed it. One time I got a broken kneecap flopping a bike and I made him lie to my parents. I said: "You tell them I fell down the marble steps serving Mass or you lose an altar boy!"' – Mario Andretti

'I started racing karts at two and a half. I couldn't brake, so my father had to hold the kart on a rope.' – Ralf Schumacher on his humble beginnings

'I was eighteen when I raced for the first time – in a Ford taxi! It was borrowed from a friend and we took the body off. After the race we put the bodywork back on and it was then used as a taxi again.' – Juan Manuel Fangio

'I started to ride a Royal Enfield motorbike at the age of ten and mashed up the front lawn.' – John Watson

'My parents had a summer house in San Remo and there I started racing with a Lambretta. I was too young to do this legally, so I changed the date of my birth and got my licence.' – Giancarlo Baghetti

'Racing seemed to pursue me. One night I was coming back from a cricket match . . . when suddenly I met three Ecurie Ecosse C-Type Jaguars. I remember thinking what a shower of madmen they were. But at the same time I felt a slight twinge of envy.' – Jim Clark

'As a navigator he was hopeless. He would read the map with it lying across the back seat while he knelt on his seat reading the directions in the opposite direction!' – Ian Scott-Watson who partnered Jim Clark in Scottish rallies in the mid 1950s

'I ran the best forecourt in the county. Then I went into the lubrication bay and made sure you could eat your breakfast off the floor.' – Jackie Stewart leaving school to work in the family garage

'I came to England in 1969 with exactly 50 quid in my pocket and this certainty that what I wanted to do was race motor cars. And another certainty, that I would one day be world champion.' – Alan Jones, from *Driving Ambition* by Alan Jones and Keith Botsford (Stanley Paul, 1981)

'Getting your bum into a car and driving a car are two very different things. Before you can drive a car, you have to have one. To have one requires ducking and diving, it takes wheeling and dealing and conniving. And that part of motor racing is the bigger part. It's like the bottom six-sevenths of an iceberg – nobody who hasn't hit one knows what it's like.' – Alan Jones

'You can throw the car sideways and see if you can get it back again. You can experiment in safety in a way you never could anywhere else. Autocross is like racing on a skid-pan.' – Jim Clark racing on grass in Scotland in the 1950s

'My philosophy of driving was to get into anything I could and go as fast as I could, and if I smashed a car up, well, I'd think about paying for it later.' – Alan Jones on his days in Formula 3

'I was a young, very fast driver. If the car had three wheels, I'd still drive it. Today, if the angle of a wheel is slightly off, I drive it into the pits. Because I am not prepared to take risks. The difference is that I now know that it hurts to take risks. Back then I didn't.' – Keke Rosberg recalling his early days in Formula 2 and Formula Atlantic, from *Keke* by Keke Rosberg and Keith Botsford (Stanley Paul, 1985)

'I was 21 at the time and was a dispatch rider during the week. They might send me on a Friday evening to somewhere like Walsall and I would get back at about midnight. Then I'd prepare the bike and head for the race track at perhaps three in the morning. You had no chance of operating like that.' – Damon Hill, racing motorbikes in his youth, from *Grand Prix Year* (Macmillan, 1995)

'I did about ten races and had one win and a few finishes, but I was very bad. Frequently I didn't even start the race, for my motorbike was always breaking down on the way to the circuit.' – Jean-Pierre Beltoise recounting his early days on two wheels

'I always try for the best. Perhaps there are Hondas in the race, then I try to be the first Cosworth. But I never really expect to win. It always seems too hard.' – Jean-Pierre Beltoise finding racing on four wheels just as much a struggle, at the wheel of a Formula 2 Matra in the 1960s

'You can't play at rowing, you have to be dedicated. You've got to concentrate too, and these and many other things which I learnt rowing helped me when I became a racing driver.' – Graham Hill

'You have to be tough as a beginner so that you can calm down later.' – Jo Siffert

'My mother was flabbergasted when she saw me come back alive. She was convinced I would be killed first time out.' – James Hunt on his intended racing debut at Snetterton in 1967, from *James Hunt: The Biography* by Gerald Donaldson (CollinsWillow, 1994). In fact, Hunt hadn't been allowed to race because his Mini had no windows

'Hunt, you'll never make a professional racing driver as long as you've got a hole in your arse!' – Nick Brittan, organiser of the European Formula Ford championship, to James Hunt after Hunt had deliberately parked his car at right angles in front of the grid to sabotage the start of a race at Vallelunga, Italy, in 1969. Hunt's fit of pique was the result of being told that he couldn't take part in the race because he didn't have the necessary medical certificate

'James always carried £5 on him so he had enough money for a protest.' – Bunty Morgan remembering James Hunt's turbulent days in Formula 3, from *James Hunt: Portrait of a Champion* by Christopher Hilton (Patrick Stephens Ltd, 1993). Hunt and her son David Morgan were involved in a celebrated altercation at Crystal Palace in 1970 when Hunt threw a punch at Morgan after their cars had collided

'The people who are going to make it are the ones prepared to jump in and put their foot right down. The only successful slow learner I've ever seen, the only one who took things steadily and worked up to the pace, was Lauda. The rest were fast from the start – fast in an unfamiliar car, fast on a circuit they'd never seen before. You have to be prepared to give it a real go.' – James Hunt on beginners, 1983

'You can't afford worries when you're in Formula 3 because you have to keep your wits about you to cope with the utter madness of it. There are some 25 drivers in the field, all as fast as each other. And nobody gives an inch. We used to come over the top in formation at 125 mph plus, jostling and banging into each other like dodgem cars. You had to be crazy to drive in Formula 3 at all. Back in 1970, I fitted the bill.' – Niki Lauda, from *To Hell and Back* (Stanley Paul, 1986)

'That first 1978 season in Formula 3 was long and difficult. I had to start following team orders and observing constructor specifications. I didn't take too kindly to this. I took even less kindly to losing. By midway through the season I was thoroughly depressed.' – Alain Prost, from *Life in the Fast Lane* (Stanley Paul, 1988)

'Johnny was so quick he'd get out in the lead and he'd get bored. He wanted to have some fun and he'd slow down to let the rest of them catch up. That used to drive me mad.' – Eddie Jordan recalling Johnny Herbert's days in Formula 3, from *Johnny Herbert: The Steel Behind the Smile* by Christopher Hilton (Patrick Stephens Ltd, 1996)

'He was bloody hopeless! He just didn't have any idea. Damon was a danger to himself and to everyone else.' – Argo team manager John Kirkpatrick remembering Damon Hill's driving debut in Formula Ford 2000 at Brands Hatch in 1983, from *Damon Hill: World Champion* by David Tremayne (Weidenfeld & Nicolson, 1997)

'I had got the reputation, fatal in England, of driving on a thin edge. Although I had not yet scratched the paint of a racing car, let alone seriously bent one, it seemed to be common opinion that I would do at any moment and that I was not the sort of chap who was wanted in a works team.' – Stirling Moss summing up his situation in 1950, from *Design and Behaviour of the Racing Car* by Moss and Laurence Pomeroy (William Kimber, 1963)

'As the race wore on, I slipped farther and farther down in the cockpit until finally I could hardly see a thing. Towards the end I had to slow down in order not to be thrown out of the car on the corners and sometimes I couldn't even reach the pedals.' – Keke Rosberg after the seat in his Formula 2 TOJ car gave way at Hockenheim in 1976, from *Keke* by Keke Rosberg and Keith Botsford (Stanley Paul, 1985)

'The relationship at that point was at its lowest. We didn't speak very much. I got on with him very poorly because he very much felt that it was Brundle and Great Britain versus Senna.' – Martin

Brundle remembering a controversial round of the 1983 Marlboro Formula 3 championship at Snetterton, from *Ayrton Senna: The Hard Edge of Genius* by Christopher Hilton (Corgi, 1997). On his home track Brundle escaped punishment for the collision which put Senna out of the race. But Senna had the last laugh by taking the championship. By the following year both men had been snapped up by Formula 1 teams – Senna by Toleman, Brundle by Tyrrell

'Everyone wanted to be a hero, to be the next F1 star.' – Jacques Villeneuve on his stint in Italian Formula 3

'Japan taught me that racing is racing and that being on the edge is what you enjoy. It taught me Formula 1 was not the only place I had to put my butt.' – Jacques Villeneuve furthering his apprenticeship in Japanese Formula 3

'Nobody takes you to Formula 1 from sports cars because you are very quick. Something else needs to transpire: that you are *better*. Once, everyone scoffed at sports car drivers and suddenly people realised that the drivers weren't that bad, suddenly people believed. That was the chance Michael took and he was wise to take it.' – Jochen Mass on Michael Schumacher's decision to drive sports cars for Mercedes in 1990, from *Michael Schumacher: Defending the Crown* by Christopher Hilton (Patrick Stephens Ltd, 1994)

'You have to have quick reactions, in effect, you are living on your reactions. It was a good training ground for the rest of my career. The tracks were just oval circuits, and the car was virtually out of control all the time.' – Jack Brabham on his days in midget racing in Australia, from *When the Flag Drops* (William Kimber, 1971)

'When I first came over there were a lot of jokes about my driving style and the way I hung out the tail of the car rather like a midget racer on a cinder track.' – Jack Brabham, from *When the Flag Drops*

'There were quite a lot of people who took themselves very

seriously – failed racing drivers who fancied themselves as champions. They were all very put out to see a sixteen-year-old getting ahead of them.' – François Cevert on his karting days

'I enjoyed karts because you drive bumper to bumper and it's real racing.' – Michael Schumacher, who spent fifteen years in karts between 1973 and 1988

'When I had my first race with Jackie Stewart and Jochen Rindt and the others, I was overawed. These people were my gods. It was enough just to race with them but then I found I could pass them. It was a revelation.' – John Watson racing in single-seaters in 1970

'He was in a Cooper-Climax and I had my old Maserati 250F, slithering around in the rain. At one point I got into a huge slide and a second later he comes past with a wave of thanks! He thought I'd moved over for him.' – Chris Amon recalling racing against Stirling Moss in New Zealand in the early 1960s, from *Grand Prix Greats* by Nigel Roebuck (Patrick Stephens Ltd, 1986)

Chapter Nine

Pit Lane Punch-Ups

Prost v Senna

'I didn't realise you wanted the championship that badly.' – Alain Prost to Ayrton Senna after Senna cut him up at the 1988 Portuguese Grand Prix

'I was absolutely sure I was going to win or have an accident because I knew that he wanted to win absolutely. You know, the problem with Ayrton is that he cannot accept not to win and he can't accept that someone might resist one of his overtaking moves. He will not accept that he has been overtaken or that he cannot overtake another car. He thinks he can't kill himself because he believes in God and I think that's very dangerous for the other drivers. I have to be careful because my life is more important than the championship.' – Prost after Senna's overtaking move at the chicane had resulted in both cars retiring from the crucial 1989 Japanese Grand Prix. But Prost had done enough to be world champion

'I no longer wish to have any business with him. I appreciate honesty and he is not honest.' – Prost cutting off all lines of communication with Senna, 1989

'If Prost gets the best start, then I'm warning him, he'd better not turn in on me because he isn't going to make it.' – Senna before the 1990 Japanese Grand Prix, the penultimate race of the season. Senna had expressed serious misgivings about the positioning of pole on the grid. Senna, on pole, was on the right-hand side of the track which was dusty whereas Prost, second on the grid, was on the cleaner left-hand side. Sure enough, Prost got the better start and Senna drove into the back of him at the first corner. Both cars were forced out, thus ensuring that the championship was Senna's

'He did it on purpose because he saw that I had a good start, that my car was better and he had no chance to win. So he just pushed me out. What he did was more than unsporting, it was disgusting. If everybody wants to drive in this way, then the sport is finished. Senna is completely opposite in character to what he wants people to believe. He is the opposite of honest. Motor racing is sport, not war. We were not even side by side. If you accept Senna's behaviour, then perhaps we will get to a situation in which people will start entering a team with one car specifically intended to push off the opposition to enable the other man to win. This man has no value.' – Prost after Suzuka, 1990

'I was coming faster than him because I had more acceleration. I think Prost made a big mistake to close the door on me in the first corner. I cannot be responsible for his actions. He is always trying to destroy people. He tried to destroy me in the past on different occasions and he hasn't managed, and he will not manage because I know who I am and where I want to go.' – Senna hits back

'I am not prepared to fight against irresponsible people who are not afraid to die.' – Prost won't let it lie

'He makes me laugh because he is the guy that complains so much and not just this year but ever since we first raced as team-mates in 1988. He complained a lot about me, then about Honda, then the following year he complained about me and Honda again. He complained about the team, and it was the team for which he won three championships. Then he goes to a new team, Ferrari, and he criticises a tyre company for supplying us with different tyres.

Then he moves on and criticises Berger, then Alesi, then his own team and management, then he ends up criticising Mansell and finishes up criticising me again. So it comes as no surprise that he criticises me over the Suzuka affair. I am used to it.' – Senna, 1990

'If you say what you feel you get banned, you get penalties, you pay money, you get disqualified, you lose your licence. Is that a fair way of working? I said what I thought and what took place afterwards was pure theatre.' – Senna attacking FISA president Jean-Marie Balestre for his refusal to move pole position to the left side of the track for the 1990 Japanese Grand Prix

'If pole had been on the good side nothing would have happened. I would have got a better start. It was the result of a bad decision. I did contribute to the accident, but it was not my responsibility.' – Senna continuing his attack on Balestre, who refused to issue the Brazilian with a licence for 1991 unless he apologised. Eventually peace – of a sort – was restored

'That's the last time he does that to me. I have no problem being on the same track as him but I will just push him off if he tries that again.' – Prost after the battle with Senna at the 1991 German Grand Prix ended with the Frenchman seeking refuge up an escape road

'I think everyone knows Prost by now. He is always complaining about the car or the tyres or the team or the mechanics or the other drivers or the circuit. It's always somebody else to blame. It's never his fault.' – Senna following the resumption of hostilities at the 1991 German Grand Prix

'It's like a 100-metres race and he wants running shoes and everybody else to be in lead boots.' – A bitter Senna after failing to land the drive alongside Prost at Williams for 1993 (Prost had a clause in his contract stopping Senna from joining him)

'Even before he joined McLaren I knew we were never going to be friends because our personalities are completely unalike. He is a very strange guy.' – Prost

Hill v Schumacher

'I don't think we would have been in this situation if Ayrton Senna had been in the car. Ayrton would have been driving circles around me. That shows what I think about Damon as a driver. He has been thrown into the number one driver position but he never really was a number one driver. With David Coulthard driving quicker than him after three races, it proves he is not a number one driver.' – Michael Schumacher having a dig at Damon Hill's driving as the race for the 1994 world championship hots up

'I think it's a half-baked attempt to destabilise me and he'll have to try better than that if he wants to do it.' – Hill responding to the criticism from Schumacher, 1994

'I went over grass and hit a wall, then I just wanted to run into the next corner. I was still in front of Damon. I drove over his front wheel. It was still my corner.' – Schumacher insisting that he had done nothing wrong in the clash with Hill at the 1994 Australian Grand Prix. The coming-together put both cars out of the race, allowing Schumacher to claim the title

'He was the champion, no doubt about that, but he had not achieved it in the way that a champion should.' – Hill choosing his words carefully following the collision with Schumacher at the 1994 Australian Grand Prix

'At the time, I couldn't believe that he would do such a thing but, with hindsight, I think I was being a little naïve.' – Hill coming to terms with the fact that Schumacher might have driven into him deliberately at Adelaide

'Michael is a great driver and is more than capable of looking after himself on the race track.' – Hill responding to Schumacher's accusation that he had 'brake-tested' the German at the 1995 French Grand Prix

'He seems to be very moody and I find it hard to get on with moody people.' – Schumacher taking a pop at Hill before the 1995 British Grand Prix

'He knows that I can beat him. That is what is upsetting him. He thinks he is the best so it upsets the balance of his mind to think that there might be someone else who has driven quicker.' – Hill fights back in the war of words leading up to the 1995 British Grand Prix

'He is so firm in his beliefs that he is like a glass: very strong in one way but any attempt to reform the structure results in the whole thing breaking.' – Hill tries to baffle Schumacher with science in the build-up to Silverstone '95

'It was a totally unnecessary thing to do. It was a crazy manoeuvre. There was no room for two cars and he came from nowhere. I just don't see the sense of doing things like this, even in front of your home crowd. You have to keep your nerve and temperament and not be a danger to anyone. I am very angry with him. I do not know what he was trying to do. It was so stupid and it spoilt a good race.' – Schumacher after he and Hill collided and spun off at the 1995 British Grand Prix

'It was not the sort of thing someone who is challenging for the championship should do. It was unbelievable. I am not worried that German fans might be angry about it when we race at Hockenheim in a fortnight because they are more intelligent than Hill.' – Benetton managing director Flavio Briatore defending his driver (Schumacher) after Hill's failed overtaking move at the 1995 British Grand Prix

'I felt that there was a genuine chance to attack him as he had taken a wide line. I believe that, and I don't think I did anything wrong.' – Hill offers his excuses

'For sure, Damon made a big mistake. He should have known that there would be some deposits on the track at this point. I knew it would be slippery, because everybody drops some oil on the first lap, so I braked early. Then I saw Damon suddenly go sideways and thought, "I can't believe this."' – Schumacher showing little sympathy for his rival's exit at the 1995 German Grand Prix. Hill spun off on the second lap while leading the race

'I am not satisfied with being driven into. Michael drove very defensively, to the point of touching wheels with me at the top of the hill. That's all well and good if it's accidental, but if it's meant on purpose, I would be pretty upset. These are F1 cars, not go-karts. Some things are acceptable, some are not.' – Hill attacking Schumacher's driving tactics following the German's win at the 1995 Belgian Grand Prix

'This is supposed to be a sport, isn't it? It seems that Michael is happy to use any means of preventing anybody else winning. I'm just not prepared to resort to similar tactics.' – Hill repeating his criticism of Schumacher's blocking tactics at Spa

'I felt a big bang and Damon crashed into me. It was not a slight touch – he really crashed into me.' – Schumacher after another collision, this time at the 1995 Italian Grand Prix

'If these guys want to carry on like that, it is OK by me. But I warn them that they must be prepared to accept the consequences, which are that they may get hurt, killed or find themselves in serious trouble.' – Bernie Ecclestone after only the intervention of marshals appeared to prevent Schumacher getting to Hill following their contretemps at the 1995 Italian Grand Prix

'Damon's biggest problem is that he doesn't appear to be in control when he is trying to overtake. He makes half-hearted attempts which land him in trouble, with no way out.' – Schumacher before the 1995 Pacific Grand Prix

'The situation now is that we are completely free to drive as we like as long as it is not deliberately dangerous. So I drove in that style and he didn't like it. But he should have no complaints; it seems that there is one rule for him and another for everybody else.' – Hill getting his own back on Schumacher by driving defensively at the 1995 Pacific Grand Prix

'We see each other at races, but apart from saying "Hello" or "Good morning", there's little that we have to say to one another. I find him cold and aloof.' – Hill on Schumacher, 1995

'I am quite happy Damon is sitting in a Williams. If there was another driver in that car it might be more difficult for me.' – Schumacher, 1996

'He tends to make mistakes under pressure. I think the reason may be that he did not have much experience before he came into Formula 1. Drivers who do have a better idea of what is possible in a fight.' – Schumacher slates Hill's driving ability again, 1996

'Whenever you get on the front row with Michael, it makes for an interesting time.' – Hill before the 1996 San Marino Grand Prix

'Michael showed his true colours and got what he deserved...I didn't think he would do anything like take Jacques off, because it would destroy his reputation...At least he is consistent.' – Hill on Schumacher's unsuccessful attempt to deny Jacques Villeneuve the world championship at Jerez, 1997

'I am human and, unfortunately, make mistakes. I do not make many, but this was a big one and I will learn from it. I see no reason to apologise.' – An unrepentant Schumacher on the same incident, 1997

'If someone wants to kill you he should do it in a different way. We are doing 200 mph down there and to move off line three times is simply unacceptable. I was lucky to get through the chicane. I can't handle an experienced man doing something like that. I shall be having big words with him.' – Schumacher upset by Hill at the 1998 Canadian Grand Prix

'We were racing for second place and I wasn't going to give it to him. He's obviously got this massive problem and overstates the case to try and defend himself. He cannot claim anyone drives badly when you look at the things he's been up to. I mean, he just took Frentzen out completely.' – Hill's reply

'What he did was Formula Ford stuff. In fact, it wouldn't be allowed in Formula Ford! Blocking at 190 mph is incredibly dangerous. That incident was one of the worst I have seen. I think it was just Damon being a prick.' – Eddie Irvine taking the side of team-mate Schumacher in the row with Hill over the 1998 Canadian Grand Prix

'His Schumacher complex becomes more and more evident over the years.' – Schumacher after Hill held him up at Suzuka, 1998

'What is this fixation – a kind of Schu fetish?' – Hill, 1998

'When we're both retired, we might talk about the past, but I won't be going round to his house and asking him if he fancies going down the pub.' – Hill, 1999

Schumacher v Coulthard

'David went very wide into the corner. I went for the gap on the inside and I was much quicker than him, but he shut the door on me. He had already done it to me in Australia, but this time I decided he would not get away with it.' – Schumacher attempting to justify his manoeuvre at the 1998 Argentine Grand Prix. While Coulthard ended up on the grass and lost valuable time, Schumacher went on to win

'The fact that a Formula 1 driver should take his foot off the accelerator at a speed of 200 mph is incomprehensible to me. I suspect that it was deliberate.' – Schumacher after running into the back of the slow-moving Coulthard in heavy spray at the 1998 Belgian Grand Prix. The collision deprived Schumacher of an almost certain victory

'Schumacher came like an animal into the pit, swearing and calling me a f . . . ing killer. I am not standing for that.' – David Coulthard after Schumacher blew his top at the 1998 Belgian Grand Prix.

'If you are lapped you should give space. Coulthard was zig-zagging. He has done that sort of thing to me before. I have to wonder whether what happened in Belgium last year was deliberate.' – Schumacher accusing Coulthard of blocking tactics at the crucial 1999 Japanese Grand Prix

'I cannot believe Michael is saying things like that. If I was weaving in front of him, it certainly was not intentional. It just shows Michael holds grudges and cannot admit mistakes.' – Coulthard's reaction to the latest Schumacher outburst

Mansell v Piquet

'You never know what's going on in his head, and often he doesn't seem to know himself.' – Nigel Mansell on the subject of Nelson Piquet, his team-mate at Williams, 1986

'All I hope is that the championship is decided on the track and not off.' – Mansell as the souring of his relationship with Piquet creates internal strife at Williams, 1986

'If Williams had kept to their contract and given me all the support I was promised, we wouldn't have ended the season like this.' – Piquet complaining that the team paid too much attention to the supposed number two, Mansell, and that was why the Brazilian had missed out on the 1986 world championship

'I didn't complain to Frank when I got shafted last year. I was a fool. I had signed for two years, so now I shut up and do my job. All I want is the same rights as Mansell.' – Piquet, 1987

'If I stay, I'll only fall out with my team. I'm not slow, but look at the times! I don't know what I'll drive at the race. The team can decide that. I'm only the driver.' – Mansell storming out of practice for the 1987 Spanish Grand Prix. Having abandoned his car and failed to weigh-in properly, Mansell was fined $3000 by race officials. He was unhappy because he thought Williams were giving preferential treatment to Piquet!

'I can afford a few other crazy races like Spain, whereas Mansell has to attack and he has to win. It's a tough life.' – Piquet gloating from the comfort of an eighteen-point lead in the championship on the run-up to the Mexican Grand Prix

'I'll be happy if Ferrari win, but Nigel doesn't agree with me. We never seem to get together on things.' – Piquet goading Mansell about the 1987 Mexican Grand Prix, knowing full well that Mansell desperately needed a win

'My team-mate tried to push me off the road twice, which I don't think was very professional.' – Mansell raging after the 1987 Mexican Grand Prix, which he won with Piquet second

'Bullshit. I'm very professional. If I want to take someone off, I do – without any problems. I didn't try to take anyone off.' – Piquet's response

'I'm pleased to have won, but someone else seems to be having an awful lot of luck. I remember the days when you got disqualified for a push start, so long as you weren't in the way.' – Mansell carping that Piquet should have been disqualified from the 1987 Mexican Grand Prix after being given a push start when he stalled. Piquet went on to win the title

'It was a successful year as far as results were concerned, but it was painful. The loudest noise in the motorhome after a race we'd won would be the complaints of our guy who finished second.' – Williams' technical director Patrick Head on the Mansell–Piquet rivalry which dominated 1987

'Piquet is just a vile man. But then I was already aware of that. For him to attack my family, which is the private side of my life and has nothing to do with my job, was out of order. I think it says an awful lot about the sort of person he is.' – Mansell responding to a scathing attack on himself and his family by Piquet in 1988. Piquet called Mansell an 'uneducated blockhead' and described Mansell's wife Rosanne as 'ugly'

'Tell Nigel I'll hold Piquet while he hits him. Families are definitely off limits.' – An unnamed British driver, 1988

'I took a lot of race wins away from Nelson, which he couldn't take. He was the number one and always had use of the spare car, but I had proved that I was able to beat him and outpace him and he didn't like it. I made him look less of a driver than he thought he was.' – Mansell, from *Mansell: My Autobiography* (CollinsWillow, 1995)

Irvine v Coulthard

'I am better than David: absolutely no doubt about it.' – Eddie Irvine, possibly angling for a drive at McLaren for 2000

'If Eddie is having difficulty finding McLaren's telephone number, it's in the Woking directory.' – David Coulthard's cool response

'For me, you have two choices: you can be humble and polite and congratulate people on their successes. Or you can have a chip on your shoulder, be gobby and have no class.' – Coulthard in a thinly veiled attack on Irvine before the 1999 Austrian Grand Prix

'I think we could have beaten DC any day of the week.' – Irvine super-confident after the 1999 Austrian Grand Prix

'He's the classic case of the male inadequacy syndrome.' – Coulthard, 1999

'I'm not trying to put myself in Eddie's mind – it's too scary to be there!' –Coulthard before the 1999 German Grand Prix

'It was gratifying that we benefited from a mistake by Irvine after all that he said about this team and our drivers.' – McLaren boss Ron Dennis quietly satisfied after Irvine slipped up at the 1999 Hungarian Grand Prix

'Although Eddie is still capable of winning the championship, I doubt he will do it.' – Coulthard after winning the 1999 Belgian Grand Prix

Senna v Irvine

'You're not a racing driver, you're a fucking idiot.' – Senna to Irvine after Irvine, on his Jordan debut, had unlapped himself at the 1993 Japanese Grand Prix. Senna, who won the race, was so angry at the impudence that he responded by hitting Irvine in the Jordan office

'I went to see him and he was like a wall. He made me lose my temper. I couldn't help it because respect is very important between drivers. The problem was he didn't even think about it, let alone say he was wrong.' – Senna

'I think the guy is a nutter. He is completely out of control.' – Irvine licking his wounds

'When Senna took a swing at me, I thought, "Here's a few quid coming..."' – Irvine

Panis v Irvine

'It was just incredible trying to overtake Eddie and it is very difficult to speak with this man even though he must have seen the blue [overtaking] flags. Maybe he has a problem with his eyes.' – Olivier Panis aggrieved after the 1997 Spanish Grand Prix

'I saw the flag, but as Jos Verstappen and I had a car to pass in front of us, I assumed they were for him.' – Irvine protests his innocence

Alesi v Brundle

'He overtook, pushed me on to the grass and then slowed. I passed him and he came racing alongside and dropped a wheel inside mine. I went flying into the air. It was crazy.' – Martin Brundle tangling with Jean Alesi during practice for the 1992 San Marino Grand Prix

'If you try to xxxx with me, I will xxxx you!' – Alesi's response – he thought Brundle had deliberately slowed in order to block him

Villeneuve v Pironi

'He let me by on lap 59 because he wanted to draft me on lap 60. And I was stupid enough to believe he was being honourable.' – Gilles Villeneuve furious after Ferrari team-mate Didier Pironi 'stole' the 1982 San Marino Grand Prix from him on the last lap

'Finishing second is one thing. I would have been mad at myself for not being quick enough if he'd beaten me. But finishing second because the bastard steals it! Jesus, that's why I'm mad.' – Villeneuve

'He was there, looking like the hero, and I looked like the spoiled bastard who sulked.' – Villeneuve describing the scene on the victory podium

'The only person to ask is Marco Piccinini [the Ferrari team boss]. He was in charge of the orders and he didn't have any for this race.' – Pironi's answer to Villeneuve's allegation that the Frenchman's overtaking manoeuvre had broken team orders

'I haven't said a word to him and I'm not going to again – ever. I'll do my own thing in future. It's war. When we get to Belgium I'll race with him as if he had a Williams or a Brabham.' – Villeneuve still seething about Pironi. They never did get to race each other in Belgium for Villeneuve was killed in practice at Zolder

'On my slowing-down lap all I could think about was not the victory, but only of Gilles.' – Pironi winning the Dutch Grand Prix later in the season

Alboreto v Danner

'I think Danner just didn't see me. I was nearly past him when he turned into me. I was up in the air.' – Michele Alboreto colliding with Christian Danner's Zakspeed during practice for the 1987 Monaco Grand Prix. Although the accident looked nasty, Alboreto escaped unharmed and had sufficient strength to storm over and give the German a piece of his mind

'I was just going up the hill, straight out of the pits, and Alboreto ran into the back of me – wallop! I'm awfully sorry for the guy, but he ought to have used his brakes. I couldn't just vanish, you know. Michele took off, came down again and there was a huge ball of flame. He's obviously furious, but so am I, quite honestly.' – Danner's version of events. Danner was subsequently excluded from the rest of the meeting for ignoring a blue flag

'I could see Danner, and it was one of those situations where you had to decide whether or not it was worth taking a chance. I decided not, but Michele went for the gap. I feel sorry for Danner.' – Ayrton Senna's view of the Monaco incident

Alboreto v Daly

'Bastardo. Bastardo. Bastardo. Next time I kill you.' – Michele Alboreto taking umbrage at Derek Daly following a collision at Tarzan during the 1982 Dutch Grand Prix at Zandvoort. Alboreto aimed a punch at Daly but missed and was reportedly restrained by the Williams pit crew from launching further attacks

'Alboreto put me off the road twice – once on the straight!' – Daly as the feud simmers on into the next race, the British Grand Prix

Piquet v Senna

'The Sao Paulo taxi driver.' – Piquet's derisory gibe at his Brazilian rival, 1986

'I'm going to call him "handbrake" now. At the start he went off the circuit, over the white line, and when he came back he just pushed his way in. I had to back off to avoid being hit by him.' – Piquet having a go at Senna after the 1987 Japanese Grand Prix

'I had to go around Piquet at the start because he was so slow getting away. I went to the right of him because if I'd gone left there might have been an accident. Alboreto was stalled there. What else could I do?' – Senna pleads his innocence

'Senna hasn't been able to get the car as he would like it this year. Maybe next year he'll do better... with help from Prost.' – Piquet taking a swipe at Senna after winning the 1987 title

Hakkinen v Schumacher

'I was pissed off with him. He wasn't being consistent. I was always having to be careful because he would brake in a surprising place and I did not want to run into the back of him. I knew I could go a couple of seconds a lap faster but I could not risk trying to overtake him.' – Mika Hakkinen after Michael Schumacher had ridden shotgun to Eddie Irvine at the 1999 Malaysian Grand Prix

'My job was to make sure Eddie had a good gap so I drove a little bit slower. That's part of the championship and the rules allow us to do that. I did not do any unfair movements on him or try and run into him.' – Schumacher conducts the case for the defence

'Schumacher drove within the regulations but it was not very sporting, was it? He lifted [off the throttle] in high-speed corners and went slow and then fast, making it impossible for Mika to overtake. I don't think it was very sporting, but it has never bothered Ferrari in the past.' – McLaren boss Ron Dennis

Prost v Arnoux

'We agreed before the race that, if we were running first and second at the end, I was to win.' – Alain Prost, claiming that his Renault team-mate, René Arnoux, had defied team orders and gone on to win the 1982 French Grand Prix at Paul Ricard

'Before the race we all decided that, if we were running first and second in the race, then Alain should win. René agreed to that. Whatever the gap between them, Prost was to win – unless the cars were being threatened by another, in which the case the order was to stay the same. But Pironi, in third place, was a long way behind. I showed René a signal to let Alain through on five occasions.' – Renault team manager Jean Sage

'If I had been five seconds, maybe even ten, ahead of Alain, I would have let him win, but I was 23 seconds in front. I was going well, and I didn't want to take the risk of easing off so much, break my rhythm, or the rhythm of the car. Pironi was not that far behind, and anyway I have not completely abandoned my own world championship hopes.' – Arnoux

'If one driver doesn't accept having at his side another driver who is fast, who can win races... Well, you can't ask the team to tell the other driver to let you past... Prost and I were engaged with the same status. At Ricard I didn't propose anything, they asked me if the case eventually arose to let him past – but nobody could imagine I would have had a 30-second lead by mid-race... If there was a chance for him to win the world championship in the last race perhaps I would have played for the team – but I say perhaps.' – Arnoux, from *Alain Prost* by Christopher Hilton (Partridge Press, 1992)

'It was the same as ever – Arnoux just didn't bother to look in his mirrors. Unbelievable!' – Prost held up by old rival Arnoux on his flying lap during qualifying for the 1988 San Marino Grand Prix

Schumacher v Berger

'Berger should concentrate on racing instead of thinking how he can criticise me. If Berger drove with the talent he shows doing his own PR, he would have won many more races.' – Michael Schumacher sniping at Gerhard Berger, 1995. Berger had criticised the decision to reinstate Schumacher's win in Brazil after he had initially been disqualified for alleged fuel irregularities

'I never criticised Schumacher. I only criticised the decision. I can live with Schumacher being angry.' – Berger's reply

Blundell v Berger

'What Gerhard did might have been acceptable in the last couple of laps in a race, but not at half distance. I shall be having a quiet word about it with him when I next see him. He certainly had some extra-wide wheels on his Ferrari...' – Mark Blundell, forced on to the grass by Berger at 190 mph during the 1993 German Grand Prix

'Although my wheels were level with the middle of his car, he chopped into me and pitched me up on two wheels. By a miracle I didn't turn over, but then the car hit a guard rail. When he got out of his car he told me that he knew I would attack at that point because I was quicker, but that fighting for tenth place was only a game!' – Blundell after another collision with Berger, this time at the 1993 Belgian Grand Prix

'I looked in my mirror and saw that he was nowhere near enough to try overtaking – then the next thing I knew he was coming over the top of me.' – Berger's explanation of events at Spa, 1993

Nilsson v Peterson

'I was right alongside him and he ran me off the road saying he didn't see me there.' – Gunnar Nilsson pushed out of the 1977 United States East Grand Prix at Watkins Glen by fellow Swede Ronnie Peterson

'He'd been behind me for many laps before he tried and he knew exactly which line I would take on the corner. I thought he was intelligent enough not to try to drive on the outside just before a right-hand corner. It was a crazy attempt to overtake.' – Peterson gives his version of events

Jones v Reutemann

'When I saw the pit signal, I thought to myself: "Right, if I give way now, I stop here on lap 57 or whatever it was, right in the middle of the track, and I leave immediately for my farm. Finish.' – Carlos Reutemann on why he disobeyed Williams team orders and refused to let team-mate Alan Jones win the 1981 Brazilian Grand Prix. A clause in their contracts stated that if Reutemann and Jones were first and second in a race with no more than seven seconds between them, Jones would be allowed to win. Near the end of the race in Rio, the team hung out a board reminding

Reutemann of the agreement but he ignored it and went on to win by just under five seconds

'It's not for nothing that the cars have those numbers on them!' – Jones pointing out the numbers one and two on his and Reutemann's cars. Jones drove number one

'Now I know the situation I shall treat him just like any other driver too and bang wheels to go past him instead of sitting back praying he's a gentleman. I don't and can't trust Carlos any more. The damage has been done.' – Jones

'I can't think of a single time last year when Carlos physically helped me to win the world championship.' – Jones rejecting a suggestion that he might help Reutemann win the title in 1981. Reutemann lost out to Nelson Piquet by one point

'Let's bury the hatchet.' – Reutemann trying to build bridges

'Yes, in your back, Carlos.' – Jones knocking them down

Hunt v Depailler

'The first thing you must do is bloody well learn to drive!' – James Hunt to Patrick Depailler after the Frenchman put him out of the 1976 United States West Grand Prix

'Hunt was driving very wild, holding everybody back.' – Depailler gets his own back two races later after the Belgian Grand Prix

Hunt v Andretti

'There is no way you can get by there. I don't know what Andretti was doing. It was his race. He had the best car. Sooner or later he was going to get by me.' – James Hunt after colliding with Mario Andretti on lap five of the 1977 Dutch Grand Prix

'James Hunt, he's champion of the world, right? The problem is that he thinks he's the king of the goddam world as well.' – Andretti to Hunt after the 1977 Dutch Grand Prix

'He was blocking me down the inside, so the only place I could try was around the outside. The first lap he put me on the grass. That was all right, legitimate. He was ahead of me. But the time we hit, I was more or less alongside him, and he's moving out and moving out. I mean, I can't just disappear. I'm *there*. Does he want me to drive through the catch fences or what? I don't ask for an inch more than is my due. He says to me, "We don't overtake on the outside in Grand Prix racing." Well, I got news for him. I'm a racer, and if I get blocked on the inside, I'll try the outside. The way he was driving, I mean, I'd expect it from an amateur but not from him. I tried the same manoeuvre with Lauda a few laps later, right? Now there's a guy with a brain in his head. He sees me there, he thinks, "If we touch, I'm out of the race," and he moves over, gives me room, and we both accelerate out of the turn in good shape. He didn't lose his place doing that. It just amazes me that Hunt didn't think about the consequences from his own point of view. There was just no need for him to ride me out there, the jerk.' – Andretti cuts loose after Zandvoort, 1977

'I was the victim of a pincer movement. Mario found himself boxed in behind Watson and he moved out, which was a pretty stupid thing to do when you're leading the world championship. All I had to do was lock a wheel and he would have been in hospital for the rest of the year, and you can't win many races from there.' – Hunt taking a swipe at Andretti at the 1978 French Grand Prix

'I passed Mario skating backwards along the guard-rails, shedding pieces of black and gold fibre-glass – he had engaged in one of his now famous first-lap overtaking manoeuvres and paid the price.' – Hunt has another pop after the 1978 Austrian Grand Prix

'I wouldn't put Andretti in the top ten in the world, at any stage in his career.' – Hunt, the final insult, 1981

Hunt v Brambilla

'We were in the middle of a real flyer, and suddenly there's bloody Brambilla almost stopped on the apex of the last corner. As I headed down to the pits, he suddenly booted it and came up behind me. I decided to give him a brake test, and we sort of got tangled up in the pit wall.' – Hunt during qualifying for the 1978 German Grand Prix

'I had fuel starvation and put up my hand to warn Hunt. As we went in the pits, he braked hard and drove me into the pit wall.' – Vittorio Brambilla who responded to Hunt's actions by charging over to his car and screaming abuse at him

Boutsen v Fabi

'What were you doing – weaving like that? Two or three times you had me on the grass.' – Thierry Boutsen to Benetton team-mate Teo Fabi after the 1987 Australian Grand Prix

'That pays you back for Portugal. You held me up there. Anyway, come back and talk to me when you've got three pole positions!' – Fabi tries to pull rank on Boutsen

Lauda v Purley

'You bloody rabbits should not be allowed in these races.' – Niki Lauda to David Purley after the 1977 Belgian Grand Prix. Lauda accused Purley of holding him up in the race.

'You wag your finger at me one more time, I'm going to break it off and stick it right up your arse!' – Purley unimpressed by Lauda's senior status

Piquet v Jones

'He deliberately drove me off the road in Belgium. He is absolutely crazy.' – Piquet after he and Jones competed for the same square foot of track at the 1981 Belgian Grand Prix

'He's a Latin. When he doesn't like someone, he tells everyone but the person concerned. I'm an Australian. When I don't care for someone, I tell them to their face. He hasn't said a word to me.' – Jones takes it all in his stride

'I've got better things to do with my time than mess about with the Piquets of this world.' – Jones

Piquet v Salazar

'Salazar also gave me trouble at Zandvoort. I was frustrated.' – Piquet after punching and kicking Chilean driver Eliseo Salazar in an incredible display of petulance at the 1982 German Grand Prix. Piquet had tried to lap Salazar's ATS and had expected Salazar to move over at the chicane. He didn't and the pair crashed out of the race

'Quite frankly Salazar can count himself jolly lucky he wasn't beaten up.' – James Hunt's view of the Hockenheim brawl. Piquet could also count himself fortunate not to sustain serious injury since he was aiming blows at Salazar's head while the Chilean still had his helmet on!

Irvine v Villeneuve

'Irvine came alongside me like a mad man. He locked his wheels and we touched. There was no way his move could have worked and I cannot believe he tried it.' – Jacques Villeneuve furious with Irvine after the 1997 Australian Grand Prix

'I was on the inside, Villeneuve was on the outside. I was clearly in front so it was definitely my corner. Jacques should have known it is impossible to overtake on the outside.' – Irvine's answer

'I think Jacques has had it. I don't think he'll win the championship this year. In fact, I don't think he'll ever win it.' – Irvine before the 1997 British Grand Prix. Four months later Villeneuve was crowned world champion

'It's the fourth time in two days that he's done that to me. It's a kind of psychological game. It just shows how far Eddie is prepared to go to help Michael.' – Villeneuve complaining that Irvine had deliberately blocked his fast laps during practice for the decisive 1997 European Grand Prix at Jerez

Mansell v Prost

'I'd love you, Alain, to come to Ferrari – you can be my number two!' – Mansell to Prost after the 1989 British Grand Prix

'I think Alain does, perhaps, lack something when it comes to *racing*... Things seem to have to be just right for Alain. He openly detests street circuits and rain, and is far from happy negotiating traffic. He is certainly not as aggressive, or alert, in attack or defence, as some other drivers.' – Mansell, from *Mansell and Williams: The Challenge for the Championship* by Mansell and Derick Allsop (Weidenfeld & Nicolson, 1992)

'In my early Formula 1 days we got on reasonably well and played golf together occasionally, but as soon as I began to beat him on the track and to pose a serious threat to him, he didn't want anything to do with me.' – Mansell, from *Mansell: My Autobiography* (CollinsWillow, 1995)

'He uses his influence to pinch the most competitive drives... When we did race on a level playing field he would rarely beat me. That's why he didn't want to compete with me on equal terms.' – Mansell, from *Mansell: My Autobiography*

'His reputation has not done him proud. Being fired from the most historic team, Ferrari, is not exactly the best way to leave motor racing.' – Mansell on Prost, 1992

'Prost disrupted things at Ferrari and upset what was a good team.' – Mansell, 1992

'I am a better and more courageous racer than he will be if he is in Formula 1 for a lifetime. He will be more of a chauffeur, making the car work for him.' – Mansell learning that Prost was to be his team-mate at Williams for 1993. Mansell elected to go Indy Car racing instead

'If I was still racing in the Williams, Prost wouldn't have won any races at all!' – Mansell, 1993

Mansell v Senna

'It was my mistake to put myself in that position with that particular driver. I've learned to be more careful.' – Mansell following a collision with Senna at the 1986 Brazilian Grand Prix

'I couldn't believe what he was trying to do, overtake on the outside at a place like that. When I saw what he was doing, I tried to get out of the way, to give him more room. My right front wheel went over the kerb yet still he moved in on me. You can only get away with these incidents for so long. We could have both been badly hurt.' – Senna on the collision with Mansell at Blanchimont during the 1987 Belgian Grand Prix which put both cars out of the race

'I had no intention of trying to pass him there – especially on the first lap. I was close behind him, and I couldn't believe how early he braked for the corner. I flicked out from behind, and was past him in an instant. I thought I'd get the corner, but he just didn't give way and slid into me.' – Mansell's view of the Spa incident. Mansell was so furious that he later paid Senna a visit

'I do not think a man is apologising when he holds you round the throat.' – Senna asked whether Mansell had come to apologise after their smash at the 1987 Belgian Grand Prix

'Someone had to do something to that guy and subsequently I have not had one bit of trouble with him. I think he will think twice about doing something silly with me again.' – Mansell on the fracas with Senna at Spa in 1987, from *Driven to Win* (Stanley Paul, 1988)

'In that position he was just not able to take the curve, he was too far in. You can't get far like that. It's a kind of suicide. Mansell risked someone else's life. If there had been a barrier, I could have ended up dead.' – Senna lashes out after the 1989 Portuguese Grand Prix

'Everyone knows there is no love lost between us.' – Mansell, the master of the understatement

'I am the only driver who is prepared to go down to the wire with Ayrton. Last year, towards the end of the season, I ruffled his feathers. I was the only challenger for his crown and he didn't like it.' – Mansell, 1992

'He will believe it is his God-given right to win the championship and that no one should challenge him. We saw that in Spain last year when I beat him and he had a real go at me. But it was a fight I wanted no part of.' – Mansell, 1992

'If I had confronted Senna, I would have flattened him. I am disgusted with the whole thing. I am glad I am rid of all this.' – Mansell after Senna put him out of his farewell F1 race, the 1992 Australian Grand Prix

'He's always complaining. It is normal for him.' – Senna unruffled

Chapter Ten

Murray Puts His Foot in It

'He's a tremendous enthusiast and he does a hell of a lot for the image of the sport.' – James Hunt on Murray Walker

'Murray is this wonderful lunatic who just cuts through all the verbiage.' – Journalist Joe Saward

'Everyone inside F1 loves him. And that is because he loves the sport. His enthusiasm is so real.' – Ken Tyrrell on Murray Walker

'Clive James called it the trousers-on-fire school of broadcasting.' – Murray Walker describing his distinctive commentating style

Murray Walker is *the* voice of Formula 1. His excitability during race commentaries is legendary but he does have a reputation for speaking before putting his mouth into gear. Here are a selection of Murrayisms:

'He's in front of everyone in this race except for the two in front of him.'

'You can see now that the gap between Mansell and Piquet is rather more than just visual.'

'And now excuse me while I interrupt myself.'

'We're looking at the man who won in '83, '85 and '86, so this could be his hat-trick.'

'This would have been Senna's third in a row had he won the two before.'

'I can't find the words to explain how mortified whoever was responsible for whatever happened must be.'

'I wonder if Watson is in the relaxed state of mind that he's in.'

'Alex Zanardi – he can talk for England, which is no mean feat as he is Italian.'

'That was exactly the same place where Senna overtook Nannini that he didn't overtake Alain Prost.'

'Schumacher, virtually pedalling his Benetton back with his fists.'

'Hakkinen continues to circulate even faster.'

'Here's Giacomelli driving like the veteran that he isn't.'

'Tambay's hopes, which were previously nil, are now absolutely zero.'

'The lead is now 6.9 seconds. In fact it's just under seven seconds.'

'The gap between the two cars is 0.9 of a second, which is less than one second!'

'Just under ten seconds for Nigel Mansell – call it 9.5 seconds in round figures.'

'He is shedding buckets of adrenalin in that car.'

'Either that car is stationary or it's on the move.'

'In case you're confused, Mansell has gone from seventh to sixth, from fourth to fifth, and is now third.'

'Alboreto has dropped back up to fifth place.'

'Warwick has overtaken Alan Jones and, in the process, moved up a place.'

'You can cut the tension with a cricket stump.'

'A mediocre season for Nelson Piquet as he is known, and always has been.'

'Mansell is almost metaphorically in sight of the chequered flag.'

'You can't see a digital clock because there isn't one.'

'Heinz-Harald, that was magnifi...no, it wasn't!'

'I'm pretty certain he's going to come in now – no he is not.'

'Into lap 53, the penultimate last lap but one.'

'We are on lap nineteen of lap nineteen.'

'This is lap 54, after that it's 55, 56, 57, 58.'

'The conditions at the Nürburgring are much better than last year's Grand Prix of Europe when the weather conditions were indescribably bad: driving rain, heavy mist and bitter cold.'

'I imagine that the conditions in those cars today are totally unimaginable.'

'...knowing exactly where Nigel Mansell is because he can see him in his earphones.'

'Do my eyes deceive me, or is Senna's Lotus sounding a bit rough?'

'And now the boot is on the other Schumacher.'

'The battle is well and truly on if it wasn't on before, and it certainly was.'

'Two laps to go when the action will begin – unless this is the action, which it is.'

'With half the race gone, there is half the race still to go.'

'I've just stopped my startwatch.'

'I make no apologies for their absence; I'm sorry they're not here.'

'The driving skill and the tactics of Alan Jones, allied to the legendary reliability of the Williams car, is paying off...Jones is in trouble.'

'Unless I'm very much mistaken...yes, I am very much mistaken.'

Index